POVERTY AND SUSTAINABLE DEVELOPMENT

POVERTY AND SUSTAINABLE DEVELOPMENT

Dr. Deepali Pant Joshi

GYAN PUBLISHING HOUSE
New Delhi–110002

Poverty and Sustainable Development
Rs. 625

ISBN : 81-212-0887-4

Published in 2008 in India by
Gyan Publishing House,
5, Ansari Road, Daryaganj,
New Delhi-110002
Phone: 23282060, 23261060
Fax: 23285914
E-mail: gyanbook@vsnl.com
Web: www.gyanbooks.com

Laser Typesetting by: Tact Computer Graphics, Delhi
Printed by : Vishal Kaushik Printer's, Delhi-93

To the sacred memory
of my father

Shri Jagdish Mohan Pant

Advocate, High Court of Judicature
at Allahabad and
Administrator General and
Official Trustee of the State of
Uttar Pradesh

"Recall the face of the poorest and the weakest man whom you may have seen and ask yourself if the step you contemplate is going to be of any use to him. Will he gain anything by it? Will it restore to him a control over his own life and destiny? In other words will it lead to self-reliance for the hungry and starving millions? Then you will find your doubts and yourself melting away"

Mahatma Gandhi

Contents

Foreword

I am happy to write this foreword to the book *Poverty and Sustainable Development* by Dr. Deepali Pant Joshi. Dr. Joshi has long experience in working in various departments in Reserve Bank of India. Her academic background combined with her practical experience in dealing with the problems associated with development makes her an ideal candidate to write a book on Development Issues.

The economic reforms introduced since 1991-92 have paid off. India is on the threshold of rapid economic growth. Achieving sustained economic growth of the order of 7 to 8 per cent annually is very much in our grasp. Development has many dimensions. Growth is one among them. But it is an important component of development. It is only a rapidly growing economy that can generate the necessary surpluses that would enable the government to meet better its responsibilities in the socio-economic arena. In short, efficiency and equity should not be posed as opposing considerations. They should be weaved together to produce a coherent pattern of growth.

Dr. Joshi has covered in this book several aspects of the Development process. She has paid special attention to issues relating to poverty and the role that credit can play in alleviating poverty. Gender concerns have also been addressed. I recommend the book to all those interested in the Indian development experience.

New Delhi

August 19, 2005

C. Rangarajan

Acknowledgements

This book would not have been possible without the blessings of my father, elders and the beneficence and grace of the good 'God Hanuman'.

The idea of taking up this work was first mooted by Gyan publishing House for me it became a challenge—response situation. With the advantage of hindsight, I can confidently assert that there can be no question of any excessive reliance on the bounties of serendipity.

As far as this work goes, I would like to formally acknowledge the debt of perennial gratitude to my family, my mother Prof. Chandra Pant, whose high standards I always strive to live upto, my ever encouraging mother-in-law Smt. Lalita Joshi, my husband Shri Rajeev Joshi and sons Paritosh and Kunal for their affection and support and for patiently bearing up with me. I also wish to thank Mr. Rabi Narayan Nath who cheerfully bore the brunt of the heavy workload. The views expressed are personal and do not reflect the views of the institution with which I am associated. Finally anticipatory thanks to the prospective readers who will take the trouble of going through the book.

Dr. (Smt) Deepali Pant Joshi

Reserve Bank of India

Introduction

Poverty alleviation has been critical to the formulation of public policy and has been central to the - National Policy Agenda for over five decades. The importance of elimination of poverty and provision of basic needs has been the fulcrum of the Planning process. The Government has addressed the issue with simultaneity on twin fronts firstly through actively pursuing economic reforms for promoting pro poor economic growth and secondly through mounting a direct attack on poverty The primary objective of the reform was to put the economy on a sustainable high growth path by establishing an incentive framework that enables movement towards the best possible allocation of factors of production across various sectors in the economy and the most efficient input combination within a production sector. It was expected that the higher growth path would be broad based enough to improve welfare of various sections of the population, particularly the poor. The economic reforms initiated in the early 1990s have definitely had an impact on our growth rates. Now the economy is on a sustainable track of 7-8 per cent growth.

As early as 1972 at the Stockholm Conference on Environment Mrs. Indira Gandhi had said that poverty is the greatest pollutant thereby drawing attention to the environmental problems of poverty as the poor use their environment to obtain their life support system and livelihoods. Agriculture continues to be critical to economic growth. Chapters 1 to 3 deal with Development themes, The Economic reforms and the 10th Plan Goals. Chapter 4 discusses The Meaning and Measurement of Poverty and strives to answer the question of how we necessarily need to make growth inclusive. Growth has to be equitable-growth with equity. If rural and urban development remains unsatisfactory, then growth loses its luster. During the past two decades, the process of poverty reduction has been significant. This has been well documented. The proportion of the population below the poverty line remained constant (at about 50 percent) till the mid-1970s but registered a decline thereafter with yearly fluctuations. The decline was remarkable in the 1980s and the 1990s - from 51 percent in 1977-78 to 39 percent in 1987-88 and further to 26 percent in 1999-2001 (Economic Survey, 2001-02). This can be attributed to higher economic growth, improvement in real wages, and proliferation of poverty alleviation programmes. The severity of poverty, reflected in the percentage of the very poor - defined as those whose total consumption expenditure is less than 75 percent of the poverty line—has declined at a faster rate than income poverty in both rural and urban areas It is likely that the incidence of poverty continues to decline and will become residual by the end of this decade. Despite the favourable declining trend, poverty remains a serious concern since children constitute close to half of the poor. Banks have since Nationalization, actively partnered the State .The Indian Social Banking experiment where Banks have through their penetrative outreach succeeded in making possible access to credit to the previously unreached poor and through their extensive branch network largely covered the unbanked areas, is truly unique.

Chapter 5 discusses the role of Banks and focuses on the importance of Rural Credit.

Chapter 6 discusses the rural Cooperative Banks. Chapter 7 delves into the overwhelming concerns with Education Health and Infrastructure. India has severe disparities in education and health. In areas with entrenched and embedded deprivation in health and education for marginalized and deprived segments of the population specially women Expanding education and health infrastructure and services is a necessity; the overall development of social infrastructure is of overwhelming importance. Social sector expenditure in India in the 1990s was low (according to the United Nations Development Programme recommended ratio) as compared to the other developing countries, and certainly as compared to East Asian countries. It is not always low as compared to what India spent in the 1980s, which depends on the indicator chosen to assess social expenditure trends. There are quite a few tasks ahead to achieve the goals of reducing poverty levels and providing health care for all. First, there is an urgent need for stepping up social sector expenditure. A substantial increase in the allocation for the social sector is likely to occur only if there are appreciable changes in the budget-making process. In that respect, movement towards decentralized planning and increasing public awareness are to be encouraged. Civil Society can play a critical role in involving a wider group of people in the process. Second, there is an obvious need for better utilization of the allocated resources. Poor implementation, misuse of funds and corruption are acknowledged in various policy documents. The delivery systems need to be addressed and reformed. The strength of the trickle-down effect is usually measured by the elasticity of headcount poverty with respect to income. There are disparities in rural and urban poverty. Clearly, the rural-urban differences in poverty reduction cannot be attributed to the differences in the growth elasticity of poverty but to the differences in their income growth. The poor are predominant in rural areas and depend mainly on agriculture for their livelihood. Poverty is both seasonal and stochastic; achieving the goal of poverty reduction depends on the growth of agriculture. To achieve more than 3 percent reduction rate of rural poverty, it is essential that agriculture grow at 4 to 5 percent per annum, especially in the regions with a high concentration of poor. Chapter 8 discusses the centrality of Agriculture in the Indian economy, Chapter 9 is an in-depth analysis of what ails Indian agriculture and also presents valuable solutions and policy recommendations on measures of redress Chapter 10 is an in depth analysis of the impact of WTO on Indian Agriculture and concludes that it is both a challenge and a valuable opportunity for Indian agriculture. Chapter 11 focuses on the successful and replicable experiment of the Rythu Bazars of Andhra Pradesh and Chapter 12 discusses the importance of water and the criticality this is going to assume in the years to come. The next six chapters deal with Gender Concerns, (chapter 13) Empowerment of women its Dimensions (Chapter 14) Credit for women, Banks Self help groups and women and the empowerment of Women, who bear the double burden of being poor and being women through the Self Help Groups. The next chapter concerns itself with the implications of regulating the incipient Micro finance movement.

This section is followed by an extensive and in depth analysis of the Banking System its strengths weaknesses emerging opportunities and the threats; its overall resilience and ability to cope with the challenge of change. The last chapter discusses policies and Programmes for employment in India.

The Government of India has all along been giving importance to direct poverty alleviation programmes. It currently commits Rs. 11,000 crore per annum on centrally sponsored schemes (CSS) including self-employment and wage-employment programmes and direct cash transfers. There are about 180 CSS administered by the Ministry of Rural Development and implemented by states that contribute about 25 percent to the total fiscal cost. In addition, some state governments have their own poverty alleviation schemes. The multiplicity of the programmes is advocated on the grounds of multidimensionality of poverty and regional variations in the efficacy of the delivery system. The recent restructuring of schemes, including the merging of a number of schemes, focusing more attention on community/group and client-oriented schemes, and involving more Panchayati Raj institutions, especially Gram Panchayats and community-based organizations in the implementation, may, to some extent, plug the loopholes. The suggestion to identify the delivery systems that work and design schemes around them is worth exploring There is, however, a need to go beyond the establishment of social safety nets; focus directly on providing employment and raising the income of the poor through explicit policy interventions. Economic growth is the best anti poverty programme and needs to be rapid to significantly improve the absolute conditions of the poor. This book argues that to have the maximum impact, there should be a necessary improvement in the relative position of the poor, so that ideally the share of the poor in the incremental income should be more than their share in the average.

Agriculture continues to be the dominant source of employment in India. It employs about 60 percent of the total workforce, even though its share in GDP has fallen to about a quarter. Indian agriculture is sustainable. The nation would be able to produce food needed for the projected population of 1.3 billion and generate some exportable surplus. This by itself would not ensure eradication of under-nutrition due to lack of purchasing power of the poor. It requires liberalization and better provision of Infrastructure. Comprehensive national food security strategy must include reforms in Indian agriculture and security of livelihood for all. However as per the National Sample Survey Organisation (NSSO) data, the incidence of open unemployment has increased from 1.96 percent in 1993-94 to 2.25 percent in 1999-2000. In absolute terms, more than 9 million persons remained unemployed in 1999-2000. The volume of total unemployment that takes into account the existence of substantial underemployment and seasonal variations in work availability has been estimated at 35 million persons in 2002 according to the Vision 2020 report prepared by the Planning Commission. The size of the labour force according to this document was 375 million in 2002 and it is expected to grow at approximately 2 percent per annum over the next two decades. . 'India Vision 2020' sets out a set of long-term economic goals for the nation realizable by optimum utilization of untapped resources. According due recognition to the changing environment and the range of new possibilities open before the people - rapid rise in educational levels, technological advancement, cheaper and faster communication, quick availability of information, and access to world market due to globalization this vision of India as a strong resurgent economy would be translated to reality. Labour force is expected to expand by 45 per cent and generation of about 200 million new jobs over the next 20 years would be a major challenge before the nation.

A significant departure from earlier government statements is the Governments advocacy of access to gainful employment as a constitutional right for the citizens through the National rural Employment Guarantee program, which is path breaking and enables all citizens 'to exercise their economic rights in a market economy'. These issues are discussed in great analytical depth and detail in the last chapter 24 of the book.

Dr (Smt) Deepali Pant-Joshi

Flat No 6,

RBI Senior Officers Flats,

Red Hills, Hyderabad-500004

1

Thoughts on Development

Economic development has been defined as a process whereby the real per capita income increases over a long period of time subject to the stipulation that the number below an absolute poverty line does not increase and that the distribution of income does not become "more unequal". The basic condition is that in the process of development the number of poor people should not increase and income inequalities should not worsen. Sustainable development is equitable development where the incomes of all increase as a result of growth impulses in the economy which help 'pull people' out of endemic poverty. Sustainable development was first articulated by the "World Commission on Environment and Development" in 1997 in its report titled "Our Common Future". As per this definition sustainable development means meeting the needs of the present generation without compromising the needs of future generations. Thus sustainable development in its wider sense means accumulation and protection of human capital through education, technological advance and physical capital (machines, tools) etc., it implies management of resources in such a way that while present needs are gratified, the quality of these resources is maintained and enhanced for future generations and builds a strong economy that benefits everyone. The income index remains an objective index of development. There are two sets of income figures used to represent economic growth. The first relates to increases in the total Real National Income of the country (national income at constant prices). As per this index an economy grows when National Income (NI) increases, a declining trend in NI is indicative of negative growth of the economy. Where NI figures are stable over a period of time, it reflects stagnation in economic growth.

The second index is per capita income that is increase in income per head. Thus, while rise in NI reflects economic growth its welfare impact is measurable only through the increase in per capita income which reflects the availability of goods and services per head. The traditional measure of development is per capita income measured in US $, this is the measure by which the world economy and international agencies rank countries. The GDP per capita defined as the total final output of goods and services produced within the country's territory can also be used instead of GNP per capita. GNP calls GDP + factors in income accruing to residents from abroad less income earned in the domestic economy accruing to non-residents. The "Big Mac" index is also a popular measure which ranks countries across the world on the units of currency required to purchase a "Big Mac" and offers a crude Purchasing Power Parity of the US $ vis-à-vis domestic currencies.

Of late, non-income indices of development are much discussed. Among them one criterion emphasizes the Physical Quality of Life Index (PQLI) that results from a certain 'use' of National Income rather than the quantity of National Income. The index incorporates the three vital components of life expectancy, infant mortality and literacy. The index has shown definite improvement over time underlining that several people have benefited, life expectancy has gone up, infant mortality has reduced and literacy has expanded.

The Basic Needs Approach (BNA) goes beyond PQLI. This approach emphasized by ILO and UNESCO involves provision for the basic minimum material needs such as consumption of food, provision of clothing and shelter and access to such essential public services as pure drinking water, sanitation, public transport, health and education. The BNA strives to achieve the objective of removing poverty and inequalities that have scarred economic development in several countries in the recent past. Since 1990 United Nations Development Programme (UNDP) has adopted the human development index which is a composite of three elements viz., per capita income, level of education and life expectancy. The per capita income, an economic indicator is used as a proxy measure for satisfaction derived from a bundle of basic goods and services. The second element is education: educational attainment is measured by a combination of adult literacy and mean years of schooling. This stresses the importance of human capital and the importance of skill formation for modern economic activities. The third element of the HDI is life expectancy and health. Life expectancy reflects the progress made in such fields as health, infant and child mortality and nutrition levels. The HDI also ranks countries inter se. For this, the current minimum value and the maximum desirable value in respect of each of the three elements of the index are taken note of. For example, for life expectancy the minimum is taken as 42 years in Sierra Leone and the maximum as 78.6 years in Japan. The index then takes the progress made from the minimum towards the maximum which is expressed in per centage terms. This is repeated for the other two indices and helps to arrive at a common denominator for ranking countries on a uniform scale. It assigns a particular value to income sufficient for human survival after which it tapers off. This implies that as the income increases beyond the cut-off point it becomes increasingly irrelevant, on the valid assumption, that rise in income beyond a certain point is subject to diminishing returns and the other two indicators become commensurably more influential in determining the index. However, this index is significant as it does not give undue importance to income but gives equal importance to the two non-income indicators of health and education. The decline in weightage of income beyond a certain point raises the importance of social indicators; this brings into sharper focus the concern with linkage of human development and economic growth, equitable development, sustainable development as opposed to mere growth. The inclusion of the social indicators in the human development index stresses the importance of the overall equality of life. This brings in the need for public/Government expenditure which needs restructuring so that there could be a greater allocation of resources for health and education. These are treated as public goods. The objectives and strategies of the planning process in India had the same undercurrent of thought. The opening sentences of the First Five Year Plan thus set the tone for Indian planning. The central objective of planning in India at the present stage is to initiate a process of development which will raise living standards and open out to the people new opportunities for a richer and more varied life.

Development thinking in the late 1940s and early 1950s was dominated by the strategy of Rosenstein - Rodan called the 'big push' strategy. Leibenstein Strategy (Balanced Growth Strategy) of critical minimum effort principally associated with R Nurkse and the strategy of unbalanced growth popularized by Hirschman. The Big Push strategy was formulated in the early forties in the context of and aimed at Industrialization of Eastern and South Eastern Europe called for the commitment of large resources for industrialization. The basis of this approach was that an industrialized economy enjoys many external economies. To reap the benefits of such a strategy, massive investment is necessary in the simultaneous development of several industries.

The second strategy of development piloted by Leibenstein was the Critical Minimum Effort Strategy. The strategy envisages a certain minimum effort in the form of deployment of investment resources of a size to achieve a substantial increase in the per capita income and self-accelerating growth in the face of a rapidly rising population. The objective was to provide a way for under-developed economies to get out of the low-level equilibrium trap of poverty. The strategy stresses the point that savings can be affected at levels of per capita income substantially higher than the substantive level. It argues that initial investment must be considerable to offset the negative effects of the Malthusian dread of rising population which can push down the economy in the poverty trap again.

The balanced growth strategy enjoyed considerable popularity. It was propounded by Lewis in 1954 it is closely identified with the work of R. Nurkse. He propounded the theory of the vicious circle of low incomes, low savings and low investment leading to low growth. The strategy envisages simultaneous investments in many and varied industries. This gives rise to diverse supplies which accord with the diverse demands of the economy hence the name balanced growth strategy. A more interesting idea was the diametrically opposite theory of unbalanced growth put forward by Hirschman and Fleming. The theory states that developed countries have not developed in a balanced way and their growth curve has not been smooth. They have grown through trade cycles. Hence keeping in view the limited resources in these countries for growth to be stimulated what is needed, is an imbalance rather than a balance among different sectors of the economy. Hence investment of limited resources has to be made either in Social Overhead Capital (SOC) such as transport, communications, water supply, etc., or Directly Productive Activities (DPA) such as production of goods and services like food, clothing, shelter, etc. Investments in either in SOC or DPA will lead to imbalances, i.e., excess or shortage. The response by the other sector to absorb excess or meet shortages will add to the total activities. As a result the economy will move to a higher level although the movement/growth path will not be smooth. In this way the growth impact is maximized.

In the 1950s and 1960s, the role of the State was considered very important. The expanded role of the State led to a complex regulatory regime and overwhelming Government controls coupled with industrial licensing to direct the 'scarce' investible resources. The Mahalanobis model outlined the strategy for long-term growth and defined the role of the State it focused on the growth of heavy industry and production of capital goods as the first priority with a view to enhancing the output of consumer goods at a later stage questions of resource availability, inflation and employment were neglected. This policy of priority for the machine goods industry of restrictions on production by the mechanized consumer goods industry self-sufficiency and no imports of foreign capital held away for four decades. In the 1980s there was a policy of foreign borrowing but on debt rather than equity account. The money so borrowed did not give enough returns to enable affordable debt servicing precipitating a forex crisis. Its assumption of a closed economy led to a strategy of import substitution rather than export promotion. The policy of import substitution came to dominate planning. As opposed to outward looking policies identified with export promotion policies identified with the import substitution process were adopted. The price of self-sufficiency was paid for in terms of relatively low growth of per capita income and of employment. Poverty remained a very serious concern. Even at a growth rate of 5 per cent, no significant reduction in poverty was effected. This raises serious concerns and while not entirety negating the trickle down Mahalnobis theory it did reflect its complete inadequacy. The proportion of people below the poverty line remained at a disquietly high level. In India the rising savings rate sustained the rising rate of investment. However, the growth rate of the economy was not commensurate with the rising levels of investment. The incremental Capital Output ratio deteriorated, this led to "inefficiency in resource use" and was a direct result of excessive protection of the economy. It is not surprising then that fiscal imbalances and a difficult balance of payments position threatened the entire structure. The country entered the1990s with unsustainable fiscal and balance of payment deficiencies. The economic reforms launched in the early 90s in India definitely represent a major paradigm shift in the management of the economy and are in a sense an extension,of the historic changes witnessed in the former socialist and developed countries practicing centralized planning. The policy of industrial licensing and the inequities it spawned was condemned as the 'license permit raj'. The 1990s led to a dismantling of the regime of indiscriminate and detailed controls. It was recognized that the control system was ineffective in achieving the desired objective, as the system of controls consisting of KAFKAESQUE rules and myriad regulations were widely abused enabling only a regime of corruption, delay and inefficiency which created monopolies.

The year 1991 marks a watershed as it led to the realization that the policy practised upto 1990 had not succeeded in becoming a growth maximizing strategy. It had led to an immiserising growth rate the so-called 'Hindu rate' of growth of 3.5 per cent over 30 years followed by a growth rate of 5.4 per cent which prevailed in the 80s. This paled in comparison to the achievements of countries in South and East Asia over a comparable period. Asian Economies known as the High Performing Asian Economies (HPAE) and several newer countries appeared to be joining the Club of newly industrialized countries, and pushing past India, leading to a question mark on the earlier models and paradigms of development.

However, it needs to be recognized that planning had fulfilled an important function in the early years. The role of the State cannot be entirely debunked. The role of the State is still necessary to ensure that markets operate as per rules and unfair practices are not adopted by the players. Planning still has relevance in that it provides a long-term perspective of the economy, identifies the thrust areas where development is required and evolves appropriate policies to achieve the desired goals. The thrust of the new economic policies adopted in the 1990s thus was to create a more competitive environment in the economy so as to improve the production and efficiency of the system. The broad objectives of planning thus continue to remain valid only the strategy of attainment of the overall goals has changed. The tasks before us are still formidable and require not only the commitment of resources but also the necessary political will to achieve these. Foremost among them is the need to ensure equitable and sustainable economic growth to lift the majority of our people out of poverty.

If we accept that the ultimate goal of development is human welfare. The foremost lesson from the development experience of the last 50 years is that the State should support rather than supplant markets by investing in physical infrastructure and human capital and by letting the markets function. The achievements in terms of growth as well as equity have been impressive in situations where the State has supplemented markets leading to the efficient use of resources through technological change and development of human capital (World Bank 1991). On the plus side we have achieved self-sufficiency in foodgrain production but are yet to graduate to a psychology of food surpluses and to emerge as a strong agricultural product exporting country. The savings rate has risen from 9 per cent in 1950-51 to 23 per cent in 1991.

On the minus side foremost is the failure to ensure social justice through effective implementation of land reforms, expansion of employment opportunities and provision of universal primary education and primary health facilities. Insufficient attention has been paid to the Social Sectors, Poverty Alleviation and Social Development. Dreze and Sen (1995) have pointed out that India's social development indicators at the commencement of reforms were lower than all the East Asian countries three decades ago which suggests that unless very significant improvement takes place in these indicators, we may not be able to achieve the target rates of growth of the economy of 7-8 per cent. It has to be clearly understood that larger investment in the social sectors, health, education and poverty alleviation are necessary not only because social development is an end to itself but also as a pre-condition to self-accelerating economic growth. Poverty alleviation does not depend merely on financial allocations but on social re-engineering. A telling critique of economic reforms is that while they have focused on Trade, Capital Markets, Industry, Agriculture and the Social Sectors represent the forgotten half of the reform process. A 'Safety Net' for the poor to shield them from the adverse effect of reforms has also not been built up. The Nehruvian Model with its dream of wiping every tear from every eye of the 1950s, Mrs. Gandhi's inspiring slogan of 'Garibi Hatao' of the early 70s promised a dream.

The Central issue...............is to expand the social opportunities open to the people. In so far as these opportunities are comprised – directly or indirectly – by the stifling of competition and its efficiency – generating advantages, and so on, the removal of these hindrances must be seen as extremely important .... Creation and use of social opportunities for all require much more than the ' freeing' of markets. While the case for economic reforms may take good note of the diagnosis that India has too much government interference in some fields, it ignores the fact that India also has insufficient and inefficient government activity in many other fields, including basic education, health care, social security, land reform and the promotion of social change. This inertia too, contributes to the persistence of widespread deprivation, economic stagnation, social inequality.

There are linkages beyond institutional credit flow, training, capacity building for empowerment of the poor. Again as Amartya Sen puts it Countries do not need to wait to become rich to address poverty which is our central concern.

This vision is absent today though the present Government has demonstrated a commitment to employment guarantee, ensuring universal primary education and health for all. In the ultimate analysis economic efficiency alone is not enough what is needed is a broad base of mass support and the necessary faith in the economic reform process stemming from the vast majority of the people grappling with social and economic disabilities and struggling to cope with the challenges of day-to-day living. Self-accelerating economic growth should now become the fulcrum of our efforts to ensure a direct frontal assault on poverty, unemployment and illiteracy to ensure development with a human face.

1991, more than a decade behind us, was India's Nightmare year when we confronted a full blown macroeconomic crisis which had been allowed to develop steadily as the internal budget deficit got out of hand, with unprecedented dependence on external borrowings in the face of depleting reserves which led as a last desperate measure, to the sale of 'family silver' when India pledged its gold abroad to avoid default on international loans. The structural reforms became an occasion to firmly place India on a firmer growth trajectory. Much has been done but the unfinished agenda also requires completion.

The Indian economy has undergone significant change since independence. Poverty has declined from 50-60 per cent to 23-26 per cent but the progress of other Asian economies is an important lesson to urge us to fulfill the tasks which still remain unfinished speedily. The crumbling of the closed economies of Soviet and Eastern Europe led to the freeing of trade in the 90s. The era of import substituting development was also discredited with the remarkable exhibition of exuberant export led growth of the East Asian economies. The currency crisis in South East Asia led to sobering reflection on the role and rule of markets. What should be the Role of the State ? The ideal form of government would still be a classical liberalism where the State is seen as a custodian of laws that facilitates unhindered pursuit of individual ends. The State should balance the needs of economic and social development to mediate so as to balance the exclusionary nature of market forces as opposed to the inclusiveness of democratic forces. Markets may exclude the poor both as producers and consumers of goods. Unbounded pursuit of markets could lead to highly unequal outcomes that are per se unequal in nature. Economic liberalization in India, with its promise of higher growth rates, has as its core the economic priorities of people employment, poverty removal, agriculture rural development investment in physical and social infrastructure education health literacy development of basic human capabilities to make possible the full realization of personality and fulfillment of potential and promise of the country.

References

1. Gerald M. Meir, *Leading Issues in Economic Development* (1984) Oxford University Press.
2. *Planning and Economic Policy in India – Evaluation and Lessons for the Future* edited by Manabendu Chattopadhyay, Pradip Mihir – Mati Rakshak.
3. Planning Commission, Government of India 1952 – Chapter 1 p. 1.
4. Paul N Rosenstein – Rodan – "Problems of Industrialisation of Eastern and South Eastern Europe" – *Economic Journal* – June-Sept. 1943.
5. H. Leibenstein – *Economic Backwardness and Economic Growth.*
6. R. Nurkse (1983)–*Problem of Capital Formation in Underdeveloped Countries*. Oxford Blackwell.
7. A. O. Hirschman – The Strategy of Economic Development.
8. *Indian Planning Objectives Strategy and Instrumentality* – Dr. C. Rangarajan.
9. *Planning is Dead, Long Live Planning – The Role of Planning in a Liberalised Economy* – Kirit S. Parekh.
10. *Facets of the Indian Economy* edited by Rakesh Mohan, OUP 2002.
11. *Agriculture Food Security Poverty and Environment Essays on Post Reform India* – C.H. Hanumantha Rao – Oxford 2005.
12. *India's Economic Reforms and Development Essays in honour of Manmohan Singh Isher Judge Ahluwalia and IMD Little* (ed.) Oxford 1998.
13. Is there life after Mahalanobois ? The Pollitical Economy of India's New Economic Policy. *The Indian Economic Review Special Number* in memory of Subhmoy Chakravarti pp. – 64 Meghnad Desai.
14. Capitalism Societies and India's Economic Development - Meghsnad Desai – Exim Bank lecture 1993.
15. *Indian Economic Development and Social Opportunity* – Dreze and Sen, Oxford.

2

The Economic Reforms Initiated in The Early 90s

India's Economic Reforms initiated in the early 1990s were in response to a severe economic crisis. In July 1991, India confronted a serious fiscal and balance of payment problem. In 1990-91, the gross fiscal deficit escalated to 8.4 per cent of Gross Domestic Product (GDP) with inflation at nearly 17 per cent. This was a direct result of policies followed in the late 1980s of extravagant borrowing without any restructuring of the economy. External debt had risen from 12 per cent of GDP in 1980-81 to 23 per cent in 1990-91. Much of the borrowing was from Non-Resident Indian (NRI) deposit at high rates of interest. Due to Gulf War there was a sharp decline in remittances from overseas Indian workers and flight of short-term NRI deposits. By mid-1990-91, India's foreign exchange reserves stood at two weeks of import coverage. The initial phase of reforms focused on macro economic stabilization as they were introduced essentially to cope with an immediate crisis.

The reforms were broad-based as they embraced reforms in industrial policy, trade and exchange rate policy, foreign investment policy, financial sector, banking sector and tax reforms. India's strategy of stabilization and structural adjustment measures produced satisfactory results. GDP growth which was 0.8 per cent in 1991-92 rose to an average GDP growth of 7 per cent during the period 1994-95 to 1996-97, industrial growth which had fallen to 0.6 per cent in 1991-92 recovered to 11.8 per cent in 1995-96 and 7.1 per cent in 1996-97. Foreign currency reserves which had fallen to almost $ 1 billion in mid-1990 are today placed at $ 141,475 billion. The build up of foreign currency reserves with the RBI has now generated a lively debate as to how best the funds can be utilized. External commercial borrowings, IMF loans and short-term deposits have declined as sources of foreign currency. Inflows of foreign investment in the form of foreign institutional investment (FII) receipts of foreign direct investment (FDI) have been rising. India's reform strategy has been to unshackle the economy and to dismantle four decades of centralized economic control. As part of reforms, we abolished industrial licensing, liberalized import rules, encouraged exports, introduced reforms in trade and exchange rate foreign investment policy, tax policy, capital markets and financial and banking sector. The reforms have had a positive and salutary effect and have been able to sustain a higher GDP growth than witnessed in the pre-reform period. Some writers appraising India's economic reforms divide the post-reform period into two phases. The years 1991-92 to 1993-94 essentially being the stabilization phase and the period from 1994-95 providing the time-frame to evaluate the longer term objective of attaining high rates of growth. On all parameters we find that there has been significant progress. The achievement of the past decades does not allow for a sense of complacency as much remains to be done. The infrastructure, agriculture, power sector and labour reforms still require attention.

As a consequence of reforms, the Indian economy has grown and stabilized. However, the reform process neglected reforms in the agricultural and social sectors, which continue to be the most crucial sectors of the Indian economy. The priorities for policy makers in the second generation reforms should be to focus on and address issues related to Rural Development, Poverty, Agriculture, Gender Concerns, Micro Finance and revitalizing the existing institutional credit delivery system.

The rapid growth of agriculture is important to achieve foodgrain security as also for household food security and to bring about equity in the distribution of income and wealth which will lead to automatic decline in poverty. High priority has to be assigned to agricultural development to ensure sustainable growth of agriculture with increased performance and productivity. A new paradigm of growth based on agriculture is to be aimed at. As agriculture triggers growth impulses in other sectors through its backward and forward linkages the agriculture sector directly impacts output, wages and employment automatically unleashing growth impulses.

The main agenda of the planning process in the last five decades, since independence has been to address the area of poverty.

Economic growth has been a paramount concern. Though there has been a deceleration in the share of agriculture in the GDP, which has now declined to 22.5 per cent of GDP. There has been no decline in the number of people who depend on agriculture for their livelihood. This number remains constant. Poor people depend on agriculture for food, income and livelihood. Hence the need for ensuring sustainable growth in the agriculture sector.

Public Investment in the irrigation sector has shown sharp decline in the 90s. Conjunctive use of surface and ground water proper on farm management of water resources is important. Proper reform management of water resources for the optimum use of irrigation potential is necessary. Use of in situ moisture management techniques such as mulching and use of micro overhead pressured irrigation systems as drip and sprinkler irrigation, water harvesting structures also need to be put in place. Participatory community irrigation management also needs improvement.

Participatory irrigation management approach has been recommended for revitalizing irrigation, under the PIM approach the distinction of water and the maintenance of canals below the distributory level are handed over to farmers who also collect charges for water themselves. There is a need for institutional and price reforms which will enable farmers to be proactive and to participate in the management of these irrigation projects. Water will in the coming decades be critical for agricultural productivity.

Indian agriculture is characterized by a predominance of small and marginal farmers. Adverse land-man ratios also negatively impact agricultural productivity. Studies of a number of States have demonstrated clearly that ownership of even a small piece of land improves the economic conditions of the landless. Consolidation of holdings all over the country is required for this updation and improvement of land records is necessary. Tenancy reforms are needed for according recognition to the rights of tenants and sharecroppers. West Bengal's move of giving protection of share croppers well known as operation 'Barga' extended the provisions for the protection of tenants to sharecroppers. Women's right to land have also to be recognized.

The Labour Laws needs to be reformed to give to the employer the right to lay-off workers with adequate compensation.

Infrastructure is another important area of reform. Roads, railways and ports need extension and improvement in the quality of service. Expenditure reduction in areas of government subsidies and employment is very necessary. State Governments should also make efforts to contain their deficits.

Fiscal deficit continues to remain a major problem. If the fiscal deficit both at the Centre and States combined is not contained it has the potential to create a major crisis which will negate all the achievements of reforms so far. The fiscal deficit is unsustainable as it also crowds out private investment and promotes inflation. When inflation rises it becomes less predictable and the increase in uncertainties affects macro-economic performance adversely. Inflation necessarily increases poverty as the prices of goods and services also rise. It is the poor and salaried classes who bear the brunt of inflation as they have no hedge against inflation. Confronted with such a situation the government can rapidly lose the consensual base which gives it the right to govern and can be upset politically.

Government has an important role to play in containing shocks to the economy caused either by inflation or supply side shocks such as droughts or changes in terms of trade. Government must control these shocks or at any rate neutralize their adverse consequences for economic growth, output consumption and investment. Macro-economic growth should be tailored to this end. Macroeconomic policies influence growth and ensure stability. Distributional interventions, attention to the social sectors like education, health and poverty alleviation are important features of macroeconomic policy which should be sensitized to both growth and poverty alleviation. Thus, the economic reforms have been successful however, fiscal prudence is to be treated as a necessary concomitant of macroeconomic policy if it is to deliver macroeconomic stability, a public good which is a necessary condition for the maximization of social welfare. Jawaharlal Nehru's words are as relevant to economic policy reforms and the economy as they were at the time of independence when he said "Long years ago we made a tryst with destiny and now the time has come when we shall redeem our pledge, not wholly or in full measure but very substantially ....a moment comes, which comes but rarely in history ..... when an age needs and when the soul of a nation long suppressed finds utterance".

References

1. *India's Economic Reforms and Development–Essays for Manmohan Singh*–edited by Isher Judge Ahluwalia and I.M.D. Little.
2. *India in the Era of Economic Reforms*–edited by J.D. Sachs, Ashutosh Varshney, Nirupam Bajpai-Oxford.

3

Managing the Finance to Meet the Goals

At the commencement of the new millennium, it is only fitting that the tenth Plan affords us an opportunity to build on the gains of the past and address the concerns of the future. Why do we need goals, goals are necessary as they enable us to pace our efforts towards the achievement of our overarching objectives. They also enable us to measure our performance and evaluate what remains to be done. Finances need to be managed so as to ensure optimum allocational efficiency and eliminate wastage. Efficiency in the use of existing resources will ensure that plan targets are attained our intention however is to manage finances in such a way that not only do we attain our goals we surpass them. Though the decades since Independence have seen significant progress on several fronts we still have much undone and many challenges to meet. We have to ensure that there is no slippage or deceleration in areas as, poverty reduction and population control. The monitorable goals are

- Reduction of poverty ratio by 5 per cent points by 2007 and by 15 per cent points by 2012.
- Providing hsigh quality employment to the addition to the labour force over the tenth plan period .
- Ensuring adequate educational opportunity all children to be in school by 2003.
- Reduction in literacy and wage gaps by 50 per cent by 2007
- Reduction in the decadal growth rate of population growth by 16.2 per cent by 2011.

- Doubling per capita incomes in the next decade to attain overall GDP growth rates of 8.7 per cent over the period of the 10th plan.

This will require effective management of finances so as to ensure sectoral growth with equity and sustainability. These are manageable goals. The first generation of economic reforms focused on industrial, trade, investment and financial sector reforms the second generation of reforms have to focus on agriculture.

Secondly, Infrastructure growth of both physical and financial infrastructure needs attention.

Thirdly, we need to strengthen our credit delivery mechanisms and the banking and financial system so as to ensure the success of institutionally mediated interventions. Rapid growth and development will also not be possible without integration with the international economy. The average ICOR in the 8th and 9th Plan has been approximately 4.0 per cent. For a 1.5 per cent per centage point increase in growth the ICOR is required to be scaled up by at least 6 per cent points and would require additional investment to promote and meet commensurable increase in credit absorption capabilities. For putting India firmly on a growth trajectory we have to tap into the opportunities offered by the Global Economy in terms of the three crucial areas of penetration into markets attracting investments and adapting the best technologies.

The banks have been partners in progress for the last three decades since Nationalistion of Banks in 1969. The outstanding priority sector advances of public sector banks increased by 16.8 per cent to Rs. 1,71,185 crore as on the last reporting Friday of March 2002 forming 43.1 per cent of net bank credit (NBC). While other priority sector advances registered the maximum rise (33 per cent) direct and indirect advances to agriculture taken together registered an increase of Rs. 9398 crore (17.5 per cent). Advances to agriculture constituted 15.7 per cent of NBC as on the last reporting Friday of March 2002. Total Priority Sector advances extended by private banks constituted 25,709 crores equivalent to 40.9 per cent of NBC while lending by foreign banks under priority sector constituted Rs. 13,414 crore, i.e., 34.25 per cent of net NBC, all figures of March 2002 details in tables V and VI). The network of bank branches has contributed significantly to both sustained growth of Indian agriclture and poverty alleviation and employment programmes.

To ensure boost to agriculture finance Public Sector Banks formulate Special Agriculture Credit Plans which are closely monitored by RBI. Under these plans banks are required to set self set targets for attainment within the year (April to March). This has led to a substantial increase in the flow of credit to the agriculture sector through the Public Sector Banks from a level of Rs. 8,255 crore in 1994-95 to Rs. 29,332 crore upto March 31 2002. There is an extensive network of bank branches which cumulatively forms an effective credit delivery mechanism. Details of branch network are given in table 3.1 below.

Table 3.1

Bank Group	*Rural*	*Semi-urban*	*Urban / Metro*	*Total*
SBI Group	5506	3947	3935	13388
Nationalised banks	13907	6769	11893	32569
Other Sch. Com. Banks	1128	1658	2145	4931
RRBs	12178	1925	359	14462
Foreign banks	0	2	169	171
Total	**32719**	**14301**	**18501**	**65521**

The agriculture sector contributes 24.3 per cent to the country's GDP. Development of agriculture would depend to a great extent on improvement in infrastructure and credit delivery. The National Agriculture Policy adopted in July 2000 envisages annual growth in agriculture of over 4 per cent per annum and highlights adequate and timely supply of credit to farmers.

Agriculture credit constitutes an important part of priority sector lending by commercial banks. A target of 18 per cent of net bank credit has been stipulated for domestic scheduled commercial banks for lending to agriculture. To ensure that the focus of the banks on credit flow to the direct category of agricultural advances does not get diluted; it has been stipulated that the lending under the indirect category should not exceed one-fourth of the agricultural sub-target of 18 per cent, i.e., 4.5 per cent of net bank credit for the purpose for computing the achievement of banks under the 18 per cent target. However, all agricultural advances under the categories 'direct' and 'indirect' are reckoned in computing performance under the overall priority sector target of 40 per cent of the net bank credit.

Public sector banks have been formulating Special Agricultural Credit Plans (SACP) since 1994-95 with a view to achieving distinct and marked improvement in the flow of credit to agriculture. Under SACP the banks are required to fix self-set targets for achievement during the year (April-March). The targets are generally fixed by the banks showing an increase of about 20 to 25 per cent over the disbursement made in the previous year. With the introduction of SACP, the flow of credit to the agricultural sector by public sector banks has increased substantially from Rs. 8255 crore in 1994-95 to Rs. 29332.39 crore during 2001-02.

Disbursements under SACP during the years 1998-99, 1999-2000 and 2001-2002 are furnished below:

Table 3.2

Year	*Target (Rs. crore)*	*Disbursement (Rs crore)*	*Percentage of achievement to target*
1998-1999	18503.51	17787.63	96.13
1999-2000	21307.62	21913.14	102.84
2000-2001	25893.32	24654.40	95.22
2001-2002	30883.12	29332.39	94.98

As announced by Government of India, during the year 1998-99, NABARD formulated a model scheme for issue of 'Kisan Credit Cards [KCCs]' to farmers enabling them to readily purchase agricultural inputs and draw cash for their production needs. The model KCC scheme prepared by NABARD containing procedure for the issue of KCCs to farmers was circulated among all scheduled commercial banks for adoption. The KCCs are issued on the basis of farmers' land holdings so that the cards can be used to purchase agricultural inputs such as seeds, fertilizers and pesticides and draw cash for production needs.

The banks were advised in June 2000 that they should consider issue of Kisan Credit Cards for limits even below Rs. 5,000 also, in order to facilitate wider coverage under the scheme. The banks have also been advised to pay interest on the credit balances in the accounts under the Kisan Credit Card scheme.

In pursuance of the Union Finance Minister's announcement in his Budget Speech for the year 2001-2002, banks have been asked to provide personal insurance package to the KCC holders, as is often done with other credit cards, to cover them against accidental death or permanent disability, upto maximum amount of Rs. 50,000 and Rs. 25,000/ respectively.

Cumulatively, 74.49 lakh KCCs have been issued by public sector banks since inception of the scheme upto March 2002. During the year 2001-02, public sector banks have issued 30.71 lakh KCCs as against the target of 33 lakh.

As announced by the Union Finance Minister in his Budget Speech for the year 2001-2002, all eligible agricultural farmers are required to be covered under the KCC scheme within the next 3 years (i.e., by March 2004). All commercial banks have been instructed accordingly. The Hon'ble Prime Minister, in his Independence Day speech (2002), has stated that efforts would be made to cover the entire population of eligible farmers under this scheme in the next two years.

With a view to promoting investment in agriculture particularly in high tech areas such as acquaculture, floriculture, pisciculture, etc., all scheduled commercial banks have been advised to set up at least one SAFB in each State (to be set up by the convenors of the respective SLBCs). So far 61 such SAFBs have been opened by the public sector banks.

The Rural Infrastructure Development Fund was set up in 1995-96 as an initiative of the Central Government to provide loans to State Governments for the creation of rural infrastructure to enable extension of finance to ensure quick completion of ongoing projects of the State Governments. Under the scheme the Central Government through budgetary allocations contributes to the Corpus Fund of RIDF. Commercial banks shortfall under priority sector lending is also deployed under the RIDF as a measure of penalty the rates of interest receivable by commercial banks on their RIDF deposits are inversely proportional to their shortfall in achieving the priority sector targets. This measure is designed to ensure that commercial banks are encouraged to lend directly to agriculture and industry as per priority sector norms. The corpus of RIDF funds 1 to 6 taken together amounted to Rs 23000 crore as on March 31, 2002. Cumulative amounts of deposits mobilized loans sanctioned and funds disbursed under RIDF as on March 312002 were Rs. 12,288 crore, Rs. 24,432 crore and Rs 13,042 crore. In terms of purpose-wise amounts sanctioned under RIDF, projects related to rural connectivity-roads bridges irrigation accounted for 90 per cent of cumulative sanctions (see tables 3.3, 3.4 and 3.5 and 5. The low disbursements under the RIDF continue to be a cause for concern to step up disbursements Panchayati Raj institutions are now eligible to implement RIDF projects. New projects have also been brought under the ambit of sponsoring through RIDF rates of interest on RIDF loans have been brought down to 8.5 per cent from 10.5 per cent. A strong and vibrant financial sector is of crucial importance to a growing economy in India the banks are partners in the development initiatives of the Government Financial Sector Reforms have focused primarily on improving the viability and stability of financial institutions keeping in view their vital role in the economy through financial intermediation.

All efforts are being made by the RBI to develop a sound and healthy financial system. There is a need for continuance of poverty alleviation programmes as the *Swarn Jayanti Gram Swarozgar Yojana*, in the rural areas the *Pradhan Mantri Rozgar Yojana* which is an All India employment generation programe and the *Swarn Jayanti Shahri Rozgar Yojana* in the urban areas.

The SGSY scheme launched in April 1999 aims at establishing a large number of micro enterprises in the rural areas of the country. The objective of the scheme is to bring every assisted family above the poverty line over a period of time by providing them with income generating assets through a mix of bank credit and government subsidy. SGSY is a holistic programme covering all aspects of self-employment such as organization of the poor into Self Help Groups, training, credit, technology, infrastructure and marketing.

Table 3.3
Cumulative Sanctions and Disbursements under Different Tranches of RIDF(As on 31 March 2002)

(Rs. crore)

RIDF	*Corpus*	*Amount Sanctioned**	*Amount Phased*	*Amount Disbursed*
1	2	3	4	5
RIDF I	2,000	1,911	1,911	1,761
RIDF II	2,500	2,620	2,620	2,250
RIDF III	2,500	2,693	2,693	2,183
RIDF IV	3,000	2,988	2,988	1,863
RIDF V	3,500	3,568	3,568	1,969
RIDF VI	4,500	4,586	3,872	1,899
RIDF VII	5,000	5,066	1,479	1,117
Total	**23,000**	**23,432**	**19,131**	**13,042**

* Excluding schemes withdrawn.

Source: NABARD.

The performance under the scheme for the year 2001-02 is as under.

Table 3.4

Year	*Total Swaroz-garis assisted*	*Bank Credit (Rs. in lakhs)*	*Govt. subsidy (Rs. in lakhs)*	*No. of SC assisted of the total swaroz-garis*	*No. of ST assisted of the total swaroz-garis*	*No. of women assisted of the total swaroz-garis*	*No. of physically handicap-ped assisted of the total swaroz-garis*
2001-02	800593	110927.52	55492.78	248021 (30.98 %)	100138 (12.51 %)	328660 (41.05 %)	5106 (0.64 %)

The SJSRY Scheme is in operation from 1.12.1997 in all urban and semi urban towns of India. Among other components, the scheme has two sub-schemes where bank credit is involved namely Urban Self Employment Programme (USEP) and Development of Women and Children in Urban Areas (DWCUA). The beneficiaries are identified by the Urban Local Bodies on the basis of house-to-house survey. Under the scheme, women are to be assisted to the extent of not less than 30 per cent, disabled at 3 per cent and SC / STs at least to the extent of the proportion of their strength in the local population.

In the year 2001-02, 168445 applications were received by banks. Of the total disbursed SC/ST accounted for 24.51 per cent, women 20.41 per cent and disabled 0.86 per cent.

The PMRY scheme was launched on 2.10.1993 and initially was in operation in urban areas. From 1.4.1994 the scheme is being implemented throughout the country. The objective of the scheme is to provide self –employment opportunities to educated unemployed youth in the age group of 18 to 35 years. In North East states the age group is 18-40. There is 10-year relaxation for SC/ST Ex-servicemen/ physically handicapped and women, in the upper age limit. To be eligible for assistance under the scheme the family income of the beneficiaries shall not exceed Rs. 40000 per annum and income of parents of beneficiary also shall not exceed Rs. 40000.

These programe may have met with only limited success but still they represent the only measure of social security or safety net which is available to the below poverty line borrower in the Indian context.

The States must necessarily put their house in order and strive to contain deficits which imperil state finances. It is imperative that the average fiscal deficit of the Centre is reduced. This should be reduced from 2.8 per cent of the GDP to 2.6 per cent of the GDP at current market prices. This projection of reduction in fiscal deficits is in alignment with the targets set in the "Fiscal Responsibility and Budget Management Bill" proposed by the government. This also needs to be accompanied by a reduction in the consolidated fiscal deficit of the Centre and States from 4.4 per cent of GDP in the baseline scenario to 3.3 per cent in the target scenario (see Tables 3.7 and 3.8 for details). Efficiency of resource use has to be assured there is considerable evidence which attests to the availability of existing stock of capital assets, which are either lying idle, or have not been used to their fullest extent. The first major area of idle capacity is in public infrastructural investment which arises as projects are launched without requisite financial provisions leading to tardy pace of completion or abandonment. Here RIDF has an important role to play.

Table 3.5

Lending to Priority Sector by Commercial Banks

Domestic Banks

	March 2000		*March 2001*		*March 2002*	
	Public sector banks	*Private sector banks*	*Public sector banks*	*Private sector banks*	*Public sector banks*	*Private sector banks*
Percentage of total priority sector lending to NBC (Target 40 per cent)	43.63	38.73	42.99	38.15	43.12	40.93
Percentage of total agricultural advances to NBC (Target 18 per cent)	15.77	8.30@	15.65	8.50@	15.81	8.53
Percentage of lending to weaker sections to NBC (Target 10 per cent)	7.22	1.73	7.28	1.70	7.30	1.82

@ Revised data. (Indirect advances to agriculture taken into account only to the extent of 4.5 per cent of NBC).

Table 3.6

Foreign Banks

	March 2000	*March 2001*	*March 2002*
Percentage of total priority sector lending to NBC (Target 32 per cent)	34.53	34.09	34.17
Percentage of SSI advances to NBC (Target 10 per cent)	10.23	10.70	11.62
Percentage of export credit to NBC (Target 12 per cent)	22.51	19.77	17.70

(Data provisional. Compiled on the basis of half-yearly ad hoc data furnished by public sector, private sector and foreign banks).

Looking ahead we again emphasise that the Theth Plan has placed in our hands a feasible blueprint for placing India on a higher growth path and ensuring sustainable development while addressing equity concerns. We have to ensure efficiency to Manage the finances to meet the Goals.

Table 3.7
Macroeconomic Parameters for the Tenth Plan–A Comparison

	Base-Line	*Target*
Average GDP Growth Rate (per cent p.a.)	6.5	8.0
Gross Investment Rate (per cent of GDPmp)	27.8	32.6
Implicit ICOR	4.28	4.08
Current Account Deficit	1.5	2.8
Gross Domestic Savings, of which:	26.3	29.8
Public Sector (of which)	2.4	4.6
Government	-0.6	1.7
Public Enterprises	3.0	2.9
Private Corporate Sector	4.9	5.8
Household Sector	19.0	19.4

Table 3.8
Fiscal Correction in the Tenth Plan–A Comparison (per cent of GDP at market prices)

	Base-Line	*Target*
Consolidated Fiscal Deficit	4.4	3.3
Gross Centre	2.8	2.6
Net Centre	2.0	1.8
States	2.4	1.5
Consolidated Revenue Deficit	2.9	0.8
Centre	1.8	0.5
States	1.1	0.3

Table 3.9

Advances to the Priority Sectors by Public Sector Banks

(As on the last reporting Friday)

Sector	*No. of Accounts (in lakh)*					*Amount Outstanding (Rs. crore)*				
	June 1969	*Mar 1999*	*Mar 2000*	*Mar 2001@*	*Mar 2002@*	*June 1969*	*Mar 1999*	*Mar 2000*	*March 2001@*	*March 2002@*
1	2	3	4	5	6	7	8	9	10	11
I. Agriculture	1.7	166	160	161	161	162 (5.4)	37,631 (14.2)	45,296 (14.3)	53,685 (15.7)	63,083 (15.8)
(a) Direct	1.6	163	157	157	157	40 (1.3)	31,167 (11.7)	34,247 (10.8)	38,003 (11.1)	44,909 (11.3)
(b) Indirect	0.1	3	3	3	4	122 (4.0)	6,464 (2.4)	11,049 (3.5)	15,682 (4.6)	18,174 (4.6)
II. Small-scale industries	0.5	24	22	23	22	257 (8.5)	42,591 (16.1)	46,045 (14.6)	48,445 (14.2)	49,743 (12.5)
III. Other priority sector advances	0.4	93	81	79	83	22 (0.7)	23,661 (8.7)	30,816 (9.7)	40,395 (11.8)	53,712 (13.5)
IV. Total priority sector advances#	2.6	284	265	273	269	441 (14.6)	1,04,094 (39.2)	1,27,478 (40.2)	1,46,546 (43.0)	1,71,185 (43.1)
V. Net Bank Credit	-	-	-	-	-	3,016	2,65,554	3,16,427	3,40,888	3,96,954

@ Data are provisional.

Inclusive of advances to setting up industrial estates, funds provided to RRBs by sponsor banks, loan to software industries, food and agro processing sector, self-help group and venture capital.

Note: Figures in brackets represent percentages to net bank credit.

Table 3.10
Deposits Mobilised under RIDF

(Rs. crore)

	RIDF -I	*RIDF -II*	*RIDF-III*	*RIDF-IV*	*RIDF -V*	*RIDF-VI*	*RIDF-VII*	*Total*
1	2	3	4	5	6	7	8	9
1995-96	350	-	-	-	-	-	-	350
1996-97	842	200	-	-	-	-	-	1,042
1997-98	188	670	149	-	-	-	-	1,007
1998-99	140	500	498	200	-	-	-	1,338
1999-00	67	539	797	605	300	-	-	2,307
2000-01	-	161	412	440	850	790	-	2,654
2001-02	-	155	264	-	689	988	1,495	3,591
Total	**1,587**	**2,225**	**2,120**	**1,245**	**1,839**	**1,778**	**1,495**	**12,288**

Source: NABARD.

Reference

Dr. Deepali Pant Joshi–*Yojana* Special Number on Xth Plan–January 2003, Vol. 10.

4

The Meaning and Measurement of Poverty

Targeting Poverty

Poverty has always been at the forefront of Public Policy and is a major evaluative concern in most societies. The mainstream approach to identifying poverty specifies a cut-off 'poverty line', defined as the level of income below which people are diagnosed as poor. The conventional measure of poverty, still widely used, proceeds from here to count the number of people below the poverty line the so called 'head count' and defines the index of poverty as the proportion of the total population that happens to be below the poverty line, (i.e., the fraction of the population identified as poor). This provides a neat and well-defined measure, and it is not hard to see why it has been so widely used in the empirical literature on poverty and deprivation.

The measurement of poverty can also be seen as consisting of two distinct though inter-related exercises, viz.

1. Identification of the poor and
2. Aggregation of the statistics regarding the identified poor to derive an overall index of poverty.

In the traditional 'head count' approach, the identification exercise is done through the use of the 'poverty line' income as a cut-off. Then, the aggregation is done simply through counting the number of the poor and calculating the proportion H the 'head-count ratio' of people below the poverty line. Both the exercises are, in this approach thoroughly dependent on seeking to define deprivation in terms of low income.

This measure treats money income as the best proxy for human welfare. Predictably, this lends to two types of errors:

1. Those defined as poor but who are not
2. Those defined as non-poor but who are actually poor. Income and Consumption Poverty are also measure on the Foster Greer Thornbecke (FGT) index which enables a calculation to be made both of the head count, i.e., the number of people below the poverty line and the poverty gap or shortfall of people below the poverty line. FGT samples are usually based on representative sample data of income or consumption. Defining minimum consumption is also not easy though food is the usual numeraire; required intake varies with age, gender, activity level and environmental conditions. Academic studies and policy concern on poverty first arose in India in the early 1960s. The first absolute poverty line was determined by Rath and Dandekar in 1966.

A working group consisting of nine distinguished academics and social workers set up by a Seminar on Planning organised by the Indian Planning Commission recommended in July 1962 that the national minimum per capita expenditure in India should be Rs. 20 at 60-61 prices. The Planning Commission noted that on the basis of available data on distribution of population accounting to per capita expenditure nearly half the Indian population in 1960-61 was below this national minimum level of Rs. 20 per capita per month and the Commission suggested a poverty line based on a national minimum consumption expenditure of Rs. 20 per capita per month at 1960-61 prices since in rural areas and urban areas at 1960-61 prices of Rs. 25 per capita per month. In 1993, the Planning Commission had set up an expert group under the Chairmanship of Professor Lakdawala which had recommended a poverty line rooted in a calorie consumption norm of Rs. 2400 calories per capita per day for rural areas and Rs.2100 calories per capita per day for urban areas. The expenditure required for the corresponding All India consumption basket for 1973-74 was treated as the poverty line, i.e., Rs. 49.09 per capita per month for rural areas and Rs. 56.64 per capita per month for urban areas. The poverty line is updated by estimating what it would cost to purchase the consumption basket at the base year 1993 at prices prevailing in subsequent years. The flaw in this model is that it does not take into account consumer preference. If the prices of some goods in the consumption basket increase poor households consumption pattern may change. They either choose to substitute that item or do away with it. Hence as a measure this is per se inaccurate. Secondly, this is very crude ratio, i.e., all those above and below the poverty line are arbitrarily determined. This ratio does not take into account the Poverty gap of the contingency of calamity, drought, cyclone, earthquake which can push a family below poverty line.

The unresolved issues on measurement are should we measure Income Poverty or Human Development? Sustainable livelihood or Social Inclusion? Current consumption or Social Exclusion? Are monetary or non-monetary variables to be assigned greater weight? If non-monetary variables are taken into cognisance how will this be quantified? The internationally accepted definition of the World Bank of poverty line at US$ one per day is not strictly applicable to the poorest countries of Asia and Africa, as poverty here is relative.

Poverty is a multi dimensional concept it means not only a lack of income but also a lack of the basic necessities for a decent life equality of opportunity, healthcare, education, sanitation and democratic and human rights. Different terms are used to define poverty.

Income or consumption poverty

Human (under) development

Social exclusion

Vulnerability

Lack of capability

Lack of basic needs

Livelihood unsustainability

Relative deprivation

In the 1970s, poverty became prominent, notably as a result of Robert MacNamara's celebrated speech to the World Bank Board of Governors in Nairobi in 1973, and the subsequent publication of Redistribution with Growth. Two other factors played a part. First was emphasis on relative deprivation inspired by work in the UK by Runciman and Townsend. Townsend, in particular, helped redefine poverty not just as a failure to meet minimum nutrition or subsistence levels, but rather as a failure to keep up with the standard prevalent in a given society.

New layers of complexity were added in the 1980s. The principal innovations were:

(a) The incorporation of non-monetary aspects, particularly as a result of Robert Chambers' work on powerlessness and isolation. This helped to inspire greater attention to participation.

(b) A new interest in vulnerability, and its counterpart, security associated with better understanding of seasonality and of the impact of shocks, notably drought. This pointed to the importance of assets as buffers, and also to social relations (the moral economy, social capital). It led to new work on coping strategies.

(c) A broadening of the concept of poverty to a wider construct, 'livelihood'. This was adopted by the Brundtland Commission on Sustainability and the Environment, which popularised the term sustainable livelihood.

(d) Theoretical work by Amartya Sen, who had earlier contributed the notion of food entitlement, or access, emphasised that income was only valuable in so far as it increased 'capabilities' of individuals and thereby permitted 'functioning' in society.

(e) Finally, the 1980s were characterised by a rapid increase in the study of gender. The debate moved from a focus on women alone women in development (WID), to wider gender relations gender and development (GAD). Policies followed to empower women and find ways to underpin autonomy, or agency began to receive greater attention.

The 1990s saw further development of the poverty concept. The idea of well-being came to act as a metaphor for absence of poverty, with concomitant emphasis on how poor people themselves view their situation. At the same time, inspired by Sen's idea of entitlements, UNDP developed the idea of human development multilayered factors which inhibited choices which focussed on the denial of opportunities and choices to lead a long, healthy, creative life and to enjoy a decent standard of living, freedom, dignity, self-esteem and the respect of others. The Sen measure of poverty and related sensitive indicators were used *inter alia* in many practical exercises in evaluating poverty in Bangladesh, India, Malaysia, United States, Brazil and several other countries.

Thinking about human development finds a counterpart in the current debate in rich countries about 'social exclusion'. This started in France in the late 1970s, but has spread widely: for example, the UK set up a social exclusion unit in the Cabinet Office in 1997. The focus again is on multiple deprivation (low income, poor housing, poor access to education, health), but also on the process by which multiple deprivation occurs. The key areas for exclusion include democratic and legal systems, markets, welfare state provisions, and family and community: rights, resources and relationships are all important.

There is a great deal of complexity in measurement of poverty. The conceptual complexity can be understood as a series of fault lines in the debate about poverty. There are nine of these:

Individual or household measures. An Early measure of poverty, (e.g., by Rowntree in England was at the household level, and much still is. Other analysis disaggregates to the individual level, so as to capture intra-household factors and different types and causes of deprivation affecting men, women, children, old people etc.

Private consumption only or private consumption plus publicly provided goods. Poverty can be defined in terms of private income or consumption (usually consumption rather than income, in order to allow for consumption smoothing over time, e.g., by managing savings), or to include the value of goods and services provided publicly, the social wage.

Monetary or monetary plus non-monetary components of poverty. So called money metric measures are often used, because they are either regarded as sufficient on their own or seen as an adequate proxy for poverty. However, there is a clear fault line between definitions of poverty that are restricted to income (or consumption) and those, which incorporate such factors as autonomy, self-esteem or participation. In Maslow's hierarchy of needs, these were seen as higher needs, which would become more important as basic needs for food, shelter, housing and safety were met. However, many current definitions deliberately blur the distinction between higher and lower needs.

Snapshot or timeline. Many surveys and poverty assessments report the incidence of poverty at a point in time. However, there is a long history of thinking about poverty in terms of life cycle experience, (e.g., Chayanov's pioneering work in the 1920s on the peasant household), seasonal stress, and shocks (illness, drought, war). In both North and South, there has been increasing attention to understanding movement in and out of poverty, what Jenkins calls 'bottoms-end churning'. Panel surveys, which track a fixed group of individuals over time, provide data.

Actual or potential poverty. Some analysts include as poor those who are highly sensitive to shocks, or not resilient. Small-scale pastoralists exposed to the risk of drought are a common example. Current income may be adequate, but vulnerability is high. Planning for these groups' means understanding both short-term coping strategies, and also long-term adaptation to livelihood stress.

Stock or flow measures of poverty. The definition of poverty as income focuses on the flow of material goods and services. An alternative is to examine the stock of resources and household goods. This may be measured in terms of physical or monetary assets (land, jewellery, and cash), or in terms of social capital social contracts, networks, reciprocal relationships, and community membership). Amartya Sen analysed the commodity bundles to which an individual was 'entitled'. As Swift has emphasised, entitlements may derive not just from current income, but also from past investments, stores or social claims on others including the State.

Input or output measures. Amartya Sen has reminded us that poverty measures as a shortfall in income essentially captures an input to an individual's capability and functioning rather than a direct measure of well-being. Writing about poverty has often assumed, wrongly, an automatic link between income and participation, or functioning, in the life of a community.

Absolute or relative poverty. The World Bank defined the first international poverty line as an income level at purchasing power parity (PPP) of $200 per capital per year, at 1970 prices or $ 1.53 at 1985 (PPP) prices Non Income Poverty line based on Calorie consumption was considered and a Poverty line equal to US $ 1 a day in consumption (at 1985 PPP) was accepted. The World Bank currently uses a figure of $US 1 per day (in 1985 purchasing power dollars) for absolute poverty. The alternative has been to define poverty as relative deprivation, for example, as half mean income, or as exclusion from participation in society. Thus, the European Union has decided that 'the poor shall be taken to mean persons, families and groups of persons whose resources (material, cultural, social) are so limited as to exclude them from the minimum acceptable way of life in the member state in which they live'.

Objective or subjective perceptions of poverty. The use of participatory methods has greatly encouraged an epistemology of poverty, which relies on local understanding and perceptions. For example, exposure to domestic violence may be seen as important in one community, dependency on additional structures in another. In practice the distinction between those just above the poverty line and those below poverty line is often blurred.

People also move in and out of poverty seasonal, cyclical or stochastic shocks are also important. Relative poverty or relative deprivations are important. Most definitions of poverty specially in the Indian context rely on the calculation of a cost of a basket of basic goods. Thus, no one measure can be selected. Ideally Targets should be there but should be easy to operationalise and implement should be, as the literature categories them SMART and EASY, i.e., target which should are stretching, measurable agreed recorded and time limited and Cost Effective, or Economic, Appropriate (relevant) Simple yearly updated, i.e., updated frequently.

Reference

Dr. Deepali Pant Joshi–*College of Agricultural Banking Journal – CAB Calling,* July-December 2003.

5
Rural Credit

In the village itself no form of credit organization will be suitable except the Cooperative Society-cooperation has failed but cooperation must succeed. All India Rural Credit survey. The founders of planning in India considered cooperation an instrument of economic development of the disadvantaged particularly in the rural areas. They saw in a village Panchayat, a village cooperative and a village school the trinity of institutions on which a self-reliant and just social order was to be built. The non-exploitive character of the cooperatives, voluntary nature of membership, the principle of one man one vote, decentralized decision-making and self-imposed curbs on profits eminently qualified them as an instrument of development combining the advantage of private ownership with public good. Cooperative banks were the first institutions that were set up with a view to providing credit to agriculturists at low rates of interest to free them from the clutches of the moneylenders and to ensure that credit reaches the farmers to enable them to meet their production needs so as to increase production and productivity in the rural areas. These objectives of policy remain unchanged todate. Cooperative banks have played an important role in the development of rural credit. Cooperative banks exist in each state of the country. Their geographical spread covers over 74 per cent of the rural sector. Over the years cooperative banks have evolved from providing loans for redemption of debts to providing investment credit and for meeting immediate short-term credit needs of seeds fertilizers etc. To meet long-term investment needs of agriculture there are State Cooperative

Agricultural and Rural Development Bank. The gross NPAs non-performing assets of the State Cooperative Agriculture and Rural Development Banks are high at 19.19 per cent for SCARDBs and 16.05 per cent for PCARDBs Development Banks, Primary Agricultural Rural Development Banks PACRDBs extend outreach to the lowest deciles. The cooperative structure now has a membership of 1.3 crore, net owned funds of Rs. 3191 crore and loans and advances outstanding of Rs.17261 crore respectively, Cooperative Banks, have a three tier interpenetrative structure with Central Cooperative Banks at the Apex District Cooperative Banks at the middle tier and Primary Agricultural credit societies at the bottom tier. As a measure of institutional strengthening NABARD provides refinance on the loans advanced by these Cooperative Banks, Cooperative Banks are now envisaged as one stop shops for meeting the needs of production credit, investment credit, indirect finance and actual credit flow to the farm sector. The Cooperative Banks have a tremendous network. Thus they are best suited to ensure flow of short-term and long term agricultural credit. As on date they have 1,04,424 outlets and the Primary Agricultural Credit Societies have 90,000 branches all over the country. Cooperative Banks borrow from and lend to their own members, ideally they should be self sufficient as far as financial resources are concerned, however in the majority of cases they are not able to generate sufficient funds to emerge as "Stand alone" economically viable institutions. The factors affecting the financial health of the cooperatives are as under.

Poor Resource Base

They are plagued by an insufficiency of resources. Recapitalization is very necessary, though again this is a difficult proposition. Until and unless the Cooperative Banks are recapitalized they will not be able to retain their micro finance intervention capabilities. The financial performance of the cooperative banks is not uniform across all the States. In some states as Andhra Pradesh, Maharashtra and Gujarat, they are very strong while in states like UP and Bihar their condition is perilous. Thus, the heterogeneity of the system prevents the design of an "across the Board" recapitalization, initiative. Some governments are also not financially strong. It may be very difficult for these state governments to contribute their share in the recapitalisation of the cooperative banks. The RBI had set up a Task Force on the restructuring of the Cooperative Credit Institutions the task force had recommended *inter alia*, that there are three major issues involved on the question of recapitalisation/cleansing of balance sheets of cooperative banks. The first one is as to who should contribute to these resources, to what extent and in what form? Whether the owners State governments alone can bear the recapitalisation burden remains a moot point. Secondly whether at all this initiative of restructuring through financial assistance restructuring, rehabilitation and recapitalisation should be extended to all the cooperative banks or extended to only a select group of cooperative banks? In the case of the exercise of the latter option what should be the criteria for selection and what are the conditionalities which should be imposed? What then would be the fate of the remaining Banks what should be done about them. A third and critical issue is to ensure that a situation which warrants such recapitalisation does not recur after a few years and how can this be ensured ? It is felt that recapitalisation could be in the form of bonds and clearly the duration of repayment should not extend beyond a timeframe of five to seven years. Beyond this period if the loans are allowed to be amortized they would be propping up inherently unviable units which would continue to be a drain on the financial resources of the system. A viability study to assess the feasibility of rehabilitation efforts is the first prerequisite of the recapitalisation exercise. Once this viability study is completed and the quantum amount of fresh fund infusion is estimated, further steps can be considered. The viability of member cooperatives and the PACs would largely determine the viability of the Central Cooperative Banks at the district level in which the PACs federate. The banks may be taken up for rehabilitation selectively and this would warrant the exercise of due care even if this takes a longer time. The Task force recommended that the revitalization package for cooperative banks may be four dimensional programe encompassing financial, organizational, operational and systemic aspects.

Secondly, the present organizational structure with its three tier hierarchies leads to high costs and negative margins. There are two ways in which the organizational structure can be simplified.

1. As suggested by the Khusro Committee the Agricultural Credit Review Committee the short-term and long-term structures should be integrated at all levels primary, intermediate district and state level. Andhra Pradesh is the only state which has affected the integration of this short-term and long-term structure.
2. The Narasimham committee had recommended delayering to reduce the high intermediation costs and to ensure provision of cheaper NABARD credit to the ultimate borrower. As a first step State Cooperative and Central cooperative Banks should consider skipping one tier and lend directly to the PACs and the ultimate borrowers where the intermediate levels are weak. There will be a reduction in the interest rate for the ultimate borrower due to reduction in the level of intermediation and secondly, it will be possible for NABARD to provide refinance even in cases where one tier of the structure is not able to borrow on account of eligibility due to the high per centage of overdues. There is also a possibility of achieving cost economies if, for instance the District Cooperative Banks are made directly eligible for refinance from NABARD. At present generally, the State Cooperative Banks approach NABARD for refinance on behalf of the DCCBs only after consolidating the demand from the individual DCCBs and obtaining the credit limits. The State Cooperative Bank in turn adds its own funds to the refinance and lends it to the DCCBs, the DCCBs repeat the same process for their member societies like the Primary Agricultural Credit societies. SCBs and DCCBs earn a 2 per cent margin for their role. If direct access to NABARD funds is allowed to the DCCBs it would significantly reduce the cost of funds to the PACS. At present the State Cooperative Banks take into account the internal resources of the DCCBs as also their own non overdue cover position while computing costs. Besides the spin off benefits of cost economies this stratagem will lead to an improvement in the resource position with cheaper and far less cumbersome procedures for raising the resources. As far back as 1981 CRAFICARD had recommended the two tier structure for

cooperative banks. This has tangible benefits. As already discussed it will serve to reduce the cost of credit by cutting down one tier and thus reduce the costs of credit to the ultimate borrower. However, as with most such issues there is also a counter argument which is premised on the view that the banks will have to open many more branches so as to absorb the trained staff of the tier which is being skipped, thus the increased overhead costs incurred in this process will effectively negate any savings effected by reducing one tier. Secondly, as Central Cooperative Banks are nearer to the Primary Agricultural Credit Societies and are relatively autonomous they are in a position to render better service than the State Cooperative Banks. The clinching argument against reducing one tier appears to be that the cost of funds to PACS may not be reduced beyond 0.25 per cent. In restructuring the Rural Credit Cooperative Institutions the major recommendations of committees Khusro Capoor Vikhe Patil are to integrate the short-term and long-term wings of the cooperative credit structure. The rationalization by removing one of the tiers to enable exploitation of economies of scale and scope in the rural structure. It would also help to address the imbalances in the Cooperative Credit Structure while the PACS are moribund higher tiers as SCARDBs, DCCBs, SCBs are healthy. In the short-term structure loans outstanding and overdues are higher at the retail levels which are the primary levels leading to a choking of credit flow at primary levels where it is most needed while the higher tier continues to enjoy financial health and solvency. These imbalances have only served to weaken the Cooperative credit structure over time. Persistent and increasing burden of overdues contributes to the high unit cost of business. The overdues and NPAs have crippled financial solvency, cramped productivity and profitability of the cooperatives. The transaction costs of the cooperative banks are also very high. Transaction costs mean management expenses, establishment and staff costs administrative costs add to overheads and the cost of funds. Poor recovery of loans lower levels of loan business result in large losses and low financial viability. Low profitability, high and growing

NPAs and low capital base are the real problems of the sector. Lack of business diversification is another problem. The cooperatives are not able to offer all types of financial services on par with commercial banks, regional rural banks and now local area banks. Money transfer facilities are of crucial importance in the rural economy but the cooperatives are not able to meet or cater to the credit needs for all purposes for a single asset. Restricted area of activities and operations is also a factor which contributes to their low profitability. Lack of professional management inhibits growth. Excessive state/central controls. As cooperatives are a state subject this leads to a high degree of bureaucratization, leading to a lack of democratic functioning within the cooperative societies which more often than not results in complete suppression of their boards. The registrar of cooperative societies enjoys overwhelming power in the present system. Mutually Aided Cooperative Societies Act is landmark legislation as it restricts the power of the Registrar of Cooperative Societies. Under the MACs act of 1995 Cooperatives registered under the cooperatives act can register afresh, i.e., reregister, provided they return and reimburse the shares held by government and enter into an agreement a memorandum of understanding with it regarding the existing loans. The adoption of the essential features of the Model Cooperative Act as recommended by the Chaudhary Brahm Prakash committee will enable bringing in necessary amendments in the State Cooperative Societies Acts and help to turn the cooperatives into member driven professional business enterprises. What do the Cooperatives need to emerge as strong efficient viable institutions first recapitalization support as the base level institutions being cash starved are completely moribund. However recapitalization alone will not be enough to strengthen the structure. Recapitalization may buttress them financially but soon it will be a case of throwing good money after bad if this is not coupled with legislative changes going hand in hand with managerial and organizational restructuring. Dual control must go in cooperative banks. Governments shareholding ranges from17 per cent to 87 per cent, government can buy shares in cooperative and become a member. As a shareholder government has the right to appoint one or more member on the Board of Directors of the cooperatives. In addition, cooperative legislation in India empowers the government to appoint managers in the cooperatives. There is a marked deceleration in credit flow to around Rs. 22706 crore of short-term credit and Rs. 5108 crore of long term credit due to mounting overdues which have cramped the processes of credit recycling. PACs are the weakest link in the Cooperative Credit Structure they should be reorganized. These weak and inefficient PACs should be merged with stronger societies. Multipurpose societies should be encouraged. The maxim of one village one society should be retained as far as possible. Managerial weaknesses need immediate redress to ensure functional autonomy. Proper personnel policies should be encouraged and adopted. Leadership is of critical importance and finally any financial institution is first as strong as the men who staff it. If they do not live up to the institutions they serve it is the Institutions which fall from grace.

Reference

Dr. Deepali Pant Joshi – Special Republic Day Number Article–*Yojana*– Vol. 46, January 2002.

6

Cooperative Banks: An Appraisal

Though the cooperatives cover almost 75 per cent of the entire countryside, the membership is still only 45 per cent of the rural families. Agricultural labourers and rural artisans constitute only 10 per cent of the total membership. The weaker sections of the rural community are still not adequately represented in the membership of cooperatives. Besides the significant regional disparities in credit availability the cooperative banks have not been able to ensure an increasing flow of production loans and investment credit in tribal, hilly and backward areas.

In the village itself no form of credit organization will be suitable except the cooperative society-Cooperation has failed, but cooperation must succeed"- "All India Rural Credit Survey".

The founders of planning in India considered cooperation as an instrument of economic development of the disadvantaged, particularly in the rural areas. They saw in a village Panchayat, a village cooperative and a village school the trinity of institutions on which a self-reliant and just social order was to be built. The non-exploitative character of the cooperatives, voluntary nature or membership, the principle of one man one vote, decentralized decision making and self-imposed curbs on profits eminently qualified them as an instrument of development combining the advantage of private ownership with public good.

Cooperative banks were the first institutions that were set up with a view to providing credit to agriculturists at low rates of interest of free them from the clutches of the moneylenders and to ensure that "credit" reaches the farmers to enable them to meet their production needs so as to increase production and productivity in the rural areas. These objectives of policy are still unchanged. Cooperative bank have played an important role in the development of rural credit. Cooperative banks exist in each state of the country. Their geographical spread covers over 74 per cent of the rural sector. Over the years cooperatives banks have evolved from providing loans for redemption of debt to providing investment credit and for meeting more immediate short-term credit needs of seeds, fertilizers etc.

To meet long-term "investment" needs of agriculture there are State Cooperative Agriculture and Rural Development Primary Agricultural Cooperative Rural Development Banks. PACRDBs extend outreach to the lower levels.

The cooperative structure now has a membership of 1.3 crore, net owned funds of Rs. 3191 crore and loans and advances outstanding of Rs.17261 crore respectively.

Cooperative banks have a three tier inter-penetrative structure with Central Cooperative Banks at the apex, District Central Cooperative Banks at the middle tier and Primary Agricultural Credit Societies at the lowest level. As a measure of institutional strengthening NABARD provides refinance against the loans extended by these cooperative banks. Cooperative banks are now envisaged as one-stop shops for meeting the needs of production credit, investment credit, indirect finance and actual credit flow to the farm sector.

The cooperative banks have a tremendous network. Thus, they are best suited to ensure flow of short-term and loan-term agricultural credit. As on date they have 104,424 outlets and the Primary Agriculture Credit Societies have 90,000 branches all over the country.

Cooperative banks borrow from and lend to their own members. Ideally, they should be self-sufficient as far as financial resources go but in the majority of cases they are not able to generate sufficient funds to emerge as "stand along" economically viable institutions. The factors affecting the financial health of the cooperatives are:

1. **Poor Resource Base.** Recapitalization is necessary to retain their micro finance intervention capability but very

difficult. The financial performance of the cooperative banks is not uniform in all states. In some states as AP, Maharashtra, Gujarat, they are very strong, while in UP and Bihar their condition is perilous; thus, the heterogeneity the system prevents the design of an "across the board" capitalization initiative. State governments are also not financially strong. It may also be difficult to find the money to capitalize the cooperative banks. The Capoor committee had clearly brought out that there are three issues involved on the question of recapitalization/cleaning of balance sheets of cooperative banks. The first one is as to whom should contribute to these resources, to what extent and in what form? Whether the owners, state government alone can bear the recapitalization burden is a moot point. Secondly whether all the cooperative banks should be taken up for restructuring financial assistance, recapitalization, rehabilitation or only a select group of cooperative banks? In the case of exercise of latter option what should be the criteria for selection and what conditionalities should be imposed? And what would then be the fate of the remaining banks? A third issue is how to ensure that a requirement of this type does not recur in the future i.e. it remains a one time measure. A timeframe of five to seven years should be imposed since sops beyond reasonable period would end up propping even inherently unviable units, which would survive in the long run and be strain on the system. Once this viability study is complete and amount of fresh funds infusion estimated, further steps may have to be considered. Viability of member cooperatives PACs would largely determine the viability of the central cooperative banks at the district level in which the PACS federate. The banks may be taken up for rehabilitation carefully on a selective basis even if the process of selection is time consuming. The revitalization package for cooperative banks may be a four-dimensional programme encompassing financial, operational organisastional and systematic aspects.

2. **High transaction Costs.** with negative margins the organization structure leads to high transaction costs. There

are two ways in which the organizational structure can be simplified.

(a) As suggested by the Khusro Committee [Agricultural Credit Review Committee] the short-term and long-term structures should be integrated at all levels, primary, intermediate, district and state level apex. Andhra Pradesh is the only state, which has effected this integration of the short-term and long-term structure.

(b) The Narasimhan Committee has recommended de layering to reduce the high intermediation costs and to ensure provision of cheaper NABARD credit to the ultimate borrower. As a first step State Cooperative Bank and CCB should consider skipping one tier and lend directly to the PACs and the ultimate borrowers where the intermediate levels are weak.

There will be a reduction in the interest rate for the ultimate borrower due to reduction in the level of intermediation and secondly, it will be possible for NABARD to provide refinance even in cases where one tier of the structure is not able to borrow on account of ineligibility due to the high per centage of overdues.

There is also a possibility of achieving cost economies, for instance the District Central Coop. Banks are eligible for refinance from NABARD for refinance on behalf of the DCCBs only after consolidating the demand of individual DCCBs and obtaining the credit limits. State Cooperative Banks in turn adds part of its own funds to the refinance and lends it to the DCCBs. The DCCBs repeat the same process for their member societies like the Primary Agricultural Credit Societies. SCBs and DCCBs get 2 per cent margin for their role. If DCCBs are able to obtain funds directly from NABARD the cost of funds to the PACs would come down significantly especially as State Cooperative Banks at present also take into account the internal resources of DCCBs and also their own Non-Overdue Cover position in computing costs. Besides the possibilities of cost economies this will lead to an improvement in resource position with cheaper and less cumbersome procedures for raising the resources.

As far back as 1981 CRAFICARD had recommended the two-tier structure for cooperative banks. This has tangible benefits. As already discussed it will reduce the cost of credit by cutting down one tier and lower cost of credit for the ultimate borrower.

However, as with most issues there is a counter-argument also. This is premised on the view that as it will be necessary for these banks to open more branches so as to absorb the trained staff of the tier that is being skipped the increased costs of overheads will negate any savings due to cutting one tier. Secondly, as Central Cooperative Banks are nearer to the Primary Agricultural Credit Societies and are relatively autonomous, they are in a position to render better services than State Cooperative Banks. The clinching argument against dispensing with one tier appears to be that the cost of funds to PACs may not be reduced beyond 0.25 per cent.

However, there are positive benefits.

In restructuring the Rural Cooperative Credit Institutions the major recommendation of various Committees from Khusro to Capoor are:

1. Integrating the short-term and long-term wings of the cooperative credit structure.
2. Rationalization by removing one of the structures/tier to enable exploitation of scope and scale of economies in the rural structure.
3. It would also address the imbalances in the coop. credit structure. While PACs are moribund higher tiers, as SCARDBs, DCCBs and SCBs are healthy. In the short term structure loans outstanding and overdues are higher at the retail levels which are the primary levels leading to a choking of credit flow at primary levels where it is most needed while higher tier continues to enjoy financial health and solvency. These imbalances have only served to weaken the cooperative credit structure over time.

The overdues and NPAs have crippled financial solvency, cramped productivity and profitability of the cooperatives. The transaction costs of the cooperative banks are also very high.

The gross NPAs (Non-Performing Assets) of the State Cooperative Agriculture and Rural Development Banks and Primary Cooperative Agriculture and Rural Development Banks are high at 19.19 per cent for SCARDBs and 16.05 per cent for PCARDBs.

Persistent and increasing burden of overdues contributes to the high cost per unit of business. The overdues and NPAs have crippled financial solvency, cramped productivity and profitability of the cooperatives. The transaction costs of the cooperative banks are also very high. Transaction costs mean management expenses, establishment and staff costs administrative costs add to overheads and the cost of funds. Poor recovery of loans, lower levels of loan business result in large losses from slate to low financial viability. Low profitability, high and growing NPAs and low capital base are the real problems of the sector.

Lack of business diversification is another problem. The cooperatives are not able to offer all types of financial services on par with commercial banks, regional rural banks and now local area banks. Money transfer facilities are of crucial importance in the rural economy but the cooperatives are not able to meet these needs. They are hampered by their inability to cater to credit needs for all purposes for a single asset. Restricted area of activities and operations is also a factor, which contributes to their low profitability.

Lack of professional management inhibits growth. Excessive state/central controls as cooperatives being a state subject leads to a very high degree of bureaucratization, leading to a lack of democratic functioning within the cooperative societies which more often than not results in complete supersession of their Boards. The Registrar of cooperative societies enjoys overwhelming power in the present system. Mutually Aided Cooperative Societies Act is a landmark legislation as it restricts the role of the Registrar Cooperative Societies. Under the MACs 1995, cooperatives registered under the Cooperatives Act can register afresh, i.e., re-register, provided they return and reimburse the shares held by government and enter into a memorandum of understanding with it regarding the existing loans. The adoption of the essential features of the Model Cooperative Societies Act as recommended by the Chaudhary Brahm Prakash Committee will enable bringing in necessary amendments in the State Cooperative Societies Acts and help to turn the cooperatives into member driven professional business enterprises.

What do the cooperatives need to merge as strong efficient viable institutions. First, re-capitalization support as the base level institution being cash starved are completely moribund. However, recapitalization alone will not be enough to strengthen the structure. Recapitalization may buttress them financially but these will soon be a case of throwing good money after bad if this is not coupled with legislative, changes going hand in hand with managerial and organizational restructuring.

Dual control must go in the cooperative banks. Governments shareholding ranges from 17 per cent to 87 per cent. Government can buy shares in cooperative and become a member. As a shareholder government has the right to appoint one or more member on the Board of Directors of the cooperatives. In addition, cooperative legislation in India empowers government to appoint managers in the cooperatives.

There is a marked deceleration in credit flows to around Rs. 22706 crore of short-term credit and 5108 crore of long-term credit due to mounting overdues which have cramped the processes of credit recycling.

PACs are the weakest link in the Cooperative Credit Structure they should be reorganized.

These weak and inefficient PACs should be merged with stronger societies. Multipurpose societies should be encouraged. The maxim of one village one society should be retained as far as possible. Managerial weaknesses need immediate redress to ensure functional autonomy. Proper personnel policies should be adopted. Leadership is also important and finally any financial institution is first as strong as the men who staff it. It they do not live upto institutions it is the institution, which falls from grace.

Reference

Dr. Deepali Pant Joshi–*Yojana,* Vol. 45–December 2001–Journal of the Planning Commission.

7

Education, Health and Infrastructure

India has evolved, over time, a functioning system of democratic governance, where power is transferred at regular intervals through elections based on adult franchise. Affirmative action by the state has expanded opportunities. On the economic front, India has done quite well in recent years by achieving a high GNP growth rate. But there are serious questions about the impact of recent GNP growth on the lives of the people and a popular demand to give a more 'human face' to the choice of the path of economic liberalization.

Investment in Human Development as a Precondition of Economic Development

One of the primary reasons why economic growth has not had an impact on the lives of ordinary people is the current state of India's backwardness in human development. The extent of human deprivation is staggering: 135 million people have no access to basic health facilities; 226 million lack access to safe drinking water; about half of India's adult population is illiterate; and about 70 per cent of its people lack basic sanitation facilities. The stark fact is that India has the largest illiterate population in the world: it has almost 2.5 times more illiterate people than the whole of Sub-Saharan Africa. Nearly one-third of the total number of absolute poor in the world live in India. What is more distressing is that while 46 per cent of India's people survive in absolute poverty, with an income of less than one US dollar a day, about two-thirds are, in Amartya Sen's words, 'capability–poor'– i.e., they do not receive the minimum level of education and health care necessary for defactualisation of human capabilities.

Education and Health

One of the principal ways of linking economic growth and human lives is to invest liberally in the education and health of the people. Wherever India has made adequate investment in the education and skill-training of its people and in strengthening its human capital, the strategy has paid rich dividends. For example, India has already gained preeminence in the 'services' industry. Computer software programmers and bourgeoning call centres have led to an outsourcing of jobs to India to the extent of promoting resentment in the developed world. India has emerged as one of the largest exporters of computer software as a result of extensive investment in skill formation in Bangalore, which has fast become India's own 'Silicon Valley'. In fact, India enjoys the great advantage of possessing a rich tradition of scientific and technological research, a large reservoir of low-paid hard-working people, the largest middle class in the world, and functioning democratic institutions. Its progress now rests on a massive investment in human development.

Priorities and Possibilities

On the occasion of completion of one year of the UPA Government, Prime Minister Dr. Singh outlined his priorities in accordance with these objectives.

"Bold initiatives are called for on the economic front. I would like to see an improvement in our public finances at all levels of government. We must reduce wasteful subsidies and divert these resources into needed social sector expenditure, investment and employment generation. There is an urgent need for restructuring of public expenditure and improving the working of ministries. Laying stress on education, he said that India would have the largest number of young people in the 21st century, a 'Knowledge Commission' was being established to study how to educate them all to convert them into economic assets apart from ensuring their health care, employment as well as leisure time activities."

Stating that it was the government's responsibility to ensure that the benefits of growth reached all sections of the society, he said, "We have to ensure that those who are adversely affected by the winds of change are able to adjust to new realities and economic opportunities. The challenge before us is to combine the economics of growth with the economics of equity and social justice. We have no option but to walk on two legs. We regard every citizen (as) a valuable social and economic asset in whom we must invest in the interests of our collective future."

Among the major challenges before the new government are:

- India must shine for all improvement in health care, education and development.
- Expansion and modernisation of the country's physical infrastructure like roads, railways, ports, airports and telecommunications.
- Social infrastructure like education and health.

Additional Gross Budgetary Support (GBS) for fulfillment of National Common Minimum Programme (NCMP) Objectives

An additional allocation of Rs. 12,000 crore as Gross Budgetary Support (GBS) has been made for the Annual Plan 2004-05 to meet the principal objectives of the National Common Minimum Programme (NCMP). Of this, Rs. 7,275 crore is to be allocated to priority areas indicated in NCMP for the Central Ministries/ Departments for new/ restructured schemes and for enhancing the scope and coverage of existing schemes. An amount of Rs. 4,725 crore has been provided as Central assistance to States/ UTs for meeting the objectives of NCMP. Additional GBS for programmes and schemes of priority under NCMP objectives, viz. education, health, rural development and drinking water supply etc. have been identified and allocations to various Central Ministries/ Departments as also the Central Assistance to the Plan of the States/UTs have since been regularized through supplementaries passed by Parliament.

Saat Sutra

The Prime Minister has identified seven sectors ("Saat Sutra") i.e.:

- agriculture
- water

- education
- health care
- employment
- urban renewal and
- infrastructure

deserving of high importance. Greater attention has been paid to the priority areas listed by the National Advisory Council, viz. SSA, Employment Guarantee Scheme (FFW-SGRY), Rural Health Mission, Mid Day Meal, ICDS/Supplementary Nutrition, and Road Network in the North Eastern Region.

The first year report card brought out by UPA Government on its performance has stressed the need to pursue reforms with a human face to lay the foundations for sustained long-term economic growth and development.

'Bharat–Nirman'

Described as a new deal for rural India, the Bharat Nirman is a business plan for developing rural infrastructure in the areas of irrigation, roads, water supply, housing, electrification and telephone connectivity.

The 42-page report card titled 'A Caring Government: One Year of the UPA Government' was released by the Prime Minister on the completion of one year in office. The first section of the report card is devoted to the social and political initiatives taken by the government to improve public welfare, while the second section deals with the policy initiatives taken to accelerate economic growth and modernise the economy. The last section deals with national security and India's engagements in international relations.

To ensure that the economy grows at least 7-8 per cent per year in a sustained manner over a decade and more and in a manner that generates employment so that each family is assured of a safe and viable livelihood.

Redeeming a Pledge to the Nation

On the eve of the departure of the British, on 14 August 1947, Jawaharlal Nehru declared: 'Long years ago we made a tryst with destiny, and now the time comes when we shall redeem our pledge'. 'The achievement we celebrate today', Nehru went on, 'is but a step, an opening of opportunity, to the great triumphs and achievements that await us.' He reminded the country that the task ahead included 'the ending of poverty and ignorance and disease and inequality of opportunity.' The overall task identified by Nehru, of 'ending of poverty and ignorance and disease and inequality of opportunity' has been quite limited.

As far as the record of social sector achievement goes, countries, which have left India behind, have pursued diverse economic policies, from market-oriented capitalism (South Korea, Taiwan, Thailand) to communist-party-led socialism (Cuba, Vietnam, pre-reform China), and also mixed systems (Costa Rica, Jamaica, Sri Lanka). As far as economic growth is concerned, their records have been diverse, and yet all of them have been able to achieve a radical reduction in human deprivation and insecurity. Despite substantial differences in economic policy, these economically diverse countries have had much in common in terms of social policies, particularly those relating to the expansion of basic education and health care, and India contrasts with all of them in this fundamental respect. There is much to learn from these countries and the commonality of their achievements in these sectors.

International Comparisons

Dreze and Sen in their monograph on "India's Economic and Social Opportunity"make clear that the comparative perspectives are important in assessing India's performance. The more effective performances (of, say, China, Sri Lanka, Thailand, or South Korea) indicate what has or has not been feasible elsewhere and provide some guidance about the yardstick on the basis of which India's record might be scrutinized. The point is not that there has been no progress in India, nor that other countries are all doing better, but specifically that India's success in removing 'poverty, ignorance, disease, and inequality of opportunity' has been markedly less substantial than that of many other countries.

The achievements of South Korea, Hong Kong, Singapore, Thailand and other countries that have made splendid use of market-based economic opportunities are indeed illuminating. What the better economically achieved performing countries did in the fields of education, health services, social security, land reform, gender relations and generally in the various areas of public action that bear on the identified social goals. The contrast between these countries and India in terms of what has been done in these fields is no less striking than the contrasts relating to economic growth and market institutions.

These international comparisons also raise an important general question about the complementarity between the opening up of economic opportunities and the social conditions that facilitate the use of those opportunities (e.g. widespread literacy). There is, in fact, some empirical evidence suggesting that the returns to educational expansion tend to increase with the expansion of market opportunities, and such a complementarity is natural to expect on the basis of general economic reasoning. Education has done much for the quality of life in, say, Sri Lanka, without doing quite so much for economic growth as such. Development is to be viewed as the expansion of human capabilities.

Education

Economic Development as Freedom

Amartya Sen defines economic development as freedom and social opportunity.

Education and health can be seen to be valuable to the freedom of a person in at least five distinct ways.

1. *Intrinsic importance.* Being educated and healthy are valuable achievements in themselves, and the opportunity to have them can be of direct importance to a person's effective freedom.

2. *Instrumental personal roles.* A person's education and health can help him or her to do many things – other than just being educated and healthy – that are also valuable. They can, for instance, be important for getting a job and more generally for making use of economic opportunities. The resulting expansion in incomes and economic means can, in turn, add to a person's freedom to achieve functioning that he or she values.

3. *Instrumental social roles*. Greater literacy and basic education can facilitate public discussion of social needs and encourage informed collective demands (e.g. for health care and social security); these in turn can help expand the facilities that the public enjoys, and contribute to the better utilization of the available services.
4. *Instrumental process roles*. The process of schooling can have benefits even aside from its explicitly aimed objectives, namely formal education. For example, the incidence of child labour is intimately connected with non-schooling of children, and the expansion of schooling can reduce the distressing phenomenon of child labour so prevalent in India. Schooling also brings young people in touch with others and thereby broadens their horizons and this can be particularly important for young girls.
5. *Empowerment and distributive roles*. Greater literacy and educational achievements of disadvantaged groups can increase their ability to resist oppression, to organize politically and to get a fairer deal. The redistributive effects can be important not only between different social groups or households, but also within the family, since there is evidence that better education (particularly female education) contributes to the reduction of gender-based inequalities.

The use of economic opportunity by one person can, in many circumstances, open up further opportunities for others, through backward and forward linkages in supply and demand. It is hard to evaluate the contributions of education except through a broad 'social choice' approach. There are similar interconnections in matters of health because of the obvious importance of externalities in morbidity, preventive care, and curative treatment. Expansion of health and education can have influences that go much beyond the immediate personal effects. Through these various interconnection, education and health can be variables of great strategic importance in the process of economic development. India's failure to have an adequate public policy in educational and health matters can be, thus, of profound significance in assessing the limited success of Indian development efforts over the last half a century. A policy reform that concentrates just on liberalization and deregulation cannot deal with this part of the failure of past planning.

Literacy is an important social achievement which has an instrumental role in facilitating other achievements. The new government initiated measures to develop a knowledge society that includes steep increase in the allocation to primary education and literacy by introducing a two per cent education cess. The Centre has plans to launch new bio-tech parks in the country, while it has approved the Technology Vision 2020 at a cost of Rs. 345 crore. In the particular field of elementary education, India stands considerably behind even the average of the poorest countries in the world.

Why Education

The effectiveness of the opening up of new economic opportunities and of expanding the possibility of good use of labour and skill may depend greatly on basic educational facilities and related circumstances.

The Role of Education in Economic Development

How does human capital or the educational attainment of the labour force affect the output and the growth of an economy? A standard approach is to treat human capital, or the average years of schooling of the labour force, as an ordinary input in the production function. An alternative approach, associated with endogenous growth theory, is to model technological progress or the growth of total factor productivity, as a function of the level of education or human capital. The presumption is that an educated labour force is better at creating, implementing and adopting new technologies, thereby generating growth.

Nonetheless, human capital accumulation has long been stressed as a prerequisite for economic growth. By treating human capital simply as another factor in growth accounting we may be mis-specifying its role. There is an alternative model which allows human capital levels to directly affect aggregate factor productivity through two channels: Human capital may directly influence productivity by determining the capacity of nations to induction. Human capital levels affect the speed of technological catch-up and diffusion. The ability of a nation to adopt and implement new technology from abroad is a function of its domestic human capital stock. At every point in time there exists some country which is the world leader in technology. The speed with which nations "catch up" to this leader country is then a function of their human capital stocks.

Economic Impact of Education

Investment in education yields returns at the individual or social level. Beyond the above "strict" or monetary impact of education, investment in human beings also has many other social values. Some come under the heading of externalities – namely, values captured by persons other than the individual investor. Others are labelled "non-market effects" and are simply means or mechanisms by which the overall impact of education is realized.

When a person becomes literate, this person will enjoy a higher lifetime consumption path, according to statistics for a large number of countries. Others will also benefit if the country has a more literate population – through lower transaction costs than if they were dealing with illiterates, for example.

Education as Opportunity

Many educated females may choose not to participate in the labour force. This does not mean, however, that such females are not more productive (relative to their less educated counterparts) in the variety of goods and services produced within the household that are not readily marketable. For example, they may provide better sanitation conditions for all members of the family and more nutritional meals. Such effects should be counted as part of the social impact of education.

Education increased the opportunity cost to a woman staying in the household and induces her to participate in the labour market. This contributes to overall efficiency in the economy to the extent that her market wage is higher than her implicit, shadow wage of being engaged in household activities.

Health status is a very important part of human well-being. Several studies have shown that literacy and other measures of education are more closely correlated with life expectancy than per capita income is. The mechanism of this relationship is that education helps determine both the level of knowledge about how to combat disease and the ease with which it can be transmitted and utilized.

The relationship between education and fertility is a very complex one, although most observers would agree that the link is negative – that increased literacy and school attendance in general delay marriage and increase the opportunity cost of having children. Consequently, families desire and have fewer children. This has been clearly demonstrated in urban areas on a global scale.

Last but not least, another often mentioned wider effect of education is that of having a more informed body of consumers and a literate electorate, leading to democratic government.

People learn from those around them, so if I have an education I improve the learning environment for my co-workers. This positive spillover or "human capital externality is not captured.

The World Bank's Education Sector Policy Paper (1980) concludes that "studies have shown that economic returns on investment in education seem, in most instances, to exceed returns on alternative kinds of investment, and that developing countries obtain higher returns than the developed ones."

Tenth Plan Goal is

(i) Ensure all children to be in school by 2003.

(ii) Ensure all children complete schooling by 2007.

(iii) Increase average literacy rate to 75 per cent by 2007.

(iv) Reduce gender disparity in literacy by at least 50 per cent by 2007.

Despite the priority accorded by the successive Plans to education, the average rate of literacy at the national level is still 65 per cent. Female literacy is even lower, around 54 per cent. Female literacy in the rural areas is only 47 per cent.

Even taking the rural and the urban areas together, female literacy falls short of 50 per cent in at least six states, namely, Arunachal Pradesh, Bihar, Jharkand, J and K, Rajasthan and UP. If female literacy rates in the rural areas alone were to be considered, another seven states would get added to this list. They are Andhra Pradesh, Gujarat, Haryana, Karnataka, Madhya Pradesh, Chhattisgarh and Orissa.

As a long-term strategy, it is essential to focus attention on universalizing access to education a the foundation level, i.e., at the primary (grades I-V) and subsequent levels. While the Gross Enrolment Ratio (GER) at the primary level has significantly improved, GER at the upper primary (grades VI-VIII) continues to be low. In fact, the ratio declined from 62.4 per cent in 1996-97 to 58.8 per cent in 1999-2000. At both the primary and upper primary levels, the drop-out rates continue to be high; 40.3 per cent for primary and 54.5 per cent for upper primary. Another disconcerting trend is that the teacher-pupil ratios for primary and upper primary declined from 1:24 and 1:20 in early fifties to 1:43 and 1:38 in 1999-2000 respectively.

Compulsory Education

Second, the 'others' to learn from are not just the countries that have experienced high economic growth (such as the four 'tigers' or Thailand, or post-reform China), but also those that have managed to raise the quality of life through other means (even in the absence of fast economic growth), such as public support for general health care and basic education.

Poverty has forced parents to send their children to work, rather than to school. It is common knowledge that children are forced to work as domestic servants, in stone quarries, the match industry, at construction sites and so on, often in activities that are highly hazardous. It is estimated that about 5.4 per cent of the children are engaged in manual work of one form or the other.

Population Size and Number of Literates (in crore) and Literacy Rate (in per cent)

Year	*Population*		*Number of*		*Literacy Rate (per cent)*
	All	*Age 7+*	*Literates*	*Illiterates*	
(1)	*(2)*	*(3)=(4+5)*	*(4)*	*(5)=(3+4)*	*(6)= (4 / 3)*
1951	36.1	28.3	5.5	22.8	19.2
1961	43.9	34.4	10.2	24.2	29.8
1971	54.8	43.0	15.6	27.4	36.2
1981	68.4	53.6	23.4	30.2	43.6
1991	84.1	67.6	35.2	32.4	52.1
2001	102.7	86.9	56.7	30.2	65.4

Note: Population aged 7+ and literacy rates are estimated for the years 1951, 1961 and 1971 while for the years 1981, 1991 and 2001, they are actual ones.

Source: Census of India Series-1 India, Paper 1 of 1981: Provisional Population Totals, Census of India Series-1, India, Paper 1 of 1991: Provisonal Population Totals and Geeta Chaubey, Literacy in India: An Examination, *IASSI Quarterly*, Vol. 16, No. 2.

References

1. Human Development Report in South Asia 1997 – Mahabub Ul Haq.
2. National Common Minimum Programme of the Govt. of India, May 2004.
3. Documents Accompanying the Budget for 2005-06 and the Budgets for the previous years.
4. Tenth Five-Year Plan- Document Planning Commission .
5. India – Economic Development and Social Opportunity – Dreze and Sen, OUP 1995.
6. Social Sector Allocation *Economic and Political Weekly*, Vol. XL No. 14, Page 1413-1417.

Health

The Tenth Plan sets out the goals of development for the coming decade. Some of these goals are in measurable terms. As far as the social sectors are concerned, the following are the goals indicated.

(i) Reduce IMR to 45 per 1000 live births by 2007 and 28 by 2012.

(ii) Reduce MMR to 2 per 1000 live births by 2007 and 1 by 2012.

The UPA Government proposes to raise public spending on health to at least 2-3 per cent of the GDP over the next five years, with focus on primary healthcare. A national scheme for health insurance for poor families will be introduced. The UPA will step up public investment in programmes to control all communicable disease and also provide leadership to national AIDS control effort.

India's Health Record–International Comparisons

First, India's health record, relatively speaking and in an absolute sense, is extremely poor. The neglect of health is inexplicable for a country so rich in resources and so generously endowed with scientific, managerial and policy-making capacities. For example, according to the Human Development Report 2004, Bangladesh, in 2002, reported a lower Infant Mortality Rate (IMR) of 51 deaths per 1,000 than India (64 deaths per 1,000 live births) in 2002. India's IMR was much higher than the IMR for Malaysia (8), Sri Lanka (17), China (20) and Thailand (24). Similarly, India's maternal mortality ratio of 540 deaths per 1,00,000 births is many times higher than the ratio in Malaysia (41), Thailand (44), China (56) or Sri Lanka (92). Second, equity and quality considerations in health have been vastly neglected. India reports wide and persistent disparities in health outcomes. For example, according to Registrar General of India (2004), in 2002 Madhya Pradesh reported an IMR of 85 and Orissa of 87 – more than ten times higher than the IMR of 10 reported by Kerala and similar to IMR levels reported by Rwanda (87) and Gambia (91). Similarly, health disparities between rural and urban areas persist. Even in Andhra Pradesh, rural IMR (71) was more than double the IMR of 35 reported in urban areas. In Karnataka, the differential was wider: 25 in urban areas and 65 in rural areas. Abnormal gaps also exist in the IMR differentials between boys and girls. In Haryana, for instance, the female IMR was 73 as against the male IMR of 54. Health achievements among communities classified as belonging to Scheduled Castes and Scheduled Tribes tend to be consistently below national averages. Third, progress and improvements in health have been disturbingly slow and patchy. In 1970, for instance, Bangladesh reported an IMR of 145-14 per cent higher than India's IMR of 127. By 2001, the situation was reversed with Bangladesh reporting an IMR that was 20 per cent lower than India's. Many states, especially in the 1990s, have witnessed slowing down and even stagnation in health outcomes. Fourth, there have been glaring failures in the management and delivery of quality healthcare. Most of the government operated rural health sub-centres and primary healthcare centres are on the verge of total collapse.

Consequences

The consequences of the neglect of health are obvious. Ill-health today has emerged as one of the most significant factors for impoverishing people. Many especially among the poor and the aged are forced to sell their assets or incur huge loans in order to cover the costs of medical treatment and care. Often, they get exploited by unethical medical practitioners in the private sector and by indifferent health professional in the public sector. It is against this background of inadequacies and failures that we should assess the spirit and contents of the announcements for health in the budget for 2005-06.

The National Common Minimum Programme announced by the UPA government underscores the urgent need to increase the levels of public spending on health from 0.9 per cent of GDP to 2-3 per cent over the next five years. It calls for extending health insurance coverage for the poor, stepping up investments to control communicable diseases and providing leadership for the control and prevention of AIDS. In response, the prime minister has announced the setting up of a National Rural Health Mission (NRHM).

The announcement of the National Rural Health Mission and the commitment in the recent budget to increase allocations for health are necessary steps in the right direction to correct India's health record.

National Rural Health Mission–Some Features

The NRHM will strive to improve the access of rural people, especially poor women and children, to equitable, affordable, accountable and effective primary healthcare. While it will provide effective healthcare to people living in rural areas across the country, special focus will be on rural populations in 18 states with poor health achievements. The Mission will take an integrated view of health by ensuring complementarity with family welfare, sanitation and hygiene, nutrition and provisioning of safe drinking water. As a result, family planning is no longer being seen as separate and isolated programme. It is positioned within the broader context of reproductive health; and reproductive healthcare is viewed as part of an integrated, comprehensive and universal primary healthcare system. The Mission will also ensure convergence by merging all vertical programmes at the district level. The success of the NRHM is predicated on three elements: (1) ensuring adequate finances; (2) establishing a cadre of well-trained and motivated health workers; and (3) improving the managerial efficiency and accountability of the health system.

Profile, Components and Strategies

The National Common Minimum Programme spells out the commitment of the Government to enhance Budgetary Outlays for Public Health and to improve the capacity of the health system to absorb the increased outlay so as to bring all round improvement in public health services. The National Rural Health Mission (NRHM) seeks to provide effective health care to the rural population, especially the disadvantaged groups including women and children, by improving access, enabling community ownership and demand for services, strengthening public health systems for efficient service delivery, enhancing equity and accountability and promoting decentralization.

The Coverage of NRHM

The NRHM covers the entire country, with special focus on 18 states where the challenge of strengthening poor public health systems and thereby improve key health indicators is the greatest. These are Uttar Pradesh, Uttaranchal, Madhya Pradesh, Chhattisgarh, Bihar, Jharkhand, Orissa, Rajasthan, Himachal Pradesh, Jammu and Kashmir, Assam, Arunachal Pradesh, Manipur, Meghalaya, Nagaland, Mizoram, Sikkim and Tripura.

NRHM a Programme of the Government of India

The NRHM is basically a strategy for integrating ongoing vertical programmes of Health and Family Welfare and addressing issues related to the determinants of health, like sanitation, nutrition and safe drinking water. The National Rural Health Mission seeks to adopt a sector wide approach and aims at systemic reforms to enable efficiency in health service delivery. NRHM subsumes key national programmes, namely, the Reproductive and Child Health II project, (RCH II) the National Disease Control Programmes (NDCP) and the Integrated Disease Surveillance Project (IDSP).

The Strategies of the NRHM

While providing a broad framework for operationalisation, NRHM lists a set of core and supplementary strategies to meet its goals.

Core strategies of NRHM include: Decentralised village and district level health planning and management, appointment of Accredited Social Health Activist (ASHA) to facilitate access to health services, strengthening the public health service delivery infrastructure, particularly at village, primary and secondary levels, mainstreaming AYUSH, improved management capacity to organize health systems and services in public health, emphasizing evidence based planning and implementation through improved capacity and infrastructure, promoting the non-profit sector to increase social participation and community empowerment, promoting healthy behaviors and improving intersectoral convergence.

Supplementary strategies include regulation of the private sector to improve equity and reduce out of pocket expenses, foster public-private partnerships to meet national public health goals, reorienting medical education, introduction of effective risk pooling mechanisms and social insurance to raise the health security of the poor and taking full advantage of local health traditions.

Provision of Health Care to Urban Population

Under the urban component of RCH II and the National Disease Control Programmes, curative and referral interventions and other programmes for urban poor would continue as before. A Task Group on Urban Health is being constituted to recommend strategies for urban poor.

The Role of Panchayati Raj Institutions (PRI) in the NRHM

One of the core strategies of the NRHM is to empower local governments to manage, control and be accountable for public health services at various levels. The Village Health and Sanitation Committee (VHC), the standing committee of the Gram Panchayat (GP) will provide oversight of all NRHM activities at the village level and be responsible for developing the Village Health Plan with the support of the Self Help Groups. Block level Panchayat Samities will co-ordinate the work of the GP in their jurisdiction and will serve as link to the District Health Mission (DHM). The DHM will be led by the Zila Parishad and will control, guide and manage all public health institutions in the district. States will be encouraged to devolve greater powers and funds to Panchayati Raj Institutions.

Key Activities for the Year 2005-06

Broadly speaking, the common activities under NRHM, which are uniformly applicable across all States/UTs over and above those proposed under ongoing programmes like RCH and National Disease Control Programmes, are as follows:

- Constitution of State and District Health Missions.
- Merger of Health and Family Welfare Societies.
- Needs and priorities.

- Finalising performance benchmarks for MoU.
- Signing of MoU between State and GOI.
- Preparation of District Action Plans.
- Upgrading two CHCs in every district to the level of Indian Public Health Standards, including the provision for two rooms in these CHCs for bringing AYUSH practitioners under the same roof.
- Formation of Rogi Kalyan Samities.
- Immunization strengthening through induction of Auto Disabled Syringes and arrangement for alternate vaccine delivery at immunization sites.
- Organising mobile medical services at district level.
- Organising Health Camp at AWW level on a fixed day in a month for assured services for women and child health care.
- Provision of household toilets.
- Strengthening institutional delivery under Janani Suraksha Yojana (JSY) through provision of escort and referral services by ASHA and subsidized hospital services for BPL women.
- Establishing systems to increase accountability of health systems to PRIs.
- Selection and training of ASHA, including provision of drug kits.
- Organising Health Melas as a platform to inform and educate the public on NRHM.
- Provision of generic drugs at village, SC/PHC/CHC level, for common ailments.

Key Performance Benchmarks for the Year

Performance benchmarks under NRHM would include performance indicators in respect of all integrated programmes. In addition, NRHM requires the following activities to be completed in Year 1:

- Constitution of State and District Health Missions.
- Merger of Health and Family Welfare Societies.
- Signing of MoU for NRHM between State and GOI.

State of Public Health

- Public health expenditure in India has declined from 1.3 per cent of GDP in 1990 to 0.9 per cent of GDP in 1999. The Union Budgetary allocation for health is 1.3 per cent while the State's budgetary allocation is 5.5 per cent.
- Union Government contribution to public health expenditure is 15 per cent while States contribution about 85 per cent.
- Vertical Health and Family Welfare Programmes have limited synergisation at operational levels.
- Lack of community ownership of public health programmes impacts levels of efficiency, accountability and effectiveness.
- Lack of integration of sanitation, hygiene, nutrition and drinking water issues.
- There are striking regional inequalities.
- Population Stabilisation is still a challenge, especially in States with weak demographic indicators.
- Curative services favour the non-poor: for every Re.1 spent on the poorest 20 per cent population, Rs. 3 is spent on the richest quintile.
- Only 10 per cent Indians have some form of health insurance, mostly inadequate.
- Hospitalised Indians spend on an average 58 per cent of their total annual expenditure.
- Over 40 per cent of hospitalized Indians borrow heavily or sell assets to cover expenses.
- Over 25 per cent of hospitalized Indians fall below poverty line because of hospital expenses.

National Rural Health Mission – The Vision

- The National Rural Health Mission (2005-12) seeks to provide effective healthcare to rural population throughout the country with special focus on 18 states, which have weak public health indicators and/or weak infrastructure.
- These 18 States are Arunachal Pradesh, Assam, Bihar, Chhattisgarh, Himachal Pradesh, Jharkhand, Jammu and Kashmir, Manipur, Mizoram, Meghalaya, Madhya Pradesh, Nagaland, Orissa, Rajasthan, Sikkim, Tripura, Uttaranchal and Uttar Pradesh.
- The Mission is an articulation of the commitment of the Government to raise public spending on Health from 0.9 per cent of GDP to 2-3 per cent of GDP.
- It aims to undertake architectural correction of the health system to enable it to effectively handle increased allocations as promised under the National Common Minimum Programme and promote policies that strengthen public health management and service delivery in the country.
- It has as its key components provision of a female health activist in each village; a health plan prepared through a local team headed by the Health and Sanitation Committee of the Panchayat; strengthening of the rural hospital for effective curative care and made measurable and accountable to the community through Indian Public Health Standards (IPHS); and integration of vertical Health and Family Welfare Programmes and Funds for optimal utilization of funds and infrastructure and strengthening delivery of primary healthcare.
- It seeks to revitalize local health traditions and mainstream AYUSH into the public health system.
- It aims at effective integration of health concerns with determinants of health like sanitation and hygiene, nutrition and safe drinking water through a District Plan for Health.

- It seeks decentralization of programmes for district management of health.
- It seeks to address the inter-State and inter-district disparities, especially among the 18 high focus States, including unmet needs for public health infrastructure.
- It shall define time-bound goals and report publicly on their progress.
- It seeks to improve access of rural people, especially poor women and children, to equitable, affordable, accountable and effective primary healthcare.

Goals

- Reduction in Infant Mortality Rate (IMR) and Maternal Mortality Ratio (MMR).
- Universal access to public health services such as Women's health, child health, water, sanitation and hygiene, immunization and nutrition.
- Prevention and control of communicable and non-communicable diseases, including locally endemic diseases.
- Access to integrated comprehensive primary healthcare.
- Population stabilization, gender and demographic balance.
- Revitalize local health traditions and mainstream AYUSH.
- Promotion of healthy life styles.

Strategies

- Train and enhance capacity of Panchayati Raj Institutions (PRIs) to own, control and manage public health services.
- Promote access to improved healthcare at household level through the female health activist (ASHA).
- Health Plan for each village through Village Health Committee of the Panchayat.
- Strengthening sub-centre through an untied fund to enable local planning and action and more Multi Purpose Workers (MPWs).

- Strengthening existing PHCs and CHCs, and provision of 30-50 bedded CHC per lakh population for improved curative care to a normative standard (Indian Public Health Standards defining personnel, equipment and management standards).
- Preparation and Implementation of an inter-sectoral District Health Plan prepared by the District Health Mission, including drinking water, sanitation and hygiene and nutrition.
- Integrating vertical Health and Family Welfare programmes at National, State, Block and District levels.
- Technical Support to National, State and District Health Missions for Public Health Management.
- Strengthening capacities for data collection, assessment and review for evidence based planning, monitoring and supervision.
- Formulation of transparent policies for deployment and career development of human resources for health.
- Developing capacities for preventive health care at all levels for promoting healthy life styles, reduction in consumption of tobacco and alcohol etc.
- Promoting non-profit sector particularly in under served areas.

Strengthening Disease Control Programmes

- National Disease Control Programmes for Malaria, TB, Kala Azar, Filaria, Blindness and Iodine Deficiency and Integrated Disease Surveillance Programme shall be integrated under the Mission for improved programme delivery.
- New Initiatives would be launched for control of Non-Communicable Diseases.
- Disease surveillance system at village level would be strengthened.
- Supply of generic drugs (both AYUSH and Allopathic) for common ailments at village, SC, PHC/CHC level.

- Provision of a mobile medical unit at District level for improved Outreach services.

Focus on the North-Eastern States

- All 8 North-East States including Assam, Arunachal Pradesh, Manipur, Meghalaya, Mizoram, Nagaland, Sikkim and Tripura are among the States selected under the Mission, for special focus.
- Empowerment to the Mission would mean greater flexibilities for the 10 per cent committed Outlay of the Ministry of Health and Family Welfare for North-East States.
- States shall be supported for creation/upgradation of health infrastructure, increased mobility, contractual engagement and technical support under the Mission.
- Regional resource centre is being supported under NRHM for the North Eastern States.
- Funding would be available to address local health issues in a comprehensive manner, through State specific schemes and initiatives.

Role of Panchayati Raj Institutions

The Mission envisages the following roles for PRIs:

- States to indicate in their MoUs the commitment for devolution of funds, functionaries and programmes for health, to PRIs.
- The District Health Mission to be led by the Zila Parishad. The DHM will control, guide and manage all public health institutions in the district, Sub-centres, PHCs and CHCs.
- ASHAs would be selected by and be accountable to the Village Panchayat.
- The Village Health Committee of the Panchayat would prepare the Village Health Plan and promote intersectoral integration.
- Each sub-centre will have an Untied Fund for local action @ Rs.10,000 per annum. This Fund will be

deposited in a joint Bank Account of the ANM and Sarpanch and operated by the ANM, in consultation with the Village Health Committee.

- PRI involvement in Rogi Kalyan Samitis for good hospital management.
- Provision of training to members of PRIs.

Role of NGOs in the Mission

- Included in institutional arrangement at National, State and District levels, including Standing Monitoring Group for ASHA.
- Member of Task Groups.
- Provision of Training, BCC and Technical Support for ASHAs/DHM.
- Health Resource Organisations.
- Service delivery for identified population groups on select themes.
- For monitoring, evaluation and social audit.

References

1. Global Equity Initiative (2004): 'Human Resources for Health: Overcoming the Crisis', Joint Learning Initiative, Harvard University, Cambridge, Massachusetts, US.
2. Government of India (2004): 'Health Information of India 2003', Central Bureau of Health Intelligence, Directorate of Health Services, New Delhi.
3. -(2005): 'The Budget 2005-06', Speech of the Finance Minister, Ministry of Finance, New Delhi.
4. Budgeting for Health–Some Considerations–A. K. Shiva Kumar–*Economic and Political Weekly*, April 2, 2005, Pages 1391-1396.

Infrastructure

The Definitional Issue

Infrastructure is an umbrella term for many activities referred to as "social overhead capital" by such development economists as Paul Rosenstein Rodan, Ragnar Nurkse and Albert Hirschman. Neither term is precisely defined, but both encompass activities that share technical features (such as economies of scale) and economic features (such as spillovers from users to nonusers). Economic infrastructure includes services from:

Public utilities–power, telecommunications, piped water supply, sanitation and sewerage, solid waste collection and disposal, and piped gas. Public works – roads and major dam and canal works for irrigation and drainage. Other transport sectors – urban and interurban railways, urban transport, ports and waterways and airports.

The Challenge

India, the largest democracy in the world, with immense cultural riches and diverse climatic and ecological regions, faces the formidable challenge of meeting the basic requirements of one billion people, who increasingly aspire for a better quality of life. These are requirements of food and other commodities, shelter, water, health, education, energy, transportation and communication. These requirements have to be met, keeping in view aspects related to environmental protection and conservation of resources such as forests, minerals and water.

Though the country has progressed immensely over the last fifty years, the challenge posed by increasing population and the consequential strain on the countries environment, resources and infrastructure is a matter of great concern. The Infrastructure needed to meet this requirement in terms of roads, ports, airports, electricity, telecom facilities, health facilities, education facilities, oil and gas, core industry, mining and oil and gas calls for huge investments in the next decade, perhaps trillions of dollars. In power sector alone, in order to sustain a GDP growth of seven per cent, the country needs 10,000 mw of capacity addition every year. This translates into an investment of the order of US $180 billion over next 10 years and US $546 billion over next 30 years in generation and transmission projects. These investments do not include investments needed to augment capacities in fuel supply infrastructure, coal mining and supply and ports and terminals in order to sustain these generation capacities.

Meeting infrastructure requirements in one sector may not be sufficient as one area is linked to another through the supply chain that ultimately delivers electricity, water and other commodities to the consumers. These links, crucial for the growth and development of the country include, power plants, electricity transmission and distribution systems, telecommunication systems, water treatment plants, ports, roads and expressways, bridges, pipelines, railways, tracks, product handling and storage facilities (coal, oil and others) etc. In addition, there are the allied requirements of trucks, ships, tankers, tankages, terminals, jetties, barges, tank wagons, truck wagons etc.

Transportation

India has a broad network of railroad lines, the largest in Asia and the fourth largest in the world. The road system comprises of about 2.9 million km of routes. The major Indian ports, including Calcutta, Mumbai, Chennai and Visakhapatnam, are reached by cargo carriers and passenger liners operating to all parts of the world. A comprehensive network of Indian-operated air routes connects the major cities and towns of the country.

Transport Sector

Railways	63,725 km
Rail Freight Traffic	409 million tons (1996-97)
National Highways	38,445 km
Ports	11 Major, 139 Minor
Cargo Handled	227.3 million tons Major Ports (1996-97)
Air Passengers	36.49 million nos. (1996-97)

Communication

India operates one of the largest telecom networks in Asia and the 12th largest in the world. Fully automatic International Subscriber Dialing (ISD) service is available to almost all the countries. The total number of stations connected to National Subscriber Dialing (NSD) is over 13,220 and this is increasing fast. The present tele-density is about 1.72 per hundred persons. In the field of International communications, progress has been made by the use of satellite communication and submarine links.

Indian Telecom Network

Switching Capacity	21.46 Million Lines
Telephone Exchanges	223,000 Nos.
Direct Exchange Lines	17.80 Million Nos.
Satellites Earth Stations	324 Nos.

The voice and non-voice telecom services include data transmission, facsimile, mobile radio, radio paging, V-SAT and leased line services to cater to variety of needs, both residential and business. A dedicated Packet Switched Public Data Network (I-NET) with international access for computer communication services is also available. ISDN service has already been introduced in the major cities. Other services like Intelligent Network (IN), Frame Relay (FR) and asynchronous transfer mode (ATM) for wide band multimedia applications will be introduced in the near future.

Finance

The requirement of capital for setting up infrastructure, a vital need for economic growth, has compelled India, in common with the governments in the developing countries to open up their markets to global capital. However, the command economy structures, centralized planning, government control and bureaucratic systems that continue to be practiced in these countries are coming in the way of private investments.

Traditionally, the government is expected to set up infrastructure facilities for public. Large government owned companies and monopsonic utilities have been discharging this responsibility. Though in this environment, the government, to some extent, were able to bring about capacity addition in the infrastructure facilities, due to the lack of market drivers, neither could existing investments be serviced nor the incremental capacities be set up. This led to poor return on investments and poor service to the consumer.

The process of privatization in India is driven by the need of meeting the increasing demand and of mobilizing additional capital to set up the infrastructure for meeting this demand.

There are two kinds of changes that were desirable. First, the changes related to deregulation–the movement towards market place-a movement, away from government controls and towards a greater reliance on market to deliver. It has become synonymous with privatization, competition and restructuring. It includes deregulation of government controlled sectors, private sector participation, divestment of and independence to government controlled companies and restructuring, unbundling and corporatization of the utilities.

The second change is related to disciplining of the market place, rules and regulations to protect the interests of the consumers and maintaining a level playing field.

Economic Reforms

The wide ranging program of economic reforms includes abolition of industrial licensing, except for strategic industries, abolition of import licensing, deregulation of interest rates, full convertibility of the rupee on current account, automatic approval of Foreign Direct Investment (FDI) in many sectors, opening of areas previously reserved only for the public sector to the private sector, realignment of direct taxes and tariffs etc.

As a result of these far reaching changes, India is moving firmly into the front ranks of the rapidly growing Asia-Pacific economic region. The FDI flows are expected to increase to US $10 billion per year from the current average of US $3 billion. Government has decided to permit automatically Foreign Direct Investments (FDI) upto 74 per cent equity for certain infrastructure sectors and even upto 100 per cent for the power sector. FDI proposals beyond that are to be considered by the Foreign Investment Promotion Board (FIPB).

GDP Growth

The awareness of the benefits of economic reforms have gained currency among the Indian public following the achievements of macro economic stability, accompanied by accelerated economic growth. Consequently, the process of economic growth has gained national consensus.

These accomplishments are no reason for complacency, however. One billion people in the developing world still lack access to clean water and nearly 2 billion lack adequate sanitation. In rural areas especially, women and children often spend long hours fetching water. Already-inadequate transport networks are deteriorating rapidly in many countries. Electric power has yet to reach 2 billion people, and in many countries unreliable power constraints output. The demands for telecommunications to modernize production and enhance international competitiveness far outstrip existing capacity. On top of all this, population growth and urbanization are increasing the demand for infrastructure.

Coping with infrastructure's future challenges involves much more than a simple numbers game of drawing up inventories of infrastructure stocks and plotting needed investments on the basis of past patterns. It involves tackling inefficiency and waste–both in investment and in delivering services–and responding more effectively to user demand. On an average, 40 per cent of the power-generating capacity in developing countries is unavailable for production, twice the rate in the best-performing power sectors in low, middle and high-income countries. Costly investments in road construction have been wasted for lack of maintenance. The concern needs to broaden from increasing the quantity of infrastructure stocks to improving the quality of infrastructure services. Fortunately, the time is ripe for change.

Major Benefits of Infrastructure

Infrastructure can deliver major benefits in economic growth, poverty alleviation and environmental sustainability–but only when it provides services that respond to effective demand and does so efficiently. Service is the goal and the measure of development in infrastructure. Major investments have been made in infrastructure stocks, but these assets are not generating the quantity or the quality of services demanded. The costs of this waste–in forgone economic growth and lost opportunities for poverty reduction and environmental improvement–are high and unacceptable.

The causes of past poor performance and the source of improved performance lie in the incentives facing providers. To ensure efficient, responsive delivery of infrastructure services, incentives need to be changed through the application of three instruments:

- commercial management,
- competition and
- Stakeholder involvement.

The roles of government and the private sector must be transformed as well. Technological innovation and experiments with alternative ways of providing infrastructure indicate the following principles for reform:

Prescription

Manage infrastructure like a business not a bureaucracy. The provision of infrastructure needs to be conceived and run as a service industry that responds to customer demand. Poor performers typically have a confusion of objectives, little financial autonomy or financial discipline and no "bottom line" measured by customer satisfaction. The high willingness to pay for most infrastructure services, even by the poor, provides greater opportunity for user charges. Private sector involvement in management, financing or ownership will in most cases be needed to ensure a commercial orientation in infrastructure.

Introduce competition, directly if feasible, indirectly if not. Competition gives consumers choices for better meeting their demands and puts pressure on suppliers to be efficient and accountable to users. Competition can be introduced directly, by liberalizing entry into activities that have no technological barriers and indirectly, through competitive bidding for the right to provide exclusive service where natural monopoly conditions exist and by liberalizing the supply of service substitutes.

Give users and other stakeholders a strong voice and real responsibility. Where infrastructure activities involve important external effects, for good or bad, or where market discipline is insufficient to ensure accountability to users and other affected groups, governments need to address their concerns through other means. Users and other stakeholders should be represented in the planning and regulation of infrastructure services, and in some cases they should take major initiatives in design, operation and financing.

Public-private partnerships in financing hold promise. Private sector involvement in the financing of new capacity is growing. The lessons of this experience are that governments should start with simpler projects and gain experience, investors' returns should be linked to project performance and any government guarantees needed should be carefully scrutinized.

Governments will have a continuing, if change, role in infrastructure. In addition to taking steps to improve the performance of infrastructure provision under their direct control, governments are responsible for creating policy and regulatory frameworks that safeguard the interests of the poor, improve environmental conditions and coordinate cross-sectoral interactions–whether services are produced by public or private providers. Governments also are responsible for developing legal and regulatory frameworks to support private involvement in the provision of infrastructure services.

Infrastructure's Role and Record

Good infrastructure raises productivity and lowers production costs, but it has to expand fast enough to accommodate growth. The kind of infrastructure put in place also determines whether growth does all that it can to reduce poverty. Most of the poor are in rural areas and the growth of farm productivity and nonfarm rural employment is linked closely to infrastructure provision. An important ingredient in China's success with rural enterprise has been a minimum package of transport, telecommunications and power at the village level. Rural enterprises in China now employ more than 100 million people (18 per cent of the labour force) and produce more than a third of national output.

Infrastructure services that help the poor also contribute to environmental sustainability. Clean water and sanitation, nonpolluting sources of power, safe disposal of solid waste and better management of traffic in urban areas provide environmental benefits for all income groups. The urban poor often benefit most directly from good infrastructure services because the poor are concentrated in settlements subject to unsanitary conditions, hazardous emissions and accident risks. And in many rapidly growing cities, infrastructure expansion is lagging behind population growth, causing local environments to deteriorate.

In India, government owns, operate and finance nearly all infrastructure, primarily because its production characteristics and the public interest involved were thought to require monopoly-and hence government–provision. The record of success and failure in infrastructure is largely a story of government's performance. In other important respects, however, the performance has been disappointing. Infrastructure investments have often been misallocated–too much to new investment, not enough to maintenance, too much to low-priority projects, not enough to essential services. The delivery of services has been hampered by technical inefficiency and outright waste. And too few investment and delivery decisions have been attentive to meeting the varied demands of different user groups, or to the consequences for the environment. Inadequate maintenance has been an almost universal (and costly) failure of infrastructure providers. Waste and inefficiency claim a large share of resources that could be used for delivering infrastructure services.

New Opportunities and Initiatives

Creating the institutional and organizational conditions that oblige suppliers of infrastructure services to be more efficient and more responsive to the needs of users is clearly the challenge. But is it possible ? Three converging forces are opening a window of opportunity for fundamental changes in the way business is done. First, important innovations have occurred in technology and in the regulatory management of markets. Second, a consensus is emerging on a larger role for the private sector in infrastructure provision, based in part on recent experience with new initiatives. Third, greater concern now exists for environmental sustainability and for poverty reduction.

Options for the Future

To reform the provision of infrastructure services, three measures are often advocated: the wider application of commercial principles to service providers, the broader use of competition and the increased involvement of users where commercial and competitive behavior is constrained.

Applying commercial principles of operation. Involves giving service providers focused and explicit performance objectives, well-defined budgets based on revenues from users and managerial and financial autonomy – while also holding them accountable for their performance. It implies that governments should refrain from adhoc interventions in management but should provide explicit transfers, where needed, to meet social objectives such as public service obligations.

Involving users. More in project design and operation of infrastructure activities where commercial and competitive behavior is constrained provides the information needed to make suppliers more accountable to their customers. Users and other stakeholders can be involved in consultation during project planning, direct participation in operation or maintenance and monitoring.

Development programe are more successful when service users or the affected community has been involved in project formulation. User participation creates the appropriate incentives to ensure that maintenance is carried out in community-based projects.

These elements apply whether infrastructure services are provided by the public sector, the private sector, or a public-private partnership. To this extent, they are indifferent to ownership. However, numerous examples of past failures in public provision, combined with growing evidence of more efficient and user-responsive private provision, argue for a significant increase in private involvement in financing, operation and in many cases ownership.

Initiatives of UPA Government (2004-05)

- All road projects to be built on Build-Operate-Transfer (BOT) concept

- First ever container Terminal Project inaugurated at Vallapadam, Kochi
- New maritime policy has been launched
- Establishment of Rural infrastructure Fund
- Implementation of education cess of 2 per cent
- Launched National Literacy Mission
- Government commitment to interlink rivers
- FDI in Airlines from 49 per cent to 74 per cent
- Launched Rural Health Mission
- Launched Rajiv Gandhi V*iduthikaran Yojana*
- Implementing irrigation projects in Andhra Pradesh
- 100 per cent FDI in construction industry.

Reforms in the Infrastructure Sector

A certain minimum investment in infrastructure is required to achieve a sustainable level of growth. In recent years, however, infrastructural bottlenecks, particularly in the areas of highways, ports, telecommunications and power have emerged as binding constraint on the realization of the growth potential of the Indian economy. In order to alleviate the constraint, numerous sector-specific measures have been initiated since the 1990s. The government has already announced a package of financial incentives.

References

1. Infrastructure for Development – World Development Report 1994.
2. India Development Report 1991-2000.
3. RBI Annual Report 2002.
4. Rakesh Mohan Committee on Infrastructure.

8

Centrality of Agriculture in the Indian Economy

The Indian economy is largely agrarian; the importance of agriculture hardly needs emphasis. Though the contribution of agriculture and the allied sector to GDP has declined to 22 per cent, the per centage of population engaged in agriculture and allied activities continues to be 67 per cent. In view of the continued dependence of two-thirds of the population on agriculture it continues to provide a ratchet to GDP growth. Growth in other sectors is not absorbing the workforce on a significant scale. Agriculture has a multiplier effect on growth. Long-term growth of the agriculture sector is necessary to achieve self-reliance at the national level, attain household food security, generate employment opportunities, and to bring about equity in the distribution of income and wealth resulting in rapid reduction in poverty levels. Though some degree of weather-proofing has occurred from the time when Indian agriculture was described as a gamble on the monsoons, agriculture still plays a critical role in determining the macroeconomic balance, especially in generating private consumption demand necessary for growth. The Fast Moving Consumer Goods (FMCG) sector is largely dependent on a spurt in the growth of agricultural income. The linkage of the agriculture sector with the growth of the economy, makes it vital for output growth, control of inflation, price and financial stability.

Sustainable growth of agriculture is essential for the following reasons:

- To put the economy on a high growth trajectory as envisaged by the 10th plan
- To ensure self-reliance and food security
- To make agriculture more remunerative for farmers
- Agriculture is crucial for poverty alleviation both in cases of chronic and transient poverty
- It is labour intensive – a source of sustenance and livelihood in the rural areas
- It is a source of employment generation in the non-farm sector through its forward and backward linkages
- It is important for the provision of raw materials, and as a consumer of finished products and industrial machinery, etc.
- Agriculture growth has a strong spillover effect on the economy in terms of its forward and backward linkages, demand linkages and employment linkages
- The contribution of agriculture to economic growth in terms of capital transfers may decline but the sector's contribution due to higher share of non-agricultural inputs in the input structure gets progressively strengthened
- The eventual impact on poverty is far more significant than the initial impact. Reduction in prices of food grains on which the poor spend most, itself leads to containment of poverty.

The Tenth Five-year Plan projects a credit flow of Rs. 7,36,570 crore to agriculture and allied activities. The estimated actual flow of credit to agriculture from formal rural financial institutions (RFI) during the first year of the Tenth Plan (2002-03) was, however, Rs. 69,560 crore or 84.8 per cent of the projected Rs. 82,073 crore (Table-1). This was despite the extensive outreach of rural and semi-urban branch network of commercial banks (about 33,000), co-operative banks (about 1 lakh) and RRBs (about

14,000). Therefore, there is an urgent need to accelerate the flow of credit to agriculture. This is a formidable challenge.

Table 1
Agency-wise Ground Level Credit Flow for Agriculture and Allied Activities

Agency / Year	*1997-98*	*1998-99*	*1999-2000*	*2000-01*	*2001-02**	*2002-03**
Co-operative Banks	14,085	15,957	18,260	20,718	23,524	23,636
Regional Rural Banks	2,040	2,460	3,172	4,220	4,854	6,070
Commercial Banks	15,831	18,443	24,733	27,807	33,587	39,774
Other Agencies	-	-	103	82	80	80
Total	31,956	36,860	46,268	52,827	62,045	69,560

Source: NABARD Annual Report, 2002-03; * NABARD data.

Domestic scheduled commercial banks are required to meet a target of 18 per cent of net bank credit for lending to agriculture under the system of directed lending. There is a further stipulation that indirect lending should not exceed 4.5 per cent of net bank credit or one-fourth of credit target of 18 per cent, to ensure that banks concentrate on the direct advances to agriculture. Indirect finance to agriculture in excess of 4.5 per cent of net bank credit is, however, taken into account while reckoning banks' total priority sector lending.

Although most public and private sector banks did not meet this target, advances to agriculture in absolute terms have steadily increased over the years:

Banks which failed to meet the target for advances to priority sector / agriculture have contributed an amount based on their shortfall to the Rural Infrastructure Development Fund (RIDF) established with NABARD since 1995-96. The nine tranches of RIDF to date have generated an aggregate corpus of Rs 34,000 crore. RIDF is used to assist state governments in quick completion of ongoing rural infrastructure projects. Cumulative sanctions and disbursements under RIDF amounted to Rs. 34,678 crore and Rs. 21,067 crore respectively till the end of March 2004. Completion of projects under RIDF is expected to improve the credit absorption capacity in the areas concerned and provide infrastructure support for agricultural production and development.

Table 2
Outstanding Credit to Agriculture by Public and Private Sector Banks

Rs crore

	March 1994	*March 2003*	*Annual Compounded Growth Rate (per cent)*
Public sector banks			
Net bank credit	1,40,914	4,77,899	14.5
Total agri. advances outstanding	21,204	73,507	14.8
Direct agri. advances	19,256	51,799	11.6
Indirect agri. advances	1,949	21,708	30.7
Private sector banks			
Net bank credit	9,545	71,761	25.1
Total agri. advances outstanding	591	11,873	39.6
Direct agri. advances	515	5,201	29.3
Indirect agri. advances	76	6,671	64.4

The target of 18 per cent of net bank credit for lending to agriculture was introduced in 1989 and banks were required to meet it by March 1990. Agricultural credit of the entire banking system, however, has not so far reached the level of 18 per cent. Private sector banks were also asked to meet the target of 18 per cent of net bank credit for lending to agriculture in 2001 within the next two years. The time frame was extended subsequently to public sector banks. Reserve Bank advised banks to step up their priority sector lending (including agriculture) so as to reach the stipulated targets by March 2003. Table 3 shows that many banks were yet to reach the required level by March 2003.

Table 3
Number of Banks Achieving Target for Agricultural Credit

As of last reporting Friday	*Public Sector Banks*		*Private Sector Banks*	
	On target	*Off target*	*On target*	*Off target*
March 2001	4	23	1	30
March 2002	6	21	2	29
March 2003	5	22	2	27

Source: Vyas Committee.

Agriculture received indirect finance from public and private sector banks to the extent of 4.5 per cent and 8.6 per cent of their net bank credit respectively. New private sector banks have lent more (12.1 per cent) than the older ones (4.5 per cent), raising the figure for *all* private sector banks (all figures as on the last reporting Friday of March 2003).

Special Agricultural Credit Plans (SACP)

As instructed by Reserve Bank, Public sector banks have been formulating Special Agricultural Credit Plans (SACP) since 1994-95 as a means of achieving marked improvement in the flow of credit to agriculture. Under SACP, banks are required to fix for themselves targets for disbursement during a year (April-March). Reserve Bank has advised banks to fix targets that are about 20 to 25 per cent higher than the disbursement of the previous year. Under SACP, the credit to agricultural sector by public sector banks increased from Rs. 10,172 crore in 1995-96 to Rs. 33,921 crore in 2002-03.

Despite its declining share in GDP, agriculture continues to be an important sector of the Indian economy. The National Agriculture Policy 2002 envisages that agriculture growth has to exceed 4 per cent a year to attain a 7 per cent overall growth rate. Both production credit and capital formation in agriculture have to be accelerated to achieve this growth rate.

Commercial banks, co-operative banks and regional rural banks (RRBs) are the main providers of agriculture credit at present under the multi-agency approach. They have established an impressive branch network over time: about 47,000 branches of scheduled commercial banks (including RRBs) and over 1,00,000 co-operative outlets in rural and semi-urban areas. Even so, the outreach of banks has remained restricted for various reasons which is caused by a weak credit delivery structure. Large parts of states such as Orissa, Chhattisgarh, Jharkhand, Bihar, West Bengal, most of the North-east and parts of Maharashtra are handicapped by weak RRBs and co-operatives in addition to branch network of commercial banks that is below the national average. The co-operative credit structure shows weaknesses in most other states except Punjab, Haryana, Himachal Pradesh and Uttaranchal.

Table 4
Disbursement of Credit to Agriculture under SACP

(Rs crore)

Year	*Production Credit*	*Investment Credit*	*Total Direct Lending*	*Indirect Lending*	*Total Disburse ment*
1995-96	4,951	4,040	8,991	1,182	10,172
1996-97	6164	4,896	11,061	1,721	12,782
	(24.5)	(21.2)	(23.0)	(45.7)	(25.6)
1997-98	7,299	5,373	12,672	2,136	14,808
	(18.4)	(9.7)	(14.6)	(24.1)	(15.8)
1998-99	8,204	6,063	14,267	3,521	17,787
	(12.4)	(12.9)	(12.6)	(64.8)	(20.1)
1999-200	9,903	6,120	16,023	5,890	21,913
	(20.7)	(1.0)	(12.1)	(67.3)	(23.2)
2000-01	11,615	6,818	18,433	6,221	24,654
	(17.3)	(1.1)	(15.0)	(5.6)	(12.5)
2001-02	15,385	7,288	22,673	6,659	29,332
	(32.5	(6.9)	(23.0)	(7.0)	(18.0)
2002-03	18,319	7,831	26,150	7,771	33,921
	(19.1)	(7.5)	(15.3)	(16.7)	(15.6)

Source: Vyas Committee (Figures in brackets indicate year-on-year growth rates).

Though the ratio of agricultural credit to agricultural GDP increased from 5.4 per cent in the 1970s to 8.7 per cent in 2001-02, the share of agricultural credit in total credit declined from 20.5 per cent to 10.5 per cent in the period (Table 3.1). This trend seems to be going counter to the changes in agriculture mentioned earlier, which would normally be more capital and credit intensive.

Table 5
Ratio of Agricultural Credit to Agricultural GDP and Total Credit

Period	*Agricultural Credit as per cent of Agricultural GDP*	*Agricultural Credit as per cent of Total Credit*
1970s	5.4	20.5
1980s	8.3	20.1
1990s	7.4	14.4
2001-02	8.7	10.5

Source: *Handbook of Statistics on Indian Economy*, 2002-03, RBI.

Increasing Share of Commercial Banks: The flow of direct institutional credit to agriculture and allied activities increased sharply from Rs. 744 crore in 1970-71 to Rs. 9,829 crore in 1990-91, at a growth rate of 7.6 per cent a year, mainly due to the increased participation of scheduled commercial banks (SCBs) in agriculture credit after the bank nationalisation of 1969. It further increased to Rs. 41,385 crore in 2001-02. The share of co-operatives dropped to 44 per cent in 2001-02 from 98 per cent in 1971-72, although their lending increased six-fold in absolute terms, while that of SCBs rose considerably from 2 per cent to 45 per cent in this period. RRBs, in existence since 1975-76, account for 11 per cent.

The inclusion of agriculture sector under the purview of WTO have thrown up challenges and opportunities. It is expected that reduction in export subsidy and domestic support to the agriculture sector by developed countries may lead to decrease in production in these countries and will offer opportunities for expansion of Indian exports.

Table 6
Decadal Average Growth Rates of Direct Institutional Credit to Agriculture

Period	Co-operatives		RRBs		Commercial Banks		Total	
	Short-term	Long-term	Short-term	Long-term	Short-term	Long-term	Short-term	Long-term
1970s	10.6	13.9	334.8	426.8	28.2	29.9	14.5	20.2
1980s	12.5	11.0	19.8	18.5	16.3	18.6	13.9	14.8
1990s	11.9	13.1	32.7	10.6	17.8	12.1	14.6	11.9

Source: *Handbook of Statistics on Indian Economy*, 2002-03, RBI.

The Current Problems Confronting the Sector

Among the major issues confronting the agriculture sector in general, perhaps, the following can be considered as the most significant challenges, which have to be met if the objectives of sustainable and high economic growth are to be attained.

The search for realization of the full growth potential of the agriculture sector leads to an analysis of the critical factors constraining agricultural growth, as given below:

1. Decline in Public Investment in Agriculture
2. Decline in Agricultural Productivity
3. Decline in Research and Development Expenditure
4. Capital Inadequacy : Need for Credit Support from the Banks
5. Decline in Irrigation and Watershed Development
6. Minimum Support Prices, Procurement, Off-take and Buffer Stocks
7. Role of Subsidies
8. Controls on Domestic Trade

In addition, the other area of concern is the preponderance of low value agriculture leading to low cost-benefit ratio and inefficient use of natural resources.

Sustainable growth of agriculture is essential to accomplish the following objectives:

1. Put the economy on a higher growth trajectory
2. Ensure self-reliance and food security
3. Equity in distribution of income and wealth
4. Rapid reduction in poverty levels
5. Make agriculture more remunerative for farmers and raise their living standards
6. Tap global opportunities

We can ensure this through a set of technological reforms combined with an appropriate incentive structure and adequate institutional and infrastructure reforms to facilitate this shift.

9

Indian Agriculture Interests and Concerns

The growth rate in the 'nineties' so far has been distinctly lower than that in the 'eighties'. Based on all-crop Index Numbers of Agricultural Production (base: triennium ending 1981-82=100), the growth rate based on semi-log (exponential) trend averaged 3.2 per cent for the 'eighties' (1980-81 to 1989-990) and 2.4 per cent for the 'nineties, (1990-91 to 1998-99).

The index numbers for area and yield are available only till 1997-98. However, it is apparent that the decline in production in the 'nineties, is on account of stagnation in the area under cultivation of foodgrains and deceleration in yield rates in respect of both foodgrains and non-foodgrain crops. The deceleration in production is sharper in the case of foodgrains than non-foodgrain crops, mainly on account of fall in the area under the former during the 'nineties. It is plausible to infer that there has been area shift from foodgrains to non-foodgrains reflecting the change in the cropping pattern during the 'eighties' and 'nineties'. The data presented in the Table AGR.A lends credence to the area shift hypothesis.

In the 'nineties, output expansion has decelerated in the case of rice, which recorded a growth rate of 1.7 per cent based on exponential trend. Wheat production has continued to grow at a noticeable rate of 3.3 per cent per annum. The yield improvements have been lower in the case of both rice and wheat in the present decade compared to that recorded in the eighties. However, the trend growth rate in wheat output has been maintained in the nineties mainly on account of renewed expansion in the area under this crop while India has touched the international yield level in the case of wheat, the yield rate of rice being far below the world average. The coarse cereals output continued to suffer as the area under cultivation declined at a rate of 2.0 per cent per annum in the nineties. In the case of pulses, the trends of the eighties have been maintained in respect of area, production and yield in the absence of any noticeable technological breakthrough. Oilseeds production decelerated in the nineties, but still recorded a satisfactory growth rate of 3.7 per cent per annum. The expansion in area has tapered off in the case of oilseeds possibly indicating limits to the compositional shift in the face of endowment consideration. While the trend growth in the case of sugarcane is by and large maintained, there is some acceleration in the production of cotton in the nineties, mainly as the area under this crop has expanded at a remarkable rate of 3 per cent per annum, in contrast to a shrinkage in the eighties.

Rabi vis-à-vis Kharif Production

Season-wise, the exponential trend growth rate of 3.4 per cent in rabi foodgrain production witnessed in the eighties was sustained in the nineties. In fact, Rabi production could have been higher but for a decline in productivity in the nineties. Thus, the decelerated growth in foodgrain production was by and large confined to kharif crops. The kharif crops recorded an exponential trend growth rate of 0.7 per cent during the nineties as against 2.3 per cent during the eighties, reflecting, primarily, the impact of continued shrinkage in the area under cultivation.

Dantwala (1967) concluded that the price factor played only a limited role in augmenting agricultural output. What was needed was improvement in non-price factors, which included, *inter alia*, technology and rural infrastructure. The aggregate supply elasticity is observed to be generally low in the agricultural sector especially in the short run. This is attested by the development programmes launched for augmenting the production of pulses and oilseeds. Despite high rise in prices, due mainly to the gap in demand and supply, no perceptible increase in the production of pulses is recorded in the absence of technology.

There is an imperative need for technological upgradation in the agricultural sector. This gap in technology is sought to be made good through the process of economic liberalisation initiated in the early nineties.

The increase in net irrigated area during the nineties as compared to the eighties may have aided rabi cultivation of foodgrains. This has resulted in achieving a substantial growth in wheat production, which is essentially an irrigated rabi crop. However, the price factor too has played a significant role in stimulating and sustaining wheat production. The increasing share of rabi production in total foodgrains production has imparted some element of stability to agricultural production in India. This has far-reaching implications for the economy in general, since a stable and growing farm sector can contribute greatly to the overall economic stability.

Minimum Support Prices, Procurement, Off-take and Buffer Stocks

The food management policy of the Government of India has all along been to ensure food security, and the public distribution system is an important mechanism for achieving this objective. In the process, the minimum support price (MSP) and the procurement of foodgrains play a significant role. The increase in support prices had contributed to a notable build-up of stocks of foodgrains with official agencies. Stocks are substantially higher than the norms prescribed for the Ninth Five-Year Plan. The narrowing of the price differential between the PDS prices and open market prices was reflected in the sluggish rise in off-take in recent years. Many recent empirical studies also suggest that there has been a secular decline in world commodity prices in the last few years. The international price of wheat is less than the domestic price and the MSP.

The minimum support price mechanism was intended to encourage higher investment and adopt high-risk new technology as also to take care of the possible hazard of high input cost. Moreover, it is considered to be an effective instrument of changing the cropping pattern in the desired direction. However, the fixing of minimum support price has thrown up an issue, namely, whether minimum support prices of crops should be fixed on the basis of import parity price or annual cost of production, a concern expressed in the Ninth Plan document. The minimum support price could impede the international competitiveness of exportable, and cannot remain unnoticed. The question is how to evolve a viable minimum support price policy that would provide adequate incentive to the farmers without impacting on the international competitiveness of the Indian products. The issue gains in importance as agricultural exports are going to be affected.

An empirical study by Jha and Srinivasan (1999) had brought out the superiority of the option of variable levies on trade as compared with buffer stocking in stabilising prices under the liberalised trade framework. Pherhaps, this option needs careful consideration, as it is being increasingly evident that stabilisation operations involving physical handing of foodgrains are fiscally expensive (World Bank, 1999). The carrying cost of buffer stocks has been estimated to be risking at the rate of 15 per cent per annum in the 'nineties.

Structural Issues

Any discussion of the structural transformation of agriculture would need to take into account the structural rigidities emanating from Government intervention and the policy initiatives taken to improve agricultural performance. These are touched upon in the following discussions.

Controls on Domestic Trade

The State intervention in the free movement of agricultural commodities had been impacting on the functioning of domestic market. Some of the restrictions placed from time to time on the free movement of agricultural commodities are spelt out below:

- The occasional physical bottling up of marketable surplus of wheat to facilitate the procurement operations of the Food Corporation of India (FCI) through minimum support price mechanism in Punjab, Haryana and Western U.P.
- The levy price (compulsory acquisition) system for rice and sugar to enable the Government to procure

the estimated requirements to feed the public distribution system (PDS) and for buffer stocking impacted on the efficient functioning of these two markets.

- The operations of FCI and the PDS are perceived to be distorting the normal regional and seasonal variations of commodity prices and production decisions by farmers relating to both timings and locations of sales of marketable surplus especially in North-West region.
- The regulatory authorities vested with the several commodity-specific viz. The Cotton Corporation of India (CCI), the National Dairy Development Board (NDDB), the Jute Corporation of India (JCI) and the Tea, Coffee and Tobacco Boards (Pursell and Gulati, 1995).

Incentive Structure

The agriculture sector during the pre-1991 period carried biases emanating primarily from protection to industrial goods, an overvalued exchange rate and controls on exports, movement and prices of agricultural goods. The thrust of the structural policy frame put in place in mid-1991 was on industrial dilicensing, liberalising the trade and foreign exchange regimes, and providing incentives to work, save and invest. This led to emergence of 'Level Playing Filed' for the agriculture sector. For example, it took a decision to grant increases in minimum support prices so as to improve the terms of trade for the farmers.

Restrictions on External Trade

Agriculture continues to be subjected to Quantitative Restrictions (QRS).

Major Policy Initiatives

Although the country has become self-sufficient in food production, the country needs to produce larger quantities than at present to keep pace with the ever-increasing population. It is estimated by the Planning Commission that the country needs to produce about 300 million tonnes of foodgrains by 2011-12, an increase of almost 100 million tonnes in less than a decade and a half.

The slow growth rate in the 'nineties could be attributable to liberalisation of input prices such as fertilisers, diesel, high-yielding variety seeds, irrigation charges and the decline in public sector investment (Box AGR. 2).

With a view to achieving 4.5 per cent rate or growth envisaged in the Ninth Plan period, the strategy has been geared to achieving the growth rate of the 'eighties' in the commodities in which the growth rate decelerated in the 'nineties' and to further improve the growth rates which became more dynamic in the early nineties.

Reforms in Water Management, Refertilisers, Seeds Policy Reforms High Yielding Varieties Programme (HYVP), these are major policy initiatives. Further.

Credit Policy Issues

The issues relating to opening up of agricultural sector and the implementation of the Agreement on Agriculture (AOA) are being debated seriously. The AOA is expected to bring about a structural change in the world foodgrain market in favour of developing countries. While, India with large agricultural base could turn out to be a major player in the world commodity market, the decelerated growth observed in the 'nineties would be a constraint to such a possibility. Again, while India can be self-sufficient in wheat production, the same cannot be said about rice. It is important to recognise that rice is an important staple food and the demand for rice is bound to go up. Since India is competitive in respect of rice, opening up of agriculture will tilt the demand for exports in favour of rice and this may pose threat to food security in the event of any short supply in global market. However, food habits would diversify from basic cereals to value added foods in the growth process, such as fruits, vegetables, milk and milk products, altering the supply and demand prospects for foodgrains in the coming years. Therefore, to capitalise on the advantages of liberation in agriculture, concerted efforts are needed to address the issue of sustainability of agriculture, expansion of irrigated areas, better infrastructural and logistic support, and improvement in bio-technology and genetic engineering, all of which would ultimately lead to the issue of raising investment in agriculture.

In this context, it is important to work out the optimal buffer stock policy. While price stabilization, and with it the stability of farmers, income follow from buffer stocking, the cost of conducting buffer stock operations should be kept within limits, from the view point of resource allocation efficiency.

The mounting input subsidy is one issue that has emerged from the viewpoint of public finance management and the need to ensure requisite public investment to take place in agriculture. There is no doubt that drastic reduction in input subsidy would impact adversely on agriculture production, whereas the rising input subsidy is likely to crowed out public investment in agriculture. In this connection, it is pertinent to point out that the attainment of 4.5 per cent annual growth in agriculture as envisaged in Ninth Five-Year Plan hinges critically on the strategies including investments that help realise the sustainability of agricultural growth (Box AGR. 3). it is pertinent to ensure that the cost of purchase of inputs would not increase sharply so as to contain the possibility of adverse terms of trade for agriculture to emerge. Sudden withdrawal of subsidy will, on the other hand, cast an impact on the different classes of farmers. Even a small reduction in input subsidy would hurt the marginal and small farmers much more than the rich farmers. It is, therefore, imperative that a balances view on sustainability of agricultural growth is taken.

Agricultural Finance

Commensurate with the attempts to augment the performance of Indian agriculture, efforts have been made over the years to address the issues concerning agricultural credit delivery system, as credit is one of the critical inputs for agricultural production. The significant developments that have emerged in the area of rural credit include, inter alia, the following :

(a) periodic review and enhancement of credit;

(b) special emphasis on the development of rural infrastructure on account of the implication for a long term sustainable agricultural growth; and

(c) Increasing momentum toward providing access to the weakest section of the rural poor to the institutional finance via micro-financing and other initiatives.

The Reserve Bank has been taking a series of steps for providing timely and adequate credit to the rural sector through NABARD. It is stipulated for scheduled commercial banks excluding foreign banks to extend 40 per cent of net bank credit to priority sector; there is also a sub-target that 18 per cent of net bank credit should flow to agriculture.

The Institutional Credit to Agriculture

It is evident that commercial banks have emerged as the predominant source of institutional credit to agriculture with its share in the total rising from 42.9 per cent in 1991-92 to 44.0 per cent in 1994-95 and to 47.5 per cent in 1998-99.

Rural Infrastructure Development Fund (RIDF)

In view of the critical importance of rural infrastructure and the lackluster growth in agriculture investment in the past, concerns were raised about the country's ability to increase production.

The sustainability of several years now, appears to have impacted the Indian agriculture. It may possibly be argued that although the public investment had been declining, the private investment had been exhibiting sustained uptrend but a bulk of this goes to boost short-term productivity by concentrating on areas like seeds, fertilisers and mechanisation rather than long-term asset building. On the positive side, the growth impulse may enhance from faovurable terms of trade. An Binswanger (1989) says, supply response to prices takes time to develop fully, sometimes as many as ten to twenty years. In a surveyor aggregate agriculture supply response in developing economies, Schiff and Montenegro (1977) opined that prices and non-price factors were complementary rather than substitutes. In other words, a high level of irrigation and other types of public investment created infrastructures enhance the impact of prices on output and vice versa.

There is a growing perception among a class of agricultural economists that it may not be possible to sustain the accelerated growth rate witnessed in the recent past, especially in the Indo-Gangetic region, which contributed about 61 per cent of total output of rice and wheat (Table GGR.F). The results of national demonstrations conducted by ICAR have brought to focus the fact that there was vast unexplored technological potential for improvement in the yield of rice in all States and the ratio of potential to actual yield is the highest (3.5 per cent) in Bihar. The emergence of rice-wheat crop system is considered over exploitative of the nature resource base and there is consequent degradation in soil health and fertility and in water supply and quality. What is more, it is apprehended that the immediate consequence of this phenomenon is the threat to sustainability of yield of both wheat and rice emanating from the intensification of rice-wheat crop rotation.

10

Indian Agriculture in the WTO Regime

Challenges and Opportunities for Indian Agriculture in the WTO Regime

India is a founding member of the World Trade Organisation (WTO), which is entrusted with the implementation of various provisions of the General Agreement on Trade Tariff (GATT). This commits member countries to an adjustment of their domestic and trade policies to meet certain WTO obligations. The new treaty has included for the first time an "agreement on agriculture", under which members are required to undertake reforms in four principal areas: (i) market access; (ii) domestic support; (iii) export competition/subsidy; and (iv) sanitary and phyto-sanitary measures.

The long-term objective of the WTO is to put in place an architecture of governance which will facilitate a framework for free and fair market oriented agricultural trading system. The purpose of WTO is ultimately to expand world trade. The key development issues for developing countries like India, are market access, developing development-friendly rules, transition issues such as helping developing countries to export, support to developing countries to face their commitments and take advantage of opportunities.

After the September 2003 Cancun Conference, there was a complete breakdown in the talks and Stuart Harbinson, Chairman Committee on Agriculture, resigned. WTO members held round the clock meetings to produce a "historic breakthrough" and

WTO members in Geneva intensified their efforts to put the Doha development agenda of the WTO back on track. In July 2004 another meeting to discuss the new package was held under the chairmanship of the General Council Chairperson Shotaro Oshima. The WTO members broadly welcomed the first draft of the package of framework agreements when they met on 19-20th July 2004 although they had reservations about some parts of the text. The key issue of contention remains agriculture.

The entire agreement has been mired in controversies since its inception. To understand its implications, it is necessary to first grasp the three pillars which constitute the agreement on agriculture. The first is increased market access, the second is reduced domestic support through subsidies, this has become the major issue of contention more in the developed world as France and European Union than in the developing world, and the third pillar is increasing export opportunities.

The concerns in India largely relate to the prospect of a threat to food security and rural employment. There are genuine concerns about the increasing dependence of the Indian farmers on corporates which would serve to impoverish and curtail traditional rights. The controversy of patents for basmati rice and neem is a case in point. The concerns about the possible adverse impact of the new trade agreement in agriculture are understandable in a country where 2/3rd of the population is dependent on agriculture for its basic livelihood. However, a number of economists have found that the WTO agreement provides us with sufficient flexibility, India will benefit from the market access and export opportunities which the agreement offers. It is evident that there are opportunities for Indian agriculture in the world trade environment. Our basic idea is to maximize the advantages without diluting in any way our policy commitment in terms of ensuring food security. The challenges are immense. Indian agriculture needs to grow at a much faster clip than in the past. A slow down in the growth rate of production and productivity in Indian agriculture can lead to stagflationary concern in the entire economy. The Uruguay discussions brought out that agriculture is a controversial topic of discussions in the

Developed countries. Although agriculture constitutes a very small per centage of the GDP of the European countries and England and France. However, these countries especially the European Union countries have heavily subsidized their agriculture. As far as developing countries like India are concerned we have only two major issues. Firstly, we want that the tariff and non-tariff barriers should be brought down with respect to agricultural products enabling us to access the rich markets of the developed countries. Secondly, greater export opportunities along with the market access should be allowed to us. As the leader of the Indian delegation at Punta del Este expressed "trade and agriculture continues effectively to be outside the mainstream of liberalization of international trade".

Market Access

Prior to the Uruguay Round quotas and other non-tariff measures restricted imports of some of the agriculture commodities. Under the new Agreement the member countries are expected to convert the quotas and other types of measures to tariffs through the process of tariffication, i.e., abolish all non-tariff barriers such as quotas, variable levies, minimum import prices, discretionary licensing, state trading measures, voluntary restraints, etc., and convert them into an equivalent tariff. Special safeguard provisions allow the imposition of additional duties when there are either import surges above a particular level or particularly low import prices as compared to 1986-88 levels. It has also been stipulated that minimum market access equal to 3 per cent of domestic consumption in 1986-88 will have to be established for the year 1995 rising to 5 per cent at the end of implementation period.

The improvement in the Balance of Payments situation enabled India to phase out the Quantitative Restrictions (QRs) and instead impose bound tariffs. Accordingly, as on 31 March 2002 QRs on most of the agricultural items were removed.

Domestic Support

The Agreement on Agriculture (AoA) classifies domestic support into two categories: support with no or minimal distorting effects on trade often referred to as Green Box trade distorting support also referred to as Amber Box.

Green Box measures include general agriculture support policies such as basic research and development, pest and disease control, infrastructure and food security, which are exempt from any reduction commitment. It also includes direct payments to producers, for example, certain forms of "Decoupled" (from production) income support, structural adjustment assistance, direct payment under environmental programmes and under regional assistance programmes.

Amber Box measures refer to price support measures aimed at farmers. These are calculated on product-by-product basis and were to be reduced by 20 per cent in developed countries by 2000 and by 13.3 per cent in developing countries by 2004.

Blue Box measures refer to permission for certain direct payment to farmers where farmers are required to limit production, certain government assisted programmes to encourage agriculture and rural development in developing countries and other support on a small scale when compared with the total value of the product or product supported (5 per cent or less in the case of developed countries and 10 per cent or less for developing countries).

The extent of subsidies a country can extend to its farm sector is calculated through Aggregate Measure of Support (AMS). The total AMS covers all support provided on either a product specific or non-product specific basis that does not qualify for exemption. The AoA does not envisage any reduction in the level of subsidies. If the total amount on account of such subsidies is lower than 10 per cent of the total value of agricultural output during the period 1986 and 1989. The AMS is to be reduced by 20 per cent over 6 years starting from 1995 by developed countries and by 13.3 per cent over 10 years by developing countries. The least developed countries have no reduction commitments.

In the case of India the calculations for the marketing year 1995-96 show the product specific AMS figure as (-) 38.47 per cent and non-product specific AMS as 7.52 per cent of the total value of production.

Export Competition

The AoA prohibits export subsidies on agriculture products unless the subsidies are specified in a Member's Lists of

Commitments. It seeks to reduce export subsidies under two heads, in physical terms and under budgetary support. In physical terms the developed countries are required to reduce the volume of goods benefiting from export subsidies by 21 per cent and developing countries by 14 per cent. In budgetary terms export subsidies must be reduced by 36 per cent by developed continues and 24 per cent by the developing countries.

The only subsidies available to exporters of agriculture commodities are in the form of (a) exemption of export profit from income tax which is not one of the listed subsidies as the entire income from agriculture is exempt from income tax; (b) subsidies on cost of rate on export shipments of certain products like fruits, vegetables and floriculture products. In the Schedule of Commitments India has indicated that it reserves the right to take recourse to subsidies (such as Cash Compensatory Support) during the implementation period.

Trade Related Aspects of Intellectual Property Rights (TRIPS)

The Agreement on TRIPS provides for patenting of all life forms including plants and micro-organisms and requires a switch over from process patenting to product patenting. Patent protection will be available for a period of 20 years for all inventions, whether of products or processes, in almost all fields of technology.

Agreement on Sanitary and Phytosanitary Measures (SPS)

This agreement sets out the basic rules for food safety and for regulating animal and plant health standards. Measures under SPS can take a variety of forms such as requiring products to come from disease-free areas, inspection of products, specific treatment or processing of products, setting of allowable maximum levels of pesticide residues, or permitted use of only certain additives in food. SPS measures, by their very nature, involve restriction on trade and the Agreement on SPS seeks to restrict the use of unjustified SPS measures for the purpose of trade protection. The Codex Alimentarius Commission – To handle the critical issues of Food Safety and quality which often result in trade barriers. The Food and Agriculture Organisation (FAO) jointly with World Health Organisation (WHO) established the

Codex Alimentarius, which in Latin means 'food code'. Its main purpose was to establish an international food standards programme to protect the health of consumers, while at the same time ensuring fair practices in food trade. It undertakes to achieve this through:

- Harmonisation of SPS standards by requiring member countries to participate in international standard setting organizations such as Codex Alimentarius.
- Requiring members to accept the SPS standards of other countries, where they can be demonstrated to be equivalent.
- Requiring members to provide scientific evidence when applying SPS measures that are different from international standards.
- Establishing procedures for enhanced transparency in the setting up of SPS standards in the member countries.

Agriculture

While reconfirming commitment to the long-term objective referred to AA, the Ministerial declaration committed to:

"Substantial improvement in market access; reduction of, with a view to phasing out, all forms of export subsidies; and substantial reduction in trade-distorting domestic support.

Special and differential treatment for developing countries to be embodied in the Schedules of concessions and commitments and as appropriate rules and disciplines negotiated so as to be operationally effective and to enable developing countries to effectively take an account of their development needs, including food security and rural development".

Reduction in Tariffs by the Developed Countries should Work to the Advantage of India rather than its Disadvantage

With the reduction in tariffs, it should be possible to enter the markets of the developed countries as well. Obviously this will depend on identifying those agricultural commodities in which India has a comparative advantage. A systematic effort must be made in this direction so that India has a share in the fast growing "dynamic commodities" in international trade.

The agreement envisages a reduction in support to agricultural production, marketing and income. It has been stipulated that aggregate measure of support (AMS) which is an aggregation of all support measures provided by the Government should not exceed 10 per cent of the total value of the agricultural products in developing countries and five per cent in developed countries. This new measure does not in any way effect India's policy of procurement and public distribution system. Explicit clarification on this subject has been provided by the agreement.

India's aggregate measure of support comes to a negative figure because the comparison is with international prices, even though some studies have questioned the negative figure. Subsidies on the capital account are excluded from the calculations of AMS. So too are extension programmes. Procurement price support is to be measured with reference to international prices which in most cases are higher than Indian domestic prices. There are many problems connected with the methodology of estimating AMS. Nevertheless, at the present moment the new rule does not in any way affect India's policies including input subsidies. At what level input subsidies should be maintained is something that India has to decide itself.

While the three measures referred to earlier are direct provisions relating to agriculture in the WTO, the indirect measures relate to intellectual Property Rights and particularly patenting of seeds. Under the TRIPS agreement, the member countries of WTO are obliged to set up international standards of protection for their innovations. Although plants and animals other than micro organisms are exempted from patents, protection for plant varieties will have to be provided either by patents or by an effective sui generic system. A sui generic system means a system that is specifically designed to protect plant varieties.

There exists already what is known as the International Union for Protection of New Plant Varieties (UPOV) convention, seeking to protect and strengthen research in plant genetics. In the Indian context, it is felt that there should be sufficient protection for "plant back seeds" rights, since over 75 per cent of Indian farmers save seeds to replant. The Agriculture Ministry has finalized the Plant Variety and the Farmers' Rights Protection (PVFRP) Bill. The sui generic system that we evolve should be unique to our situation.

In the July Doha agenda a number of major net importing countries objected to the proposed ceilings (or "caps") on tariffs, cuts on tariffs on all products and expansions on all tariff quotas. They considered the flexibility given to protect their sensitive products to be inadequate.

On the other hand a number of developing countries complained that the more specific "comfort" given to the richer countries for their sensitive products was not matched by the vaguer flexibilities to be given to developing countries. The agriculture negotiations chair, Ambassador Tim Groser, had suggested that it would be more appropriate to negotiate the flexibilities for developing countries (under "special products" and "special safeguards mechanisms") after the developed countries' flexibilities had been settled–several developing countries said the two should not be linked.

The failure of the Cancun Ministerial Meet has put brakes on the progress of negotiations on agriculture in World Trade Organization (WTO). Lack of consensus among key WTO members in the Ministerial did not allow WTO to endorse an official 'modalities text' [1] on which Members could carry the negotiation forward. The impasse continued even after the Ministerial as WTO was forced to postpone a meeting on farm trade negotiations which was scheduled to take place on Oct 6-9, 2003. In a statement made in Geneva, Stuart Harbinson, Chairman, Committee on Agriculture (CoA) said: "in order to allow a period for reflection after the Cancún Ministerial Conference, the Special Session of the Committee on Agriculture, which was initially scheduled to take from 6 to 9 October 2003, is postponed until further notice."

Another disruption in the progress came when, during the first week of November, Stuart Harbinson resigned from the chairmanship of the WTO. It might be recalled that Harbinson was instrumental in the successful facilitation of a draft outlining a new agriculture negotiating mandate, adopted by Members in 2001 at Doha. According to Bridges Weekly, the General Council

(GC) Chair, Carlos Perez del Castillo indicated that a new chair will not be elected before 2004.

In spite of these setbacks, since mid-November, there have been some initiatives to bring the negotiations on agriculture back on track. During 20th-21st November 2003, a group of around 30 key WTO members held informal "green room" consultations on agriculture. Another discussion on agriculture was held during 15th-16th December 2003 as a part of WTO General Council meeting mandated by last September's Cancun Ministerial. During these talks, the European Union delegation asked for extension of the 'Peace-Clause' beyond 31st December 2003. The Peace Clause (Article 13 of the Agreement on Agriculture) protects countries using subsidies which comply with the agreement from being challenged under other WTO agreements. It is to be remembered that because of the protection granted by this clause, it is difficult to impose countervailing duties on subsidized imports of agricultural commodities. As mandated in the Uruguay Round Agreement on Agriculture, the peace clause is due to expire at the end of 2003. Most developing countries and countries belonging to the CAIRNS group are against the extension of this clause. Given the preponderance of subsidies in the agricultural sector of developed countries, it is not surprising that the EU is asking for an extension of this clause.

The reluctance of developed countries to cut down their subsidies became evident once again when the EU delegate refused to reveal its position on abolition of export subsidies and stated that it could not respond to this demand until it had concluded its internal consultation on the post-Cancun talks. According to Third World Network, trade diplomats are interpreting this as a sign that the EC is not yet prepared to offer a date for the elimination of export subsidies.

As far as tariff reductions on agricultural goods are concerned, a new study tabled by India in this meeting highlighted that the tariff reduction formula proposed by WTO in the draft Ministerial Declaration circulated in Cancun would hurt developing countries. It might be recalled that the so called 'Derbez text' or the second revision of the draft Cancun Ministerial Text, contained a "blended approach" to tariff reduction under market access. This approach was initially proposed in the joint submission by the US and the EU and was later adopted in the official Cancun Ministerial draft. According to this arrangement, WTO Member countries would have to reduce tariffs under three categories: first, tariff lines to be cut by an average overall per centage; second, tariff lines to be reduced more drastically under a "Swiss formula" (where the higher the tariffs, the higher are the per centage cuts); and thirdly, some tariffs to be reduced to zero or near zero.

To estimate the likely outcome of this approach, India presented a simulation based study, using estimates based on tariff profiles of developed and developing countries. The results of this study show that under the aforementioned methodology, developing countries would have to undertake significantly deeper tariff reductions than developed countries. The study suggests that because the blended formula is linked to each country's tariff structure, given the difference in tariff profiles of different countries, the application of the same or a similar formula would have different impacts on different countries. The study estimates that the developed countries would have to make an approximate cut of about 30 per cent under the blended formula. However, for developing countries, tariff reduction obligation would be between 30 per cent to 70 per cent, depending on their respective tariff profiles.

Given the disconcerting conclusions of the study, India appealed to the WTO Secretariat to undertake a more detailed simulation based study to estimate the impact of the blended formula based tariff reduction schedule on each WTO Member country. Though most developing countries supported this call by India, some developed countries, were not happy with the suggestion of carrying out the simulation studies. After the General Council Meeting, Carlos Perez del Castillo conceded that "the blended approach" in the Derbez text has been the "subject of concerns by a number of developing countries" and that further work is needed on "this or other formulas".

Apart from these developments, a noteworthy feature of post-Cancun negotiations is that the Derbez Text, which faced strong opposition from developing countries during the Cancun

Ministerial, is slowly gaining some acceptance among key WTO Members. For example, at a recent summit of the Asian-Pacific Economic Cooperation (APEC) in Bangkok, the 21 APEC Members, including the US, Japan, China and Australia had agreed "to build on Chair Derbez's text of 13 September". Also, during the General Council meeting of WTO, Brazil, a prominent member of the G-21 group, was of the opinion that the Derbez text could be a starting point for the discussions. However, Brazil also pointed out that much work in many areas of the text needs to be done. According to Brazil, the provision for special and differential treatment in the Derbez text is inadequate and it has to be significantly revamped. It also criticized the text by pointing out that on the issue of domestic support, the Derbez text is extremely lenient as it allows developed countries to continue with trade distorting domestic subsidies. According to Brazil, the Derbez text should include prohibitions against shifting of subsidies from amber to blue to green boxes.

But some members, such as India, have expressed serious objections about the Derbez text being accepted as the only basis for further agriculture trade talks. According to reports published in the *Bridges Weekly* newsletter, the Indian Ambassador to WTO K.M. Chandrasekhar has indicated that India would prefer a hybrid approach under which various "positive" elements from different texts, such as the Harbinson draft modalities and the various drafts Cancun Ministerial declarations would be combined.

Apart from these developments there was no major breakthrough in the negotiations after the Cancun ministerial. In most major issues countries stuck their positions expressed during the Cancun ministerial and there were hardly any movements forward. The Chairman of the General Council, told journalists after the meeting: "There was no negotiating mood. There is the persistence of difficulty on the big issues. The positive thing is that discussions went on. But there is no basis for any new text at this stage."

Some New Developments in 2004

In 2004, there seems to be a renewed interest about resuming the multilateral trade talks. In a letter dated 11th January

2004, US Trade Representative Robert Zoellick has urged members of the World Trade Organization to restart the Doha round trade talks. In this letter, Zoellick emphasizes that the focus of the renewed multilateral talks should be on the key areas of interest and recognizes "that an ambitious result in agriculture is essential for this negotiation to proceed and succeed". To outline USA's current position on some key areas of negotiations on agriculture, he points out that:

1. USA demands total abolition of export subsidies in agriculture by a certain date. According to Zoellick, as export subsidies are most trade distorting measures, final elimination of these subsidies is going to be the biggest step forward for the negotiations on agriculture. Along with total abolition of export subsidies, he also proposes to eliminate the subsidy component of export credit programe and to discipline the special privileges of State Trading Enterprises.
2. Regarding domestic subsidies, the letter suggests that amber box subsidies should be reduced substantially. Zoellick also proposes that there should be a cap on blue box subsidies. The US trade representative has not talked about imposing any cap on green box subsidies. It can be mentioned here that a significant proportion of subsidies given to the farmers in USA are given either through the Green Box measures or through the export credit route. It is not surprising that imposing stricter disciplines on these measures have been underplayed or sidestepped in Zoellick's proposals.
3. About market access for agricultural products, the letter indicates that the USA is not averse towards a 'blended approach' (an approach which will be a blend of Swiss formula and the Uruguay Round type linear tariff reduction formula) provided some conditions are met. He puts forward three conditions, they are: (a) the tariff reduction formula should create substantial market access both in developed and developing countries, (b) there should be an in-built provision to cap on tariff peaks and (c) there should be a common tariff reduction formula for all WTO Member countries.

It is notable from this communication that USA is against the suggestion that there should be different tariff reduction formulas for developed and developing countries.

The response from EU to Zoellick's letter was on predictable lines. In their speeches at Strasbourg on 13th January, both Franz Fischler and Pascal Lamy said that EU is willing to accept a framework for negotiating modalities only if : (a) amber box subsidies are disciplined more than blue box subsidies and (b) all forms of export support must be disciplined. These responses are no different from the stance taken by the European Union since the current round of negotiations started in 2000. The responses of other prominent WTO members are still awaited, but it appears that in spite of the recent initiative of the US Trade representative to "explore every avenue to make 2004 not a lost year, but a year of accomplishment for the Doha Agenda and the WTO", negotiating positions are not moving any closer towards convergence than they were after the Cancun Ministerial meet.

The developing countries' key issues in the Doha agenda are market access in agriculture and special safeguards for their farmers, resolving the remaining problem in TRIPS and health, SDT, market access to textiles, and labour movement in services.

Opinion on the timing and the pace of liberalization and its likely implications is sharply divided. Those who support liberalization of agricultural trade argue that India has a strong comparative advantage in agriculture over most of the developed world and the WTO-induced trade liberalization has made agricultural exports more attractive and remunerative. This advantage is said to be strong in the case of high value crops such as fruits, floriculture products and vegetables, basmati rice, and cotton. Opening up trade in these crops has already shown that there is considerable potential to promote export of such crops. On the other hand, those opposing globalization of Indian agriculture assert that liberalization of agricultural trade would destabilize prices and expose Indian markets to violent fluctuations in the international market. It is also feared that liberalization of agricultural exports would change the crop pattern away from food, and result in steep hikes in foodgrain prices which would jeopardize the food security of vulnerable sections of the population. One-third of the country's population is below the poverty line and cannot afford to buy adequate food grains even under existing price structures.

Thus, in conclusion we find that globalization in trade and investment through harmonization of national laws will be the major impact of the WTO. The contribution of knowledge as a factor of production is being increasingly given central importance in economic development. The Indian strategy to make the most of WTO aims at making efforts to ensure that Indian agriculture becomes not only globally more competitive but also domestically more progressive by using knowledge as a strategic resource so that agriculture sustains the livelihood of millions of poor households dependent upon it in an environmentally sustainable manner. As it stands today the WTO agreement will not come in the way of our public policies to enhance the productivity of our agriculture or to ensure food security which continues to be our over riding goal. Maintenance of our public distribution system is also not effected. In sum WTO presents immense opportunity for the development of Indian agriculture.

Reference

Dr. Deepali Pant Joshi – *CAB Calling Journal* – October-December 2004, Vol. 28, No. 4.

11

Rythu Bazars–Learning from Andhra Pradesh

The Rythu Bazar of Andhra Pradesh presents an interesting model and represents successful intervention by the State. Rythu Bazars have been an immense success and benefits have accrued to both consumers and farmers who interface through them.

These Bazars were first established in 1999, outside the purview of the Agricultural Market Committees, managed by Estate Officers under the control of Joint District Collectors. About 97 Rythu Bazars are functioning in Andhra Pradesh. They were envisaged to provide better marketing avenues for the quick sale of perishable agricultural produce as also to help bridge the gap between farmers producers and consumers.

Andhra Pradesh is the second largest producer of fruits vegetables and flowers in the country. The absence of market yards and proper infrastructure promoted inefficiencies in markets and led to conspicuous losses through poor handling and a lack of storage facilities. Estimated losses in the handling of fruits and vegetables were around 35 per cent through the traditional marketing channels. Much to the dissatisfaction of the producer and the consumer the traditional marketing system failed to emerge as a equitable medium for commodity exchange. Farmers complained of non-remunerative pricing, exorbitant commission charges and lack of facilities consumers remain unhappy with the inferior quality, high prices and weighment malpractices. Small farmers are not able to bargain for better prices in the wholesale markets. Inefficiency in these markets results in problems of multiple handling, loss in quality and gap in producer and consumer prices. The proliferation of retailers each handling increasingly small quantities leads to an increase in the Overheads leading to high margins on produce. This also isolates small retailers who are denied the benefits which arise from the economies of scale which flow naturally from large-scale marketing. Sadly, the provision of marketing facilities for agricultural commodities in urban areas has not moved in tandem with urbanisation. As a consequence farmers who live in the villages which surround the urban settlements commute regularly to urban centres to market their produce, leading to ad hoc and unorganised marketing and also to frequent distress sales. The Rythu Bazars are controlled markets to redress these deficiencies. They have succeeded in ensuring remunerative prices to the farmers and providing fresh vegetables to the consumers on a daily basis, facilitated prompt realisation of sale proceeds to farmers without any deductions, curbed rampant malpractices, by providing vegetables with correct weighment to the consumer. Most importantly they have succeeded in providing a direct interface between the farmers and consumers – eliminating intermediaries from the system. Farmers from a cluster of 10-15 predominantly vegetable growing villages willing to participate in the Bazar are identified by the Horticulture department. Each Rythu Bazar ensures the provision of certain minimum facilities- Adequate number of sheds for farmers to store and sell their produce, adequate arrangements for storage of unsold produce including refrigeration facilities like the Zero Energy Cool chambers, Provision of tamper proof weighing scales for all farmers, arrangements for periodic removal of garbage and regular cleaning of the market. A sanitised atmosphere and high cleanliness are maintained in the Bazar. maintenance of cleanliness and sanitary conditions are entrusted either to an SHG, a local body or outsourced to a private agency and is paid for through income generated by auction of parking space, market canteen and lease of private nurseries Rythu Bazars are located on Government owned land identified by the district collectors who identify a location convenient and easily accessible for both farmers and consumers. The criteria for setting up of a Rythu Bazar are the availability of at least one acre of land in a strategic location and the identification of 250 vegetable growing farmers, willing to participate in the Bazar. Critical to the success of the Rythu Bazar are the establishment of marketing linkages between the buyers and sellers. Farmers are identified by a three man team comprising the Agriculture Officer, Market Research Officer and Horticulture consultant. They finalise and publish a schedule of visits to the neighbouring villages. They have a farmer wise, village wise, mandal wise inventory for the variety and quantity of the different vegetables sold in the Rythu Bazar. On their visits to the villages they convene meetings with vegetable growing farmers, the farmers are briefed about the advantages of the Rythu Bazars. They are encouraged to go in for cooperative marketing. They are given seeds at subsidised prices. The horticulture consultant also provides expertise to farmers towards the production of off season vegetables and holds training sessions for the vegetable growers. In meetings the farmers are told about the provision of horticultural services, seed supply at subsidised rates transportation arrangements pricing mechanisms and the elimination of middlemen in order to motivate them to come forward. After the meeting the three member team visits the village, the fields of the farmers wiling to join and issues them photo identity cards on the spot. Within a week of issue these are replaced by laminated identity cards. The cards have pertinent details as the name of the farmer, his postal address extent of land under cultivation type of vegetables cultivated photograph of the farmer as also of the group members these are attested by the Horticulture Officer. Tenant farmers are also eligible for identity cards on field verification. Farmers are split up into groups which are allowed to self select their members. Each group can send one or more of its members by rotation for sale of produce in the Rythu Bazar. The benefits extended to self help groups are extended to these groups. The Joint District Collectors ensure adequate transport arrangements for the farmers to and from the Bazar in consultation with the Andhra Pradesh Road Transport Corporation after ascertaining the specific requirements from the Estate Officer and the Farmers. The estate Officers are appointed on a monthly contract basis they are paid Rs. 4000 per month and are responsible for daily allotment of space, space is allotted on a first come first served basis and on rotation. To prevent monopolies no farmer is allowed to occupy the same shop continuously and nor can shops e reserved by retaining stock overnight. The estate officer is actually responsible for the entire upkeep and maintenance of the Bazar. He also ensures the formation of Price fixation Committees, the actual fixation of prices and ensures that sales take place at the prices fixed he provides weighing scales to farmers on a daily basis and collects them in the evening. For price fixation every day's wholesale market and retail prices are collected and prices in between the two, the wholesale and the retail prices are fixes. The price differential between the wholesale market and the retail outlets in perishables is sometimes nearly double. In the retail market the consumer suffers high prices. To combat these variations the system of price fixation has been devised in the Rythu Bazars. If the prices in the Rythu Bazar are higher than the local market rate there is no incentive to the consumer and if the prices fixed are lower than the wholesale market rates, there is no incentive to the farmer. Keeping this in view, the prices are generally 25 per cent above the wholesale price and 25 per cent below the retail prices. Networking among Rythu bazaars enables the fixation of realistic prices and also helps farmers and SHGs to take advantage of the prevailing prices in different markets. The Rythu Bazars are fully equipped with communication facilities. Telephone, fax and computers are provided in all Rythu Bazars. Each Rythu Bazar has a computer operator cum assistant on a consolidated salary of Rs 2500 per month and the price data are completely computerised. The estate Officer furnishes daily reports of transactions in the Rythu Bazar weekly and fortnightly reports on prescribed proforma are also submitted. The Joint District Collector conducts periodic meetings with the Estate Officers, farmers and consumers to assess the needs and concerns of the Producer/ seller arrangements. They also hold weekly meetings with the estate officer and inspect at least one rythu bazar each week and monitor its performance over time. This also leads to better coordination between Departments of Agriculture, Horticulture, Revenue, Marketing and Transport for improved functioning of the Rythu Bazar. About 97 Rythu Bazars are functioning where approximately one lakh quintals of vegetables are sold per week, benefiting nearly six thousand farmers the total turnover of vegetables and other essential commodities is about 7.5 crore per week. Rythu Bazars represent a successful direct marketing innovation. They have brought about a direct interface between the consumer and producer eliminating the middlemen, improving margins and assuring better prices, while the producers of perishable goods around the cities and urban towns are able to get the benefit of direct selling to the consumers. Rythu Bazars have, therefore, increased the returns to producers, while ensuring the provision of vegetables fruits to the consumers at economical prices. A win-win situation in sum for all the stakeholders Infrastructure efficient management market intelligence and support have made these Bazars viable for the farmers State Governments of the adjoining states of Orissa and Tamilnadu are trying to replicate the successes of the Rythu Bazar in Andhra Pradesh. The concept of the Rythu Bazar evolved and successfully innovated by Andhra Pradesh serves as a viable easily replicable model across the country for the establishment of a alternate market structure of benefit both to producers and consumers which by promoting the interests of both greatly optimises the efficiency of markets.

Reference

Dr. Deepali Pant Joshi–CAB Calling–April-June 2004.

12

Neeru Meeru–Water and You

In terms of assets, land and water rights are obviously the most critical for the rural poor and perhaps the most difficult to alter. Yet in recent years new approaches have been forged for agrarian reform using collaborative, sometimes market-based approaches that often involve Civil Society in the realm of participatory Public Policy. Competition for water is already emerging as a source of tension between groups, states, communities. Access to water in the coming years will be even more problematic. Greater resources and new technologies will have to be mobilised together with the direct involvement of the poor farmers, to bring about more equitable and sustainable solutions to the complex issues of water use and water stress. Human capital and the capacity to work are among the most important assets the poor possess. Unfortunately, past deprivation has often left them inadequately equipped with the skills required to adapt to modern technologies and markets. Enhancing these skills and building the human capital of the poor is particularly important, as it has a positive externality in terms of their economic productivity. The basic issue is the need to enable the poor to exercise a stronger role in both official and non-official institutions that affect their lives, especially at the local level.

The Andhra experience with water users associations has shown that progress in decentralisation and devolution of authority to local institutions is useful when poor groups are efficiently organised to take part effectively in such institutions. Water is vital to most production. Water is also vital to consumption. Low quality and quantity drinking water harms health and indirectly productivity, largely among poor rural communities these have least water security in production and consumption partly for want of water yielding assets (taps/wells). Hence they have less, worse or more unreliable water than others and women of poorer communities have to go long distances to fetch water. Water is the greatest scarce resource which we need to conserve with care. It is water which sustains all life forms. Industry, economy, the common people, people need water for livelihood water is also the most easily expended resource. One which is coming under severe stress due to the growth of population. Peoples participation is necessary for the success of all efforts recognising this AP has launched the "Neeru -Meeru Programe literally translated it means "water and you". The A.P. Government has created a state led Water Conservation Mission since May 2000. A prioritisation of areas has been undertaken and the mandals which suffer greater water stress have first been taken up for attention.(The mandals in Category -1 are those with water levels > 20 m, category 2, water levels 15-20 m, Category 3, water levels 10-15 m. Category 4, water levels 5 to 10 m and category 5 water level, 5 m. The identification is done by the ground water department.) In addition to this habitations which experience scarcity of drinking water and villages located in high water stress mandals are given greater attention. Neeru-Meeru helps harvest rain water to improve ground water discharge. What marks out the programe distinctively is the high level of peoples mobilisation and involvement which it has created. Neeru Meeru works are taken up by the water users associations, SHGs, *Samithis*, and groups of people mainly these are, building chains of tanks to link the existing tanks to harvest the surplus flow of one tank into the linked tank by developing feeder channels and strengthening tanks, Building sunken pits, check dams to revive flow in rivulets, creating Diversion Weirs, building sub surface dykes and utilise the abandoned dried up wells by diverting water to the wells from the farmers own lands for recharge of the dried up wells. The groups are all involved in this effort Vana Samrakshana Samithis, Water Users Associations, Yuva Shakthi, SHG and DWCRA (Development of Women and Children in the Rural Areas). To further encourage and facilitate the peoples participation, the Government has set up committees at state, district, constituency, municipal mandal and Gram Panchayat levels which co-opt NGOs and members from the Water Users associations. Forest, Rural Development, Minor Irrigation and Water departments represent the involvement of the Government machinery in this process. Its success however can be attributed largely peoples initiatives.

Andhra Pradesh also has a "water conservation mission" its objectives are to develop a clear vision and strategy for water conservation and its sustainable utilisation, ensure promotion of cost-effective measures for water conservation and utilisation in the state. Innovations have been readily adapted by the people simplified procedures have been devised to enable "water audit" at village level which can enable the taking of judicious decisions. This programe has contributed to increase in ground water levels and enhancement of productivity. Andhra Pradesh is the first state in the country which has piloted a forward looking Act. The Andhra Pradesh Water, Land and Trees Act 2002. The main objectives are to promote water conservation and tree cover and to regulate the exploitation and use of ground and surface water for protection and conservation of water resources. Water is becoming scarcer and less reliable with increasing pressure of population ground water tables are falling. Water subsidies are steered to thirsty crops and to the rich, who control most of the water yielding assets. Thus, given the importance of water resources and control for the rural poor, every effort is being made to enhance the amount, efficiency and poverty impact of water and water resources. In the ensuing decades water constraints will tighten due to increasing urbanisation and perhaps climate change. Water Users Associations are important so also drainage, breeding water economising crops. Focussing water benefits on the rural poor which involves getting water assets to them and saving water by asset choices that use labour specially in the slack season as against capital Complementary policies should aim to save farm water by labour using methods, and to shift control over water and water yielding assets to the rural poor. The poor can gain more from water or water yielding assets by either redistribution or improved efficiency, overall efficiency of water use in agriculture is low increasing efficiency means reducing spillage, leakage, infiltration, evaporation, clogging of water with weeds, failures of drainage and impediments to water and aquifer recharge through mistimed or mislocated irrigation or drainage. In A.P. public works with slack season labour help in irrigation and drainage maintenance. Water Users Associations promote efficiency also in the use of water which leads to more water for the poor. This is also advanced by better integration between water and crop research, extension and delivery systems. The poor are also helped to invest in their own wells, pumps and so on, with credit, technical assistance, input distribution extension and provision of hydrological data. The WUA of A.P. have made ownership of irrigation equipment feasible for even the landless .Water Users associations have members which may be few or many but are generally found to be close and homogenous. The institutional arrangements can be local and quick and women are generally able to participate to a larger extent They help to keep water yielding assets especially degraded large scale public irrigation systems well managed, responsive to users and sustainable. Meeru Neeru helps to use technology appropriate to the service level demanded by a community and practicable to operate, maintain and repair with locally available energy. Recognising the critical importance of water and giving due centrality to peoples efforts. Meeru Neeru programe has created appropriate institutions and incentives for all stakeholders, enabling the state "Water Safety Net" to act effectively. The A.P. State has shown the way as a successful model worthy of emulation.

13

Gender Concerns

Sociological Perspective on Women

Women account for 407.8 million (including girl children) as per the 1991 census and constitute 48.1 per cent of the country's total population. Depending upon the developmental needs of the individual age groups, the entire female population has been categorized into five distinct sub-groups:

1. Girl children in the age-group 0-14 years, who account for 153.85 million (37.8 per cent) and deserve special attention because of the gender bias and discrimination they suffer from such a tender age;
2. Adolescent girls in the age group 15-18 years, who account for 38.70 million (9.5 per cent) and are very sensitive from the viewpoint of planning because of the preparatory stage for their future productive and reproductive roles in the family and society;
3. Women in the reproductive age group of 15-44 years, numbering 183.67 million (45.1 per cent) who need special care and attention on account of their reproductive needs;
4. Women in the economically active age group of 15-59 years, who account for 226.04 million (55.5 per cent) and have different needs like those of education/training, employment, income generation and participation in the developmental process, decision making etc; and
5. Elderly women in the age group 60+, numbering 27.17 million (6.7 per cent) who have limited needs mainly relating to health, emotional and financial support.

When we consider upliftment of women through design and delivery systems of credit we are essentially limiting ourselves to the fourth category, i.e., to half of the population of women, i.e., 226.04 million economically active human beings. From the economy's point of view it becomes imperative not to neglect this tremendous human resource and to bring them in the economic mainstream.

The focus is also on women in the unorganized sector who remain invisible. For almost three decades the Self-Employment Women's Association (SEWA) has helped organize women's cooperatives to agitate for their rights in the unorganized labour sector, where around 94 per cent of India's female labour is placed, for promoting the organisation of women to demand better pay and working conditions.

The principles of gender equality, equity and protection of women's rights have been the prime concerns in Indian thinking right from the days of Independence. This is reflected in the Constitution of India and various developmental policies initiated in this country.

While Article 14 confers equal rights and opportunities on men and women in the political, economic and social spheres, Article 15 prohibits discrimination against any citizen on the grounds of sex, religion, race, caste etc; and Article 15(3) empowers the State to take affirmative action and positive discrimination in favour of women.

Similarly, Article 16 provides for equality of opportunities in the matter of public appointments for all citizens. Article 39 explains further that the State shall direct its policy towards providing to men and women equally the right to means of livelihood and equal pay for equal work.

Article 42 directs the State to make provisions for ensuring just and humane conditions of work and maternity relief.

Article 51(A)(e) imposes a fundamental duty on every citizen to renounce the practices derogatory to the dignity of women. To make this de-jure equality into a de-facto one, special legislations have been enacted from time to time in support of women.

The Current Situation

Developmental policies and programmes, both in the women-specific and women-related sector, put into action through various Five Year Plans, have brought forth a perceptible improvement in the socio-economic status of women in the country.

The following paragraphs give an account of important achievements in the core sectors of health and demography, education, employment, decision-making, political participation, etc.

Health and Demography

Expectation of life at birth for females has risen steadily from 31.7 years in 1951 to 59.7 years in 1989-93 and finally overtaken the male life expectancy of 59.0 years during the same period, as detailed in Table 13.1.

Table 13.1
Life Expectancy at Birth (in years)

Year	*Female*	*Male*
1951	31.7	32.5
1961	40.6	48.9
1971	44.7	46.4
1981-85	55.7	55.4
1987-91*	58.6	58.1
1989-93*	59.7	59.0

* Based on the Sample Registration System (SRS) Estimates.
* *Source: Census of India*, 1991– Final Population Totals Paper 2 of 1992, Government of India, New Delhi, 1993.

In the year 1996 female life expectancy was 62.1 years, which shows considerable improvement since the year 1951 when it was 31.7 years.

Similarly, the Mean Age at Marriage for females has also increased from 15.6 years in 1951 to 18.3 years in 1981, while the effective age at marriage stood at 19.4 years in 1995.

The Child Marriage Restraint Act of 1976, which raised the age of marriage for girls from 15 to 18 years, has helped prevent child/early marriages amongst girls and the consequent early pregnancies and birth of premature babies.

Acquiring higher/continuing education and greater employment by women has also played a role in raising their age at marriage as per the details given in Table 13.2.

Table 13.2
Mean Age at Marriage during 1951-1995 (in years)

Year	*Female*	*Male*
1951	15.6	19.9
1961	15.5	21.3
1971	17.2	22.4
1981	18.3	23.3
1991	19.5*	N.A
1995	19.4*	N.A

* Mean age at effective marriage.

Source: Sample Registration System (SRS)–Fertility and Mortality Indicators for respective years, Registrar General of India, New Delhi.

Further, while the Crude Birth Rate (CBR) has declined from 40.8 in 1951 to 27.5 in 1996, the Crude Death Rate (CDR) has gone down from 15.6 in 1970 to 8.9 in 1996.

Similarly, the Total Fertility Rate (TFR) has also declined from about 6 in the early 1960's to 3.5 in 1994.

Yet it remains that the average Indian woman bears her first child before she is 22 years old, and has little control over her own fertility and reproductive health

The maternal mortality that stood at a very high rate of 437 per one-lakh live births in 1993, as per the National Health and Family Survey, is a matter of great concern.

This high rate of maternal mortality is attributable to the following major causes, as indicated in Table 13.3, which are both treatable/preventable through effective health and nutrition interventions:

Table 13.3
Percentage Distribution of Cause–Specific Maternal Deaths–1995

Cause	*Percentage*
Bleeding of Pregnancy and Puerperium	28.9
Abortion	17.6
Anaemia	17.0
Toxaemia	9.9
Puerperium Sepsis	8.5
Malposition of Child	4.0
Non Classifiable	14.1

Source: Survey of Causes of Death (Rural), India and Annual Report (1995), Office of the Registrar General of India, New Delhi.

Indian women spend 16 years of their life in pregnancy or lactation, deliver 6 children out of which 4 survive. Maternal mortality accounts for 2.5 per cent of all female deaths in India, and 12.5 per cent of deaths of rural women between the ages of 15-45.

As is evident from the table, the highest numbers of maternal deaths in 1995 were due to bleeding during pregnancy and Puerperium, which are preventable through better reproductive health care.

Abortion which is the second highest accounted for 17.6 per cent of total maternal deaths in 1995, although abortion was legalized as early as in 1972 as a health measure through the Medical Termination of Pregnancy (MTP) Act, 1971, still illegal abortions continue to be performed by unauthorized persons and untrained persons under unhygienic and unsafe conditions because of the non-availability of MTP services within the easy reach of most of the rural population.

The Sex Ratio, which illustrates the survival ratio of women, has been exceptionally unfavourable to women, besides being on a declining trend right from the beginning of this century, except for a marginal rise in 1951 and 1981. The sex ratio, which was 946 females per 1000 males in 1951, has declined further to 927 in 1991, as shown in Table 13.4.

Table 13.4
Sex Ratio (1951–1991)

Year	Sex Ratio
1951	946
1961	941
1971	930
1981	934
1991	927

Source: *Census of India, 1991* – Final Population. Totals. Paper 2 of 1992, GOI, New Delhi, 1993.

Thus there are far fewer women than men in the country. These missing women were either aborted before they were born, or they died before reaching adulthood. The majority of these deaths occurred from easily preventable diseases.

Literacy and Education

Literacy and education are the most essential inputs for empowerment of women. The gains in the women's education, has been reflected in the increase of female literacy rate from 7.9 per cent in 1951 to 39.3 per cent in 1991.

Though the gains in the educational status of women have been impressive, gender justice in education still continues to be a distant goal, with 60.7 per cent of women being illiterate.

Table 13.5
Literacy Rates (1951–1991)

Year	Female	Male
1951	7.9	27.16
1961	15.34	40.40
1971	21.97	45.95
1981	29.85	56.50
1991	39.3	64.13

Source: Census of India of respective years; Office of the Registrar General of India, GOI.

The enrolment of girls at the primary level has also increased from 5.4 million in 1950-51 to 47.9 million (provisional) in 1996-

97, representing a nine-fold increase. Correspondingly, the enrolment of girls at the middle level has also increased from 0.5 million to 16.3 million and at the higher secondary level from 0.2 million to 9.8 million, indicating an increase by more than 32 times and 49 times, respectively during the same period.

Similarly, the number of women/girls in the higher education, which includes colleges, universities, professional colleges of Engineering, Medicine and Technology, has also increased from 13.60 lakh (33.2 per cent) in 1990 to 21.39 lakh (35.5 per cent) in 1997, as per the details given in Table 13.6.

Table 13.6

Enrolment of Girls at Graduate/Post Graduate/ Professional Courses during 1990-91 and 1996-97

(Figures in lakhs)

	1990-91		*1996-97*	
Levels	Girls	Total	Girls	Total
Graduate (B.A./B.Sc/B.Com)	11.40 (34.7)	32.87	18.20 (37.4)	48.72
Post Graduate (M.A./M.Sc/M.Com)	1.16 (32.8)	3.54	1.65 (30.5)	5.41
B.ED./B.T.	0.40 (44.2)	0.92	0.50 (43.1)	1.16
B.E./B.Sc(Eng.) B. Arch.	0.26 (10.9)	2.41	0.49 (14.9)	3.28
M.B.B.S.	0.28 (34.3)	0.84	0.43 (35.4)	1.21
Ph.D./D.Sc./D.Phil.	0.10 (26.2)	0.33	0.12 (29.2)	0.41
Total	13.60 (33.2)	40.91	21.39 (35.5)	60.19

Note: Figures within the parenthesis indicate per centage to total.

Source: Selected Educational Statistics–1990-91 and 1996-97, Dept. of Education.

The drop-out rates, which have a direct bearing on the school retention rates, have also shown a definite declining trend both in the case of boys and girls at all levels of school education during the last decade 1986 to 1996.

However, the dropout rates in the case of girls have always remained higher than those of boys. This is because even when girls are enrolled in schools, fewer girls than boys manage to stay in school for a full ten years. In 1991 the overall dropout rates for boys were 59.00 per cent whereas in the case of girls it was 68.00 per cent. Most of these girls are working in the homes and fields of either their parental or marital families.

Work and Employment

According to the 1991 Census, the female Work Participation Rate (WPR) registered an increase from 14.2 per cent in 1971 to 22.3 per cent in 1991. But, at the same time, it was much lower than the male work participation rate with both urban and rural differentials and with much wider regional variations ranging from as high as 34 per cent to as low as 4 per cent amongst the major States.

Data on the Work Participation Rate is given as per Table 13.7.

Table 13.7
Work Participation Rates (1971–1991)

Years	*T/R/U*	*Females*	*Males*	*Persons*
1971	Total	14.22	52.75	34.17
	Rural	5.92	53.78	35.33
	Urban	7.18	48.88	29.61
1981	Total	19.67	52.62	36.70
	Rural	23.06	53.77	38.79
	Urban	8.31	49.06	29.99
1991	Total	22.27	51.61	37.50
	Rural	26.79	52.58	40.09
	Urban	9.19	48.92	30.16

Note: 1. Excludes Assam and J & K.

2. 1971 figures are totals of workers and non-workers with secondary work whereas 1981 and 1991 figures are totals of main and marginal workers.

Source: *Census of India*, Series-I, Registrar General of India, New Delhi.

The Table 13.8 attempts to give the distribution of women work force in the organized and unorganized sectors in comparison to their male counterparts:

Table 13.8
Labour Force in the Organised and Unorganised Sectors in 1991

(Figures in Millions)

Sector	*Female*		*Male*		*Total*	
	Actual	*per cent*	*Actual*	*per cent*	*Actual*	*per cent*
Organised	3.78	4.2	22.95	10.2	26.73	8.5
Unorganised	85.99	95.8	201.41	89.8	287.40	91.5
Total	89.77	100.00	224.36	100.0	314.13	100.0

Note: Computed based on the Census data and of the DGE & T, GOI, New Delhi.

Of the total women workforce of 89.77 million (28.6 per cent) in 1991, their share in the organized sector is only 4.2 per cent, while the rest of the 95.8 per cent are in the unorganized sector where wages are lower and there are no legislative safeguards even to claim either minimum or equal wages along with their male counterparts, leave aside the other benefits that the women in the organized sector enjoy.

Invisibility of Work

Women's work is undervalued and unrecognized. Women work longer hours than men, and carry the major share of household and community work that is unpaid and invisible. A woman's economic activities are invariably related to family occupations like agriculture, animal husbandry, forestry, weaving, construction labour, and cottage industries. Thus, women's personal contribution gets merged with the family and becomes invisible. Even when she gets wages, which are generally low, she is at best seen as providing supplementary income to the family. The reality, however, is that women's income is used for the survival needs of the family. Domestic chores are arduous and unrecognized.

The Table 13.9 gives the occupational break-up of women both in the rural as well as the urban areas.

Table 13.9
Distribution of Main Workers by Industrial Category, 1991

Total / Rural / Urban	*Industrial Category*	*Percent Main Workers*		
		Persons	*Males*	*Females*
Total	Cultivation	38.7	39.9	34.6
	Agricultural labour	26.1	20.8	44.2
	Livestock, Forestry, Fishing, Hunting and Plantations, Orchards and allied activities	2.1	2.1	2.1
	Mining and quarrying	0.6	0.7	0.3
	Manufacturing, Processing, Servicing and Repairs in Household Industry	2.4	2.1	3.5
	Manufacturing, Processing, Servicing and Repairs in Non-household Industry	7.6	8.8	3.8
	Construction	1.9	2.3	0.7
	Trade and Commerce	7.4	9.0	2.2
	Transport, Storage and Communications	2.8	3.5	0.3
	Other services	10.3	10.8	8.3
Rural	Cultivation	48.4	51.6	38.9
	Agricultural labour	31.6	26.0	48.5
	Livestock, Forestry, Fishing, Hunting and Plantations, Orchards and allied activities	2.2	2.3	2.1
	Mining and quarrying	0.5	0.5	0.3
	Manufacturing, Processing, Servicing and Repairs in Household Industry	2.2	1.9	2.9
	Manufacturing, Processing, Servicing and Repairs in Non-household Industry	3.6	4.0	2.3
	Construction	1.0	1.3	0.3
	Trade and Commerce	3.3	4.0	1.1
	Transport, Storage and Communications	1.2	1.6	0.1
	Other services	6.0	6.8	3.5

Cont....

Total / Rural / Urban	Industrial Category	Percent Main Workers		
		Persons	Females	Males
Urban	Cultivation	4.9	4.9	5.1
	Agricultural labour	6.7	5.4	15.5
	Livestock, Forestry, Fishing, Hunting and Plantations, Orchards and allied activities	1.7	1.8	1.5
	Mining and quarrying	1.1	1.2	0.7
	Manufacturing, Processing, Servicing and Repairs in Household Industry	3.1	2.5	7.5
	Manufacturing, Processing, Servicing and Repairs in Non-household Industry	21.9	23.1	14.1
	Construction	5.1	5.3	3.3
	Trade and Commerce	22.0	23.8	10.0
	Transport, Storage and Communications	8.3	9.2	2.0
	Other services	25.1	22.8	40.4

Source: Table C-1, Census of India 1991 Industrial Category, Part IIB–Primary Census Abstract.

Census 1991 reveals that 34.6 per cent rural women are cultivators, 44.2 per cent fall in the category of agricultural labourers and 1.2 per cent are engaged in livestock, forestry, fisheries and other allied activities. Only 20.8 per cent of men are engaged as agricultural labour in the rural areas where majority of women work force is deployed it is necessary to introduce women friendly technology. Hence any technological innovations would lead to more displacement of women than men. A wide disparity can also be seen in trade and commerce where only 2.2 per cent of women are engaged as against 9.0 per cent of men. 3.5 per cent women were working in the manufacturing, processing, servicing and repairs in household industry as against 2.4 per cent of men. The situation however gets reversed in the non-household industry where only 3.8 per cent women are involved as against 8.8 per cent of men.

In the urban areas a noticeable feature is that nearly 40 per cent of women are engaged in other services whereas only 22 per cent of men are working here.

Representation of women in the government account for only 13.7 per cent, their representation at the decision-making levels through the three Premier Services in the country viz. Indian Administrative Service (IAS), Indian Police Service (IPS) and Indian Foreign Service (IFS) has accounted for only 5.8 per cent in 1987. Although, the same has been increased marginally to 7.5 in 1997, yet it stood at a very low ebb as per the data given below, requiring both affirmative action and special interventions to help raise the number of women at various decision-making levels.

Table 13.10
Representation of Women in Premier Services (1987-1997)

Service	*1987*			*1997*		
	Total	*Female*	*per cent*	*Total*	*Female*	*per cent*
IAS	4204	339	7.5	4991	512	10.2
IPS	2418	21	0.9	3045	67	2.2
IFS	480	53	10.0	575	71	12.3
Total	**7102**	**413**	**5.8**	**8611**	**650**	**7.5**

Source: Ministry of Home Affairs; Ministry of External Affairs: Department of Personnel, GOI, New Delhi.

The problem of unemployment, especially amongst the educated women, has become a matter of great concern in the recent past. The rate of unemployment amongst urban females which stood at 5.4 per cent in 1990-91 has become very significant when compared to 0.4 per cent amongst rural females during the same year. The same trend is visible even in the National Sample Survey Organisation (NSSO) data based on the current weekly status of unemployment, which stood at 5.3 per cent for urban females and 2.1 per cent for rural females in 1990-91. While the number of women on the Live Registers of Employment Exchanges has increased from 5.5 million in 1988 to 8.4 million in 1996, the educated unemployed women (Matriculates and above) in 1992 stood at 5.4 million.

The landmark achievement of both 73rd and 74th Constitutional Amendments in 1993 brought forth a definite impact on the participation of women in the grass-root democracy through the Panchayati Raj Institutions (PRIs) and Local Bodies. In the recent elections of PRIs held during 1993-95, women have achieved participation even beyond the mandatory requirement of 1/3rd of total seats in States like West Bengal (35.1 per cent), Kerala (36.4 per cent) and Karnataka (43.4 per cent). In fact, these amendments are expected to achieve effective participation of women in grass-root democratic institutions and its processes, both as individuals and as representatives of interest groups.

In the State Legislative Assemblies, although the number of women has increased from 102 (2.5 per cent) in 1977 to 162 (3.9 per cent) in 1997, the same stands at a very low ebb. Similarly, the number of women in the Lok Sabha has also increased from 22 (4.4 per cent) in 1952 to 41 (7.5 per cent) in 1998 as shown in Table 13.11, but the same continued to be very low.

Table 13.11
Representation of Women in Parliament (1952–1998)

Year	*Lok Sabha*		*Year*	*Rajya Sabha*	
	Females	*Males*		*Females*	*Males*
1952	22	475	1952	15	201
1980	28	514	1984	24	209
1991	39	486	1990	24	221
1996*	39	501	1996	19	219
1998	41	543	1998	18	218

* Provision as on 20.8.1996.

Source: Election Commission of India.

The status quo, referred to above, can only change when women's concerns gain political prominence and a fairly representative number of women are in position not only at grass-roots level, but also at the state and national levels to convert them into a political will. This calls for affirmative action on the part of the Government.

Violence against women, both domestic and at work place, continues its existence as is evident from the increasing incidence of rape, dowry-related cruelty and murders.

As per the data published by the National Crimes Record Bureau, New Delhi, out of the total 1,15,723 cases related to women and registered under IPC in 1996, rape accounted for 14,846 (12.8 per cent), dowry deaths 5513 (4.8 per cent) and cases of torture 35,246 (30.5 per cent).

The visual media has also not played a very positive role as it continues with gender stereotyping thereby making these stereotypes deeply enmeshed in the Indian psyche. This, in fact, has been rendering invisibility to many aspects of women's contribution to society. Media needs to be used more positively to project women.

References

1. *Census of India 1991.*
2. Census of India of respective years: Office of the Registrar General of India.
3. Selected Educational Statistics – 1990-91, Department of Education, GOI.
4. Ministry of Home Affairs, Ministry of External Affairs, Dept. of Personnel, GOI.
5. Election Commission of India Statistics.

14

Empowerment of Women: Its Dimensions

Introduction

The concept of empowerment has to be studied in a broader perspective. Empowerment means not only economic empowerment but also social as well as political dimensions. Empowerment of women refers to women gaining an increased access to financial, natural and intellectual resources. It means women acquiring the confidence, knowledge, information and skills to understand and intervene in economic, social and political structures and processes and gives them the authority to take decisions in matters which affect them, as well as the nation. It enables access to information which in turn leads to the making of informed choices.

Gender: The Concept

Empowerment and disempowerment in India is related to access and constraints to access. Also in Indian society access - who gets what - is closely related to gender. In fact the question of access is fundamental to the social construction of gender. This is due to the gender differences that are made to exist in the society.

The term "gender" is used to describe a set of qualities and behaviour expected from men and women by their societies. A person's social identity is formed by these expectations. These expectations stem from the idea that certain qualities, behaviour, characteristics, needs and roles are 'natural' for men, while certain other qualities and roles are 'natural' for women. As Simon de Beauvoir in the opening sentence of her path-breaking work 'The Second Sex' declared "One is not born, one becomes a women through a gradual process of socialization and acceptance of societal norms".

Gender is not biological – girls and boys are not born knowing how they should look, dress, speak, behave, think or react. Their "gendered" masculine and feminine identities are constructed through the process of socialization, which prepares them for the social roles they are expected to play. These social roles and expectations differ from culture to culture and at different periods in history. They can and do change.

Gender relations in India (as everywhere else) are patriarchal – that is, they reflect and perpetuate a hierarchy where women are subordinate to men. Women's subordination is reflected in inequality and differences between women and men within the family and community, as well as in all social, economic, cultural and political interactions and relationships between people.

Patriarchy makes women powerless in many ways – by convincing them of their own inferiority to men; by limiting their access to resources and by restricting their opportunities to participate in decisions, which affect their own lives.

These different forms of control buttress each other in reinforcing hierarchical structures and have resulted in the exclusion and marginalization of women from social, economic, and political processes. Women's subordination is reflected both in women's socio-economic condition (like their levels of health, income and education), as well as in their position, or degree of autonomy and control over their own lives.

To examine the gender differences it is necessary to start with the biological differences. Women bear children and in general are a little smaller than men. Society subjects these differences into cultural constructions that have social and economic consequences.

First, there is a Strong Inside-outside Dichotomy

Part of the cultural definition of the 'female' in India is her association with what Lakshmi Holmstorm terms the 'Inner

Courtyard'. In myth and legend women are associated with the mystique of the inner courtyard, the inside, the home and courtyard where the family is cared for. This is in contrast to males who belong outside in the field and the bazaar where livelihoods are earned and economic and political power is transacted. Since education, health care, and labour force participation all involve interaction with the "outside", girls and women face special barriers in these areas.

The definition of the "inside" and the precise boundaries of where a woman can operate vary greatly according to the economic status of the household, its place in the caste hierarchy and the social norms prevailing in their community and region. These boundaries vary for the same woman at different stages of her life. The mapping of the inside and the outside for each individual woman is therefore subject to change, and hence the definition of certain spaces as "inside" is really a conceptual rather than a physical matter.

Thus the fact that women bear children is interpreted to mean that women belong inside the four walls of the home. Purdah (female seclusion) is one manifestation of this. In India Purdah is observed in certain communities such as high caste Rajputs and certain Muslim groups; Haryana and Rajsthan/ Hyderabad lead the group with 75 and 60 per cent of women observing (Purdah) veil in the family.

In general thus women get associated with the household and the family, whereas men are associated with markets, politics, and everything else outside the household. Women's access to information, economic resources, capacities, opportunities, therefore, are all mediated and limited by men.

Second, Smaller Physical Stature can be Linked with Gender Violence

The economic and political invisibility of women caused by the inside-outside dichotomy creates vulnerability for women. Violence then can be seen as the ultimate enforcer of gender-based social exclusion.

All this leads to much weaker bargaining power for women. How societies construct the meaning of differences between men and women obviously has huge consequences for the welfare of women, children and although this has yet to be proved, the welfare of society, including men. A country would want to move from the equilibrium of inefficient economic situations in which these physical differences are reinforced by society as disadvantages to cultural constructions that interpret female and male roles in ways that don't lead to disparities. Responsibility for children doesn't mean blocked access mediated by a benevolent dictator. Smaller physical stature doesn't mean vulnerability to violence. The Autonomy Index shows that most women since have no independent access to their money, have no say in financial decision making of the family's access to health or education and also in savings decisions.

Here we should try and build a critical understanding of the causes and processes of disempowerment.

Sources of Women's Disempowerment

Marriage and kinship systems

The key elements of patrilineal system–patrilocal residence, patrilineal inheritance, a gender division of labour and norms of female seclusion–affect women to varying degrees. In all patrilineal communities women face restrictions on where they can live and whether they can inherit property. Typically women leave their parental home at the time of marriage to join their husband in his home and return to their parental home or move to a third locale only under dire circumstances. And typically very few women inherit land from their husbands or still fewer from their fathers. The net result of this patrilineal system is a structured dependence of women on men: that is, women are conditioned to be economically and socially dependent on male kin and have limited direct independent access to resources and markets.

Household and Extended Family

Within their own marriages and their immediate families, many women have limited power to bargain for their rightful share of property, maintenance, healthcare, or even food and to resist beatings (and other forms of maltreatment) by their husbands.

Within their husband's extended family women have even less bargaining power.

Patron-client Relationship

Many low-income women depend on– and thereby get locked into client relationships with– local patrons: wealthier residents of their village or slum who provide them with employment (for low wages), loans (with high interest), advice and arbitration (often in the patrons interest), or political protection (in return for political support). Women are often particularly dependent on patrons for access to credit and employment because they lack direct independent access to formal financial and labour markets.

Community Groups and Local Councils

Most community groups and local councils are dominated by the local male elite. Unfamiliar with the law or with their rights as citizens, the women often lack voice and representation in local institutions. As a result the women often rely on these groups for advice or counsel, for arbitration of local conflicts, for representing their grievances or demands to local government and for extracting goods and services form government. However, many times these local elites are themselves are often the sources of local corruption or exploitation.

Wider Economy and Markets

In the wider economy or markets, women face other forms of unequal poor relations. Women often have limited direct access to employment or economic opportunities outside the home due to norms of female seclusion and dependency. Because they do not own property to offer as collateral, women have limited access to loans from formal financial institutions and are charged particularly high interest rates in the informal financial markets. Another feature of the informal financial market is that what is generally pawned to pawnbrokers is what is seen as women's property: namely jewellery and utensils.

Further many labour markets are segmented along gender lines so that women who work outside their homes are often in the lowest paid and most insecure jobs. In Madras, women (and children) comprise the lowest rung in the hierarchy of construction workers: both female and child labour are called *chitals* (small persons). If women try to move up the hierarchy (to take up more skilled jobs), they face resistance and harassment by male masons and by the male trade unionists: both the masonry subcontracting system and the construction workers' union are male dominated.

We thus get a picture of the various contexts, roles and relationships in which women lack power. To help us understand this complexity, the sources of women's disempowerment are presented in a table form:

Table 14.1

Sources of Women's Disempowerment[3]

	Women-Intensive	*Women-Exclusive*
Social	Dependence on elite	Dependence on male kin
	Dowry	Divorce or desertion
	Poor housing	Patrilocal residence
	Poor infrastructure	Gender division of labour
	Class violence	Gender violence
	Social isolation	Norms of seclusion
		Limited bargaining power/mobility
Political	Lack of consciousness	
	Lack of representation	
	Lack of organisation	
	Lack of voting rights	
	Limited bargaining power	
	Anti-poor politics	Male-biased policies
Economic	Limited asset base	
	Limited access to resources	
	Limited employment	Male-biased recruitment
	High interest loans	Limited access to loans
	Indebtedness	
	Limited bargaining power	
	Imperfect markets	Gender-stratified markets
	Unfair or high prices	
	Environmental degradation	
	Exploitation	Gender exploitation

These sources have been divided into two broad categories.

- First, there are those which arise because women are members of low income households, or disadvantaged groups but which women, because of their gender, experience more intensely than the men of those same households or groups: what we have called *women-intensive* sources.
- Second, there are sources, which arise primarily because of women's gender or, in other words, because of gender stratification rather than other forms of stratification (such as caste or class): what we have called *women-exclusive* sources.

Within these categories, the reported sources of women's lack of power have been grouped according to whether they arise in the social, political and economic spheres of women's lives. Of course, none of the compartments in this matrix is watertight or mutually exclusive.

In summary, the lack of power of low-income women arises from a conjunction of two primary systems of stratification–*class and gender*-, which intersect with, and mutually reinforce, one another through local, social, political and economic institutions.

A third axis of stratification is also quite pronounced: namely, *social status* as institutional class systems among Hindu communities and parallel social class systems in other communities.

The Major Aspects of Empowerment can be explained as follows:

Economic Empowerment

Economic empowerment can be defined as 'economic change/ material gain plus increased bargaining power and/or structural change which enables women to secure economic gains on an on-going and sustained basis'.

The following are the constituents of economic empowerment:

- Financial interventions (increased access to credit)
- Enterprise development (increase access to skills/ business/management training and improved technologies/production packages)

- Marketing strategies (increased access to markets)
- Bargaining (for higher wages/better working conditions/job security)

Economic Empowerment

It is the starting point in the upliftment of women. In order to bring about an economic change in the lives of women it is essential to provide them with the financial access as well as access to other backward and forward linkages. A holistic approach is necessary to bring about a change and sustain it. Improved access to credit can help raise the productivity and incomes of women entrepreneurs.

Social Empowerment

This refers to factors regarding women which lead to improvement in their status. Such factors are education, health, nutrition, housing and shelter, environment, violence against women, hygiene and sanitation etc., these factors required to be improved significantly to improve the status of women. Economic empowerment is meaningless without social empowerment.

Political Empowerment

In order to achieve emancipation of women in the true sense then political awakening of a woman is essential. Only when she is represented in the policy making and at decision taking level then she will be influence the formulation of policies and programmes for women. In India, several measures have been taken to achieve this. There is a 33 per cent reservation at the Panchayat Raj institutional level. Unfortunately the Women's Reservation Bill has been mired in controversies ever since it has been tabled and any further action has got political overtones.

Hence, we can say that economic empowerment is a necessary condition for the upliftment of women but not a sufficient one. Emancipation of women is complete only when a holistic concept of empowerment is achieved.

References

1. Lynn Bennett, Social Development Sector Unit, South Asia Gender and Development Workshop–April 2, 1998 (Gender and the Household).

2. Carr, Chen, Jhabvala, *Speaking Out: Women's Economic Empowerment in South Asia,* Vistaar Publications, 1998.
3. Lycette and White, 1989; Ardener and Burman eds., 1995.
4. World Bank Discussion Papers (117) "Developing Financial Institutions for the Poor and Reducing Barriers to Access for Women", Sharon L. Holt and Helena Ribe.

15
Credit for Women

Credit plays an important role in the upliftment of women. Credit however is not a panacea and is likely to remain debt if it is not supported by markets and infrastructure. Thus a holistic approach is required to empower women economically.

Women when provided with financial services would have access to more capital at lesser cost (low interest) than before. Women when provided with inputs, training, and technology would result in women having better quality inputs at lower costs and improved skills and knowledge, which in several cases leads to, improved productivity.

The net result would be that women members enjoy higher net profits from their enterprises; profits which can be used for consumption, savings and investment.

Any developmental programme that is directed towards upliftment of women must relate to the special nature of women's work and their specific credit needs. Only then women would be able to make full use of the opportunities extended to them.

Women's Access to Credit

Women have been facing problems in reaching out to the formal banking system for credit. Credit to women has the following dimensions:

Timeliness of Credit

Credit should be made available when it is required by women. Most women entrepreneurs require credit chiefly for working capital purposes. If the credit is not available at the onset of the working capital cycle then the business and production would get seriously affected.

Adequacy of Credit

What women want is adequate credit and not necessarily subsidized credit. Adequacy of credit thus assumes grave importance. Women are more than willing to pay relatively high interest rates for adequate access to credit.

Credit Needs of Women

Women require credit for a variety of purposes. Depending on the level of income and the occupation that they are involved in, their credit needs differ.

Minimalist Credit Needs

These are the needs of women who are below the poverty line. Their requirement of credit is for survival only. Credit given to such women is utilized primarily for consumption purposes. This is one deterrent for financial institutions to lend to poor women, since if credit is utilized for consumption then the problem of repayment arises.

Repayment Needs

Besides consumption needs, women also require credit for repayment purposes. When a poor woman approaches financial institution for credit she is already heavily in debt with the informal credit lending system such as the moneylenders. Hence the credit is utilized for repaying the earlier debt. This is a reality that no financial institution can ignore.

Entrepreneurial Needs

Credit is also required by women for their entrepreneurial development. Credit is primarily given to women so that they engage in income generating activities, which can be sustained on a long-term basis. In fact credit is the basis on which a productive venture can take off. Entrepreneurial needs consist of the following:

- The initial set up cost
- Capacity building needs

- Day-to-day working capital requirements

The policies of government as well as the initiatives taken by other institutions aim to fulfill this basic entrepreneurial credit need of women. Even though consumption needs and repayment needs are a reality that no financial institution can ignore, due to the fungibility of funds in the household these needs lose their criticality. The credit that is given to the woman gets utilized partly for consumption and repayment purposes and partly for entrepreneurial purposes. In this way the funds are fungible in the sense that women borrowers may use the loan to meet immediate debt payment or consumption needs and yet still manage to organize the resources needed to invest in a productive activity that enables them to make timely repayments. As long as the household's financial management permits repayment, the actual use of the loan may not be important.

Women however face several constraints in access to credit. These constraints are as follows:

The factors, which act, as constraints to the access of credit for women are both of supply and demand.

On the Supply Side

High transaction costs and controlled high interest rates generally inhibit poor women's access.

High transaction costs are largely the result of the high unit costs of administering small loans to a highly dispersed and possibly illiterate clientele and the increased risks that arise because poor women lack collateral and a formal credit history. Few banks are set to handle the additional constraints associated with small-scale lending.

These disincentives are aggravated by government *regulation of interest rates,* which leads to the rationing of credit. Rationed credit tends to go to those with wealth and influence–not poor women. Formal lenders have strong incentives to favour larger, more accessible clients.

On the Demand Side

Poor people's access to formal credit has been constrained by

- Collateral requirements,
- High borrower transaction costs,
- The limited education that makes application procedures difficult,
- Social and cultural barriers, and
- The nature of their work.

These constraints– some of which are strictly gender-related– are worse for women.

Collateral Requirements

Women have particular trouble meeting this requirement. Property and other assets that can be used to meet collateral requirements are usually in a man's name. In India traditions severely impede women's ability to become titleholders of land and other assets. Also states like Uttar Pradesh and Gujarat have statues that prevent women from inheriting agricultural land.

And types of valuables to which women have access are often deemed unacceptable by formal financial institutions.

This includes women's small-scale businesses that do not have the documentation of formally registered enterprises, and valuables such as jewellery that are often accepted by moneylenders and pawn brokers but rarely by formal banks.

Borrower Transaction Costs

The non-interest costs of acquiring formal loans can be substantial. The total borrowing costs for small women borrowers generally exceed nominal interest payments. These costs include transportation costs, bribes, legal and title fees, paper work expenses, time lost waiting in line, and dealing with these demands. Also costs increase when formal loans are not disbursed quickly. Thus the non-interest costs contain the opportunity costs in terms loss of a days work that a women borrower has to incur every time she visits the bank.

Education Limitations

Poor women have a relatively low level of literacy and numeracy, which make it difficult for them to overcome even the procedural barriers of taking out a formal loan. Poor women's higher illiteracy rate than poor men's, and their general lack of experience in public and contractual transactions make it difficult for them to deal with formal credit services. As a result, many poor women have trouble completing the complicated application forms and financial statements that banks require. And their limited experience with formal credit institutions adds to the problem.

Social and Cultural Barriers

Social and cultural constraints may also restrict women's demand for, and access to credit. In many areas it is considered inappropriate for a woman to travel alone the long distance between her rural home and a bank in a town, or to offer the occasionally necessary bribe to a male official in charge of credit application. More, importantly, women are commonly excluded from local organisations that provide information or extend credit.

The Types of Business Women Engage in Affect their Access to Credit to a Certain Extent

First, because women have limited access to physical and human resources, their businesses tend to be among the smallest and have low profit margins. Their concentration in smaller, lower profit activities makes women bigger credit risks for commercial lenders.

Second, women tend to keep their businesses close to their home to minimize conflict between their multiple roles as wage earner, mother, homemaker, and so on. These multiple responsibilities restrict the time and mobility of the women. Hence women are generally unable to pursue long distance wholesale trade. Because of these constraints on their mobility and time access to credit becomes a problem.

Institutional Framework of Credit Delivery

Informal sources of finance. This is the most common source of credit for women. A key element of the informal sources is the low transaction costs. Transaction costs are lower because

- The informal financial agents know their clients better than formal banks, which reduces their cost of information.
- Their administrative and staff overhead is lower.
- Also their interest rates are not regulated so they can adjust to market changes.
- And they are not subjected to reserve requirements.

At their best the informal sources of credit have a number of potential advantages:

- Low transaction costs due to proximity of borrower and lender;
- Immediacy of loan disbursement;
- Willingness to extend small loans;
- Flexible repayment schedules and minimal and flexible collateral requirements because of familiarity of borrower and lender.

Women commonly use a range of informal credit sources:

Moneylenders and Pawn Brokers

They are usually familiar to the borrowers being the loan traders, or landowners. Loans are given with less or no collateral and there is flexibility of repayment. However the rate of interest charged is extremely high. Pawn brokers are specially attractive to poor women because they take jewellery, ornaments or gold as collateral. However informal lenders rarely accept deposits or provide long term loans. Also exploitation is a serious threat to women.

Friends, Relatives and Shopkeepers

Women tend to rely heavily on friends, relatives for both emergencies and routine borrowing needs. Women rely on them more for trustworthiness and safety than for proximity or convenience. Interest is seldom explicitly charged and repayment is generally according to situation of the borrowers. However relatives and friends are limited as sources of finance.

Rotating Savings and Credit Societies (ROSCAS)

These associations provide savings-based credit to low income/ middle-income women. ROSCA is based on the following basic principle: the members contribute a fixed amount into a pool and the total amounts are distributed to each member at fixed intervals on a rotating basis. For the first member to receive the funds, the money can be considered as a loan, whereas for the last it is more a matter of receiving savings. ROSCA's usually have a fairly homogeneous composition. Their membership is small, the result of self-selection, and based on mutual trust, which minimizes the risks involved. ROSCAs however have difficulty meeting members' needs when loans are synchronized as they are, for example, at the beginning of agricultural production cycles. Nor do they typically pay interest. In India, such ROSCAs are very commonly observed in states like Kerala, Karnataka, Tamil Nadu, etc.

Informal sources even though very convenient thus have a number of disadvantages for poor women

- Moneylenders and pawnbrokers give credit to women, often using jewellery as security – but poor women are less likely to have even jewellery.
- Rates of interest from moneylenders and pawnbrokers on unsecured or "risky" loans are generally higher than secured loans.
- They are isolated from larger markets, which curtails lenders' access to funds and reduces competition.
- They also have limited ability to provide term finance and large loans, or to mobilise savings.

And it has been argued that as long as women rely on informal markets they will remain outside the economic mainstream.

Formal Sources of Credit

Formal sources of finance are generally regulated by the government or/and the Central Bank. The advantages of formal finance lie in scale. Large systems tend to gather relatively small deposits from households and others in their hinterlands, which they lend to firms in relatively larger amounts in money centres, facilitating investment. They provide a large bundle of services, minimizing transaction costs and creating economically rational interest rates over time and space.

However as we consider the nature of micro credit extended to poor women the situation changes considerably.

Formal finance has *low interest rates and "high" transaction costs*. Interest rates are low because large reservoirs of household savings are effectively tapped and risk management is mastered to a high degree. Transaction costs are high because of the nature of large systems and because of structural factors that are often heavily influenced by government policy.

An important source of transaction costs is the gathering and processing of information required to screen loan applicants who are not known to lenders. Borrowers have to be monitored and extensive documentation is required. Specialised, skilled staffs are also required. The transaction costs of deposit-taking are also important. These include part of the cost of branch networks, maintaining and managing large amounts of noninterest-earning cash, and record keeping.

The costs of putting a Rs.100, a Rs.1000, a Rs.10,000 and a Rs.1,00,000 loan on the books are not greatly different. This prompts lenders to favour larger borrowers. This is the reason why poor women as borrowers do not constitute a priority. Borrowers also incur transaction costs in applying for loans. Information must be provided, documents must be obtained, and time and effort expended. For large borrowers the transaction costs of formal loans are trivial, while for small women borrowers taking very small loans they are large. Poor women are additionally discouraged from obtaining formal credit because transaction costs of applying for credit are incurred before the outcome of their application is known. Material sums, time and effort can be spent in applying for a loan, only to have the application rejected.

These differing characteristics determine the frontier between formal and informal credit markets. Poor people and women especially tend rationally to gravitate toward informal transactions.

Nevertheless formal credit delivery system has grown by leaps and bounds in India. It has reduced the dependence on informal finance which though convenient is exploitative in nature.

In India, formal credit to women is disbursed through:

- Programes chanelled through the banking system and
- Programes chanelled through second tier institutions such as NABARD, RMK, SIDBI.

Programmes Chanelled through the Banking System

The Government of India has made available credit facilities to women under Central Government sponsored poverty alleviation and self-employment schemes:

Prime Minister's Rozgar Yojana (PMRY)

Government of India is implementing a subsidy linked self-employment scheme for providing employment to educated unemployed in the age group 18 to 35 years in the rural and urban areas through setting up micro enterprises under the scheme. There is no separate target for women but preference is to be given to women beneficiaries and other weaker sections. Loan applications under this scheme are treated under the priority sector and have to be disposed of within a specified time frame to ensure adequate and timely availability of credit. The minimum educational qualification required under this scheme is standard VIII pass. The beneficiary is required to bring in 5 per cent as margin money and the Government provides subsidy of 15 per cent of the project. Statistics have shown that under the programme only 13.1 per cent of the loan disbursed to women.

Swarna Jayanti Shahari Swarozgar Yojana (SJSRY)

This scheme is in operation from 1.12.1997 in all urban and semi-urban towns of India. Among other components, the scheme has two sub-schemes where bank credit is involved namely: Urban Self-employment Programme (USEP) and Development of Women and Children in Urban Areas (DWCUA). Under the scheme, women are to be assisted to the extent of not less than 30 per cent, disabled at 3 per cent and SC/STs at least to the extent of the proportion of their strength in their local population. The scheme is funded on a 75:25 basis between centre and state.

Under USEP, under employed and unemployed urban youth whose annual family income is below the poverty line and who are educated upto ninth standard and who have been included in the ULB list are to be assisted with bank loans. Projects costing upto Rs.50,000 are to be financed by banks. Subsidy will be provided by the government at 15 per cent of the project cost subject to a maximum of Rs.7,500.

Under DWCUA, women beneficiaries may take up self-employment ventures in groups. The group should consist of atleast 10 urban poor women. The group is entitled to a subsidy of Rs.1,25,000 or 50 per cent of the project cost whichever is less.

Swarna Jayanti Gram Swarozgar Yojana (SGSY)

This is a restructured programme launched from April 1999 replacing the existing schemes like Integrated Rural Development Programme (IRDP), Training of Rural Youth for Self-Employment (TRYSEM), Development of Women and Children in Rural Areas (DWCRA), Supply of Improved Toolkits to Rural Artisans (SITRA), Ganga Kalyan Yojana (GKY).

SGSY is a holistic programme of micro-enterprises covering all aspects of self-employment, viz., organisation of the rural poor into Self-help groups and their capacity building, infrastructure build up, technology, credit and marketing. The objective is to bring every assisted family above the poverty line in three years by providing them income generating assets through a mix of bank credit and government subsidy.

The scheme is to funded on 75:25 basis by the centre and states and will be implemented by the District Rural Development Agencies (DRDAs) through Panchayat Samities.

SGSY will particularly focus on the vulnerable groups among the rural poor. Accordingly, the women for atleast 40 per cent, SC/STs will account for at least 50 per cent of the Swarozgaris, and the disabled for 3 per cent.

There is no ceiling on the size of the loan amount. Group activities will be given preference. Major share of assistance will be for 4-5 cluster activities identified at the block level.

Subsidy will be uniform at 30 per cent of the project cost subject to a maximum of Rs.7,500/-.

Since the target under SGSY for women is atleast 40 per cent that the targets are achievable.

Programmes chanelled through Second Tier Institutions:

In India, there are three second-tier institutions which channel funds to women through microfinance institutions at concessional interest rates.

Rashtriya Mahila Kosh

Rashtriya Mahila Kosh (RMK) was set up by the Department of Women and Child Development, Govt. of India, as an organisation registered in 1993 under the Societies Registration Act 1860. It was set up with the main objective to promote and undertake provision of credit as an instrument for socio-economic change for the development of women.

This is the first and only one apex microfinance organisation for women set by the Government of India. RMK was provided a corpus of Rs. 31 crores to fulfill its objective. The aim was not to replace the banking sector but to fill the gap between what the banking sector provides and what the poor need.

In order to achieve its objective RMK is working through a set of Intermediate Microfinance Organisations (IMOs) functioning at the intermediate level and thrift and credit groups or the SHGs of the borrowers at the grass-root level.

The SHGs are the foundation of microfinance service delivery system which provides the poor women an opportunity to come together to save and access credit facilities and a platform to find an expression to their needs, develop confidence and awareness and access other social development opportunities. At the intermediate level RMK credit facilities are available to NGOs, Women Cooperative Societies, Women Development Corporations etc., however bulk of RMK credit funds have overwhelmingly been routed through NGOs.

As on 31 March 2000 the number of IMOs working with RMK reach 712 spread in various corners of 20 states. Upto end March 2000 RMK credit facilities have reached 3.60 lakh women.

RMK Schemes

RMK schemes have been designed in a sequential manner –IMOs and ultimate borrowers are expected to start with the smaller loan schemes and slowly graduate to the larger loan schemes as they gain experience and increase their own outreach.

RMK borrowers are expected to form into groups, start with their own savings, and to take the first loans from their own savings to meet their immediate consumption needs, before taking loans from RMK–groups must learn to save before they can learn to borrow–RMK has found that it is best to think in terms of a sequence in which the very poor, by borrowing for consumption, are able to gradually reduce their income vulnerability and get into a position where they can think of riskier investments in working capital, hiring of extra-family labour, and ultimately fixed capital–such a sequence helps the poorest to successfully overcome the barriers of self-exclusion, social exclusion and institutional exclusion that currently block their access to loans.

These loan schemes, in preferred sequence, are:

(a) ***SHG Development Scheme.*** Interest free loan of upto Rs.100,000 to organisations for formation, promotion and development of SHGs, where no SHGs exist.

(b) ***Loan Promotion Scheme.*** For initial credit facility of upto Rs.500,000 to IMOs having, at least one year experience in thrift and credit management. The aim is to promote and encourage smaller organisations to build up their confidence in handling credit and thrift programmes more effectively and efficiently.

(c) ***Main Loan Scheme.*** Credit is provided for on lending to Self-Help Groups/ women beneficiaries for undertaking income generating and other activities by providing credit limits to IMOs having, at least three years experience of Micro- finance/SHGs as per their capability and potential.

(d) ***Revolving Fund Scheme.*** The objective of this scheme is to provide lumpsum funds to any single organisation having adequate infrastructure and a good track record in implementing RMK assisted programmes. An added advantage is the flexibility to revolve the recoveries for financing new self-help groups/members.

(e) ***Marketing Assistance Scheme.*** The main objective is to support marketing of the products of micro enterprises of women's groups.

The common features of all loan schemes are as follows:

- Group loan mechanisms
- Repeat loans are encouraged to ensure that the borrower is brought above the poverty line
- The loans can be given to rural/urban women whose family income is below the poverty line income as defined by Government of India.
- The loans can be given for income generation activities or for acquisition of assets, which will yield income.
- The loans can be given through various Intermediate Micro finance Organisations like: NGOs, suitable State Government agencies or corporations, Women's Cooperatives (with at least 33 per cent women members and working in profit for at least two years), etc.

Criteria for NGO Eligibility.

- Should be registered for at least 3 years;
- Should have experience in thrift and credit management for atleast 3 years and loan recovery levels of about 90 per cent and this should be appropriately reflected in the audited accounts of last 3 years.
- Should have clause in bye-laws giving powers to borrow or raise loans from outside agencies;
- Should have essential staff and infrastructure;

There are no collateral or security requirements.

Method of Disbursement

The IMO should disburse to final women beneficiaries preferably through women's Self Help Groups (SHGs).

Interest Rate:

RMK → IMO	8 per cent on reducing balances
IMO → SGH	12 per cent on reducing balances
SHG → beneficiary	Upto 17.09 per cent which is linked with interest rates fixed by State Bank of India on unsecured loans on the closing date of the last financial year (i.e. 1998-99)

Small Industries Development Bank of India (SIDBI)

SIDBI was set up on April 2, 1990 as a wholly owned subsidiary of IDBI, under an act of the Parliament, viz., Small Industries Development Bank of India Act, 1989. The objectives of SIDBI are to serve as the principal financial institution for promotion, financing and development of industry in the small scale sector and to co-ordinate the functions of the institutions engaged in promoting, financing or developing industry in the small scale sector.

SIDBI has developed a number of schemes and programmes for women with the twin objective of:

- Providing training and extension services to women entrepreneurs through a comprehensive package sited to their skills and socio-economic status.
- Extending financial assistance on liberal terms to enable them to set up industrial units in the small-scale sector.

Mahila Udyam Nidhi (MUN)

This scheme was launched in the year 1990 with SIDBI as its sponsoring agency. This scheme provides equity support to women entrepreneurs for setting up projects in Tiny/Small Sector and rehabilitation of viable sick units. Being the refinance scheme, the assistance under MUN is channelised through prime lending Institutions. The objective of this scheme is to provide soft loan (quasi equity) assistance to women entrepreneurs. The project should not exceed Rs.10 lakh and service industries are also eligible for assistance. Also SIDBI provides soft loan assistance of upto 25 per cent of the project cost with a ceiling of Rs.2.5

lakh per project to meet the gap in the equity. The soft loan is provided at nominal services charges of 1 per cent p.a.

Upto the March 2001 the cumulative assistance under MUN aggregated Rs.1772 lakh of sanctions and Rs.1435 lakh of disbursements, benefiting more than 2200 women entrepreneurs.

Mahila Vikas Nidhi (MVN)

This scheme was launched with the objective of bringing about economic empowerment of women, especially rural poor, by providing them avenues for training and employment opportunities by facilitating creation of infrastructural and training facilities for the purpose. A special development fund has been created for extending support by way of a judicious mix of loan and grant to accredited Voluntary Organisations (VOs), for taking up activities such as setting up Training-cum-production centres (TPCs), skill upgradation programmes, extension of marketing assistance etc., which would ensure that women are provided with training and employment opportunities. Such TPCs relate to diverse activities like sericulture, spinning, weaving, knitting, etc.

Micro Credit Scheme (MCS)

SIDBI has taken the initiative of encouraging informal lending channel by carving out MCS in the year 1994. MCS envisages fund support to well managed NGOs/VOs to on-lend to rural poor with emphasis on women for setting up of their own micro-enterprises. The assistance is channelised in small amounts and members are encouraged to plough back their savings to the group corpus fund, with a view to building borrower's equity.

Under MCS, the cumulative sanctions for the period ended March 2001 aggregated Rs. 8105 lakh channelised through 169 NGOs/MFIs across 24 States/UTs benefiting over 4,42,000 rural poor, of which more than 90 per cent are women. Further, 150 capacity building programmes have been supported with an assistance of Rs. 91 lakh for providing training to 2,750 participants from NGOs in the areas of credit usage, management, monitoring and administration of credit programmes.

Trade Related Entrepreneurship Assistance and Development (TREAD)

TREAD was launched in 1998 and is sponsored by the Government of India and supported by UNDP. It seeks to economically empower women through the development of entrepreneurial skills; elimination of constraints faced by women and strengthens trade support networks. Under the programme, it is envisaged that an integrated package of assistance would be provided to micro-financial intermediaries and end users of credit, whereas the loan requirement would be provided by SIDBI.

As at end-March 2001, 14 NGOs were provided grant assistance under this scheme.

SIDBI Foundation for Micro Credit (SFMC)

SIDBI foundation for micro credit was launched on November 27, 1998 on all India basis, with an initial corpus of Rs. 100 crore. The new approach not only envisages financial assistance but also strives to build and strengthen the management capabilities of the micro finance practitioners for achieving sustainability, economies of scale, desired outreach, etc.

Distinctive features of SIDBI foundation are multi channel credit dispensation routes through apex-NGO's, self help group federations, specialized co-operatives etc., focus on encouraging micro finance product innovations, enhanced flow of assistance to the micro finance sector, reorientation in the security and collateral requirement, simplification in procedures for availing assistance and rating of micro finances institutions and non-governmental organisations.

Women Entrepreneurship Development Programmes (WEDPs)

These are conducted not only with the objective of training a target group in entrepreneurial traits, but it also endeavors to see that on completion of the programme, the trainees are motivated and guided in setting up their own enterprises.

Upto March 2001, SIDBI has supported a total of 1317 Ads of which 285 were women based benefiting 7,100 women.

Marketing Assistance

SIDBI created a marketing finance and development department and formulated a comprehensive scheme for providing financial assistance to undertake marketing activities. It also created a marketing development assistance fund (MDAF) the total corpus of which on March 2001 was Rs.55 crore. Out of this fund a Marketing Fund for Women (MFW) has been set up with an earmarked amount of Rs. 2.5 crore for providing marketing assistance to women entrepreneurs involved in marketing of products manufactured by women entrepreneurs to increase their reach, both in domestic and international markets.

Refinance Scheme for Women Entrepreneurs

The cumulative assistance provided during the period 1999-2001 including both special scheme for women entrepreneurs and women entrepreneurs assisted under refinance scheme aggregated Rs.552.39 crore of sanctions and Rs.432.51 crore disbursements benefiting 17,332 women.

National Bank for Agriculture and Rural Development (NABARD)

Refinance support: NABARD provides refinance to State Cooperative Banks, SCARDBs, RRBs and commercial banks against their lendings both under farm and non-farm lending sectors. The refinance schemes are gender neutral.

Promotional Support. As a necessary adjunct to the refinance (Credit) support provided by NABARD, it also provides promotional support to select NGOs promotional agencies, etc., with a view to increase the credit flow in the rural non-farm sector. In the connection, due emphasis is led on development of women.

NABARD has introduced the following three exclusive promotional schemes for development of rural women.

A. Assistance to Rural Women for Non-Farm Development (ARWIND)

A single window scheme was introduced in October 1993, to encourage and support individual or group enterprises promoted by rural women with umbrella support by NGOs for meeting both promotional and credit needs of women entrepreneurs. By the end of March 2001 cumulative number of projects sanctioned stood at 103 involving grant-cum-revolving fund assistance of Rs. 2.70 crore, benefiting around 9100 rural women.

B. Assistance for Marketing of Non-Farm Products of Rural Women (MAHIMA)

'MAHIMA' a scheme aimed at developing a 'niche' or 'pro women' market and to help the agencies engaged in marketing of products produced by rural poor women was introduced in November 1997 as a part of the National Bank's initiatives to promote credit for women through promotion of Rural Non-Farm Sector (RNFS). Under the scheme, by March 2001, NABARD has been able to support 14 agencies involving promotional grants assistance of Rs. 0.43 crore.

C. Women Development Cells

A series of research studies and some action research projects carried out by NABARD led to the evolution of "Self-Help Groups (SHG)–Bank Linkage" model as a cost effective mechanism for providing financial services to the unreached and underserved poor and women.

A SHG is a small economically homogeneous and affinity group of rural poor voluntarily coming together:

- To save small amounts regularly
- To mutually agree to contribute to a common fund
- To meet their emergency needs
- To have collective decision making
- To resolve conflicts through collective leadership and mutual discussion
- To provide collateral free loans with terms decided by the group at market driven rates.

For selection of SHGs for the linkage with banks, NABARD has set out simple and specific guidelines for the use of bankers and NGOs.

- The group should be in active existence for atleast a period of six months.

- Have successfully undertaken savings and credit operation from its own resources.
- Democratic working wherein all members feel that they have a say is evident.
- Maintaining proper accounts/record.
- The banker should be convinced that a group has not come into existence only for the sake of participation in the programme and availing benefits. There should be a genuine need to help each other and work together among the members.
- Members preferably have homogeneous background and interest.
- Interest of the NGO or the SHG promoting institution concerned, if any, in the group is evident and the agency is helping the SHGs by way of training and other support for skill upgradation and proper functioning.

Broadly, three different models have emerged under the SHG linkage approach in the country.

- *SHG-Bank linkage Model-I*–where the NGO acts as a promoter and facilitator in bringing the SHGs to the door step of the bank branch which directly provides loan to the SHGs in proportion to the savings.
- *SHG-Bank linkage Model-II*–where the NGO acts as a financial intermediary in the sense that it promotes the SHGs, trains them and also provides them loan after availing the same from the bank in proportion to the savings of the SHGs.
- *SHG-Bank linkage Model-III*– where the banks themselves promote SHGs without any assistance from the NGOs and also provide loan to the SHGs in proportion to the savings of the groups.

Each of the three models can be qualitatively assessed to arrive at the strategic significance and scope for wide scale adoption. Criteria for evaluation may include factors like:

- Transaction cost of lending for the banks.

- Transaction cost of borrowing for the SHGs and poor.
- Risk of funds and guarantee of repayment.
- Load (costs) of co-ordination and management.
- Ease of adoption by all stakeholders.
- Smoothness and ease of providing credit to the poor and its repayment.
- Quick replicability.
- Social and economic impact on SHG movement.
- Extent of social investment required.

India's economy has experienced profound changes in the recent decades with changes in the regulatory and institutional landscape much of the traditional underpinnings of the economy have altered. The priorities of issues which merit attention have still not changed substantially though a newer set of questions and issues may have come into prominence. Economic reforms initiated in the early 90s have led the country to a sustained trajectory of growth sustainable growth at 8 to 9 per cent appears within react and we must overcome obstacles to this attainment.

This book's essays on Development Theme presents a comprehensive and contemporary treatment of the defining issues in the country chapters in this volume range over issues of macroeconomic performance, poverty, rural credit, effective credit delivery through the institutional credit delivery channels of cooperatives and RRBs, Gender Concerns, The promise of microfinance. Each of these subjects is deftly handled. The issues are presented indepth critically analysed sectoral insights are provided and they are linked to the functioning of India's economy today and policy options for long term growth prospects presented. The chapters are lucidly argued and simply presented in non-technical language accessible to the general reader, without of course, any compromise on academic rejour. The book it is hoped would contribute to policy making or at any rate to the debate on public policy. The presentation is objective and non-ideological. The only brief held is to underline the need for rapid economic growth and development, which is the only panacea for the challenges confronting the country, growth with a human face which necessarily ensures the welfare of women and the weaker sections where vibrant financial delivery models partner in the march to progress in the decade of development.

Economic growth at 8 per cent to 9 per cent over a decade will combat poverty. There is a dream of the economy which is always tantalizingly so near and yet so far – the dream of being the new miracle economy. Trumpets, drums and cymbals have announced the arrival of the new era – we need to live up to the promise.

In the area of social improvement post independence India has been able to eliminate famines child and infant mortality has declined. However, 300 million people out of 3 still live in poverty. The life expectancy is 63 years a decade behind in developing countries. Illiteracy is still a curse. Women tend to have lower literacy levels a girl is one third less likely to attend secondary school than a boy. As Mahatma Gandhi had expressed it 'lives in the villages' thus most of India's rural poor live in rural areas and are engaged in agriculture thus a viable sustainable long-term strategy for poverty eradication becomes increasing incomes of those engaged in agriculture as agriculture continues to absorb the majority of the workforce. The reforms of the 1990s definitely generated better terms of trade for agriculture. Though public investments in agriculture declined, its adverse effect on farm incomes was more than offset by increased subsidies on agricultural inputs electricity, irrigation, fertilizer and price supports. However, as the reforms concentrated on the liberalization of the industry the terms of trade shifted in favour of agriculture helping private investment grow faster than output in the sector. Agriculture is in need of major reforms to transform it into a dynamic engine for growth.

Poverty rate declined in the 1980s and 1990s the fraction of population below the poverty line dropped from 54 per cent in 1983 to 36 per cent in 1989-90, in rural areas and from 38 per cent to 35 per cent in urban areas. Over the period 1991-97 urban poverty declined, but rural poverty has remained broadly unchanged.

The figures tend to mask tremendous inter-regional disparities in poverty levels and in rates of change. The accurate measurement of poverty ratios continues to be a challenge. A chapter has been allotted to the Meaning and Measurement of Poverty which studies its theoretical and conceptual underpinnings. National Sample Survey (NSS) which lists the number of households that report they cannot obtain two square meals a day, continues to be a source of data, shows a considerable drop in the figures. The original poverty line defined in 1960-61 concerned food needs hence the disparity in estimates raises pertinent questions about how the poverty line needs to be adjusted to account for changing demography, food habits and relative food prices. Poverty alleviation programmes, though with a gender bias, have failed to address the serving needs of women. Poverty alleviation programmes invariably lose their effectiveness through leakages i.e. transfers to the non-poor, the poor can be identified by proxy indicators as occupation, asset holding, literacy rates, etc.

The financial sector has to play a critical role in a liberalized economy. We have to rethink the role of banks in India's economy. Thus an entire section is devoted to banks it stresses the new and emerging challenges before banks, banking reforms are obviously important ranging over issues from new strategies for prudential regulation to coping with Basle II norms. Indian banks especially the nationalized banks, cooperative and Regional Rural Banks present a framework for regulation riddled with conceptual and practical problems and the unique moral nag and that arises from State ownership.

16

Banks to the Fore

"Within the framework of a democratic polity, our laws, development policies, Plans and programmes have aimed at women's advancement in different spheres. From the Fifth Five Year Plan (1974-78) onwards, there has been a marked shift in the approach to women's issues from welfare to development. In recent years the empowerment of women has been recognized as the central issue in determining the status of women.

The National Commission for Women was set up by an Act of Parliament in 1990 to safeguard the rights and legal entitlements of women. The 73rd and 74th Amendments (1993) to the Constitution of India have provided for reservation of seats in the local bodies of Panchayats and Municipalities for women, laying a strong foundation for their participation in decision-making at the local levels. The national policy for women, 2001 is a step in building up a strong women's movement. The goal of this policy is to bring about the advancement, development and empowerment of women.

The Ninth Five Year Plan is committed to women's empowerment. The principle of gender equity is enshrined in the Indian Constitution in its Preamble, Fundamental Rights, Fundamental Duties and Directive Principles. The Constitution grants not only equality to women, but also empowers the State to adopt measures of positive discrimination in favour of women."

Feminisation of Credit

Women constitute half the world's population and make up one-third of the labour force. In India, although literacy levels have registered an increase, majority of women are still illiterate, without any access to property and credit. But the poorest women try their best to save whatever little money they can secretly, say, under the mattress. They are so poor that they do not have anything to offer as security for loans and shy away from approaching banks for loan assistance. Sadly, they feel comfortable in approaching money-lenders and pawn brokers to meet their day to day requirements.

It is high time that banks realize that women need not only a wide spectrum of financial services, but also adequate and timely access to them. That women tend to be much more prompt in repayment of loans as compared to males. That they desperately require support and help, particularly in the form of credit to enable them to set up income generating projects, which will enable them to make a living on a sustainable basis.

The Banking Division of the Ministry of Finance in consultation with the Reserve Bank of India (RBI) and other institutions ascertained the problems faced by women entrepreneurs in order to help overcome the hurdles being faced by them in access to bank credit and credit plus services. Some of the problems are:

- Genuine difficulty in identification of women borrowers and establishing direct dialogue with prospective women borrowers, who normally do not come to banks.
- Cumbersome and time-consuming documentation and procedures of the banks and funding agencies in processing of loans.
- Urban bias of branch managers and officials of banks.
- Lack of region/area based approach for development of women.
- Absence of credit at doorsteps and in time.
- Unequal inheritance laws and practices and control over property and incomes by men.
- Women entrepreneurs are by and large engaged in a few selected activities and operating at small scale. Their lack of wide market exposure restricts the level of operation to suit the local limited demand.

On the basis of these findings, a 14-Point Action Plan has been drawn for implementation by public sector banks, which includes redefining of Banks' policies/long-term plans, setting up women's cells and designating an officer in each branch exclusively to handle flow of credit to women, simplification of existing procedural formalities, orientation of Bank officers/ staff on gender concerns, publicity campaign for creating awareness about credit facilities, entrepreneurship development programmes for women, motivational strategies to enthuse Bank staff to achieve targets for women, a proper data collection and monitoring system, involving NGOs, Self-Help Groups.

With a view to meeting the credit needs of women in the tiny and SSI sector within the existing institutional framework, the RBI has taken measures recently by increasing the limit for non-obtention of collateral security from Rs.1.00 lakh to Rs. 5.00 lakh, raising of composite loan limit from Rs. 5.00 lakh to Rs. 10.00 lakh, raising of the limit of projects for equity support under the National Equity Fund Scheme of SIDBI from Rs. 15.00 lakh to Rs. 25.00 lakh.

The RBI has also helped draft a number of credit facilities for women entrepreneurs under various Central Government sponsored poverty alleviation and self-employment schemes, some of which are as indicated below:

Prime Minister's Rozgar Yojana. The Government of India is implementing a subsidy-linked self-employment scheme for providing employment to educated unemployed in the rural and urban areas in the age group of 18 to 35 years through setting up micro enterprises under the scheme. There is no separate target for women but preference is to be given to women beneficiaries and other weaker sections. It is observed that about 80,000 women borrowers have been sanctioned loans by banks to avail of self-employment during the last three years under the scheme. The minimum educational qualification fixed is to pass Std. VIII. The beneficiary is required to bring in 5 per cent as margin money and Government provides subsidy of 15 per cent of the project cost. The ceiling on subsidy is Rs.7,500/ in States/Union Territories other than North Eastern Region where the ceiling is up to Rs. 15,000.

Swarnajayanti Gram Swarozgar Yojana. The objective of this scheme is to bring every assisted family above the poverty line in three years by providing them income generating assets through a mix of bank credit and government subsidy. The monthly income from activity to be undertaken should not be less than Rs.2,000 net of repayment to the bank at least in the third year.

It is a holistic programme covering all aspects of self-employment such as organization of poor into Self Help Groups, training, credit technology, infrastructure and marketing. The scheme will be funded on 75:25 basis by Centre and States and will be implemented by DRDAs through panchayat samities.

Swarnajayanti Shahari Rozgar Yojana. This is operational in all urban and semi-urban towns of India. Among other components, the scheme has two sub-schemes where bank credit is involved, namely Urban Self Employment Programme and Development of Women and Children in Urban Areas (DWCUA). Women are to be assisted to the extent of not less than 30 per cent. It is funded on a 75:25 basis between Centre and State.

Under DWCUA, women beneficiaries may take up self-employment ventures in group. Each group should consist of at least 10 urban poor women. The group is entitled to a subsidy of Rs.1,25,000 or 50 per cent of the project cost, whichever is less.

Differential Rate of Interest Scheme. Here, banks provide finance at concessional rate of interest of 4 per cent per annum to the weaker sections of the community, including SC/ST women for engaging in productive and gainful activities so that they could improve their economic conditions.

Self Help Groups. This is a cost-effective mechanism for providing financial services to the unreached and underserved poor and women. Self Help Groups are small economically homogeneous and affinity groups of rural poor voluntarily coming together to save small amounts regularly, to mutually agree to contribute to a common fund, to have collective decision-making and to provide collateral free loans with terms decided by the group at market driven rates.

Broadly, three different models have emerged under the Self Help Group-bank linkage approach in the country:

Model I– Where the NGO acts as promoter and facilitator in bringing the SHGs to the door step of the bank branch, which directly provides loan to the SHGs in proportion to the savings.

Model II– Where the NGO acts as financial intermediary in the sense that it promotes the SHGs, trains them and also provides them loan after availing the same from the bank in proportion to the savings of the SHGs.

Model III– Where the banks themselves promote SHGs without any assistance from the NGOs and also provide loan to the SHGs in proportion to the savings of the groups.

With over 4.5 million poor households accessing bank services, including micro-credit, through their 263 thousand SHGs, the SHG-bank linkage programme is now perhaps the largest micro finance programme of the world in terms of its out-reach. The year 2000-01 witnessed a two-fold jump in the outreach of this programme, both in physical and financial terms.

Support for Setting Up of Women Development Cells. Under this scheme, assistance in the form of grants is being extended to meet 50 per cent of the pay and allowances forming part of the salary of key personnel (lady officer) to be appointed in such cells by the Regional Rural Banks and Cooperative Banks, subject to a maximum of Rs.75,000 per cell per annum. So far 91 such cells have been set up in 15 States.

Apart from these and many other schemes, the Ministry of Finance, in consultation with the RBI and other institutions, has suggested certain measures to improve the mindset of our people, some of which are to tackle gender bias, to help banks take initiative for reaching out to women, simplification of procedures, publicity campaigns/awareness programmes, entrepreneurship development programmes and marketing facilities for women, free technical training facilities for poor women, specialized branches for women.

As Kofi Annan, Secretary General of the United Nations, rightly put it–"When the poorest, especially woman receive credit, they become economic actors with power. Power to improve not only their own lives, but in a widening circle, to impact the lives of their families, their communities, and their nations." Several steps have been initiated at the Indian Government and other banking institutional levels for strengthening women entrepreneurial capabilities, skill training and making available counselling and consultancy services so as to help them to settle in income generating activities. If this is implemented well, women's empowerment would soon become a reality leading to gender parity in a few years.

Reference

Dr. Deepali Pant Joshi–*Rural Credit Journal,* May-June 2002.

17

Credit, SHGs and Women The Andhra Pradesh Way

A silent revolution is sweeping through Andhra Pradesh through its networks of self-help groups (SHG). The state has demonstrated that empowerment (based on the SHG model can have far reaching spin-offs. It has blazed a new path and shown clearly that the poor benefit materially from access to credit. That they are willing and able to service loans on a commercial basis.

The uniqueness of the SHG approach lies in its simplicity. Groups which self-select 15-25 members are organised with the help of an animator, a trainer. This role fulfilled by a non-government organisation (NGO) which acts as a social intermediary a 'bridge between the NGO and the bank, and also helps financial intervention through the bank. SHG members are encouraged to make small, affordable and regular contributions to a savings fund managed by the groups.

Once a reasonable corpus is collected, the group is encouraged to provide petty loans for its members. The group decides the priority of needs as to who should get the loans first and determines the rates of interest. Membership of the group gives women a sense of self-worth. It confers on them a voice in their families and in their larger society and also ensures the economic and social upliftment of women.

Once the group builds up a stake through regular contribution to its corpus, it is also given revolving credit. Though interest rates are set by the group, they are lower than the rates charged by the moneylender by two–three per cent per month which means 24-36 per cent per annum.

The velocity of turnover is quite rapid as repayments are prompt. This leads to disbursement of loans which are three to four times the quantum of savings. A loan can average between Rs. 500 and Rs. 1,000. Supplementary doses of assistance are provided 'for those who have only been able to avail of a nominal sum during the first borrowing cycle.

For landless women, assistance is provided for taking animal husbandry programmes or cottage and village industries. For women who have taken land on lease and those who own land, assistance is provided for land- based activities. This represents a demand-driven approach to credit. This is also a participatory approach, and gives rise to democratic empowerment among SHG members.

The involvement of women in SHGs has also changed the behaviour of their men-folk. They have started helping them in domestic tasks, and have started sharing responsibilities within the home. Not Just that the access to and control over resources by women has empowered them towards asserting their own rights.

Though gender division in decision-making still persists in the project-districts, there is definitely an increase in the intra-household decision making powers of women. This empowerment has percolated into decisions regarding credit activities, children's activities, and health care of family members and use of family assets. NGOs also play a central role in the formation of groups and in project activities.

In Andhra Pradesh, Velugu was launched in 2000. It was introduced on a pilot-basis in six districts aided by the World Bank. Velugu provided additional funds which enabled skilled animators to be hired, thus reducing dependence on the free services provided by NGOs. It financed a 'community investment fund' for building small local infrastructure as sheds for weavers, etc. After the success of the pilot-project, Velugu 2 has been launched in every mandal of the state.

Under the umbrella of Velugu, all SHGs are encouraged to form 'federations of village organisations' which in turn federate into Mahila Mandal Samakhyas. The model is highly cost effective:

lender transaction-cost could be further reduced if the option of institutional lending to groups for lending to individuals rather than directly to individuals within groups is considered. This is attractive for banks.

However, this requires the exercise of great care in so far as group dynamics is concerned particularly with regard to loan distribution within the groups to ensure that the poorer women are not marginalised. It is necessary not to lose sight of the fact that pro poor, equitable and transparent financial operations through built-in savings and lending practices contribute to the efficient functioning of the groups and to the collective engagement of the group in socially productive activities.

SHGs have successfully created a number of successful income generating opportunities. Loans have enabled women to manage their activities independently and to have greater control over their assets and incomes. The assumption that women would generally make wise choices due to their expertise and knowledge of local markets conditions has been justified by healthy repayment rates.

SHGs in Andhra Pradesh have achieved much and heralded an era of social change with respect to empowering women in rural communities. Its strongest point centres around the formation of cohesive women's groups who have developed the habit of systematic savings. It has helped consolidate their bargaining power and decision making responsibilities towards the overall development of their communities.

The distinct features and success in enabling women to overcome the double burden of being poor and being women are indicators of the need to replicate the model to empower women in other states. There are valuable lessons to be learnt from SHGs of Andhra Pradesh.

Reference

Dr. Deepali Pant Joshi–*Financial Express*–February 2004.

18

SHG–Empowering Poor Women

SHG approach is a process oriented project, which lays great emphasis on the qualitative and socio-economic aspects of development of women rather than setting mere statistical targets. NGOs and commercial banks come together to work to achieve common objectives related to socio-economic development of women leading to their empowerment. SHG approach is a participatory, people centred and process oriented approach. Facilitating empowerment of poor is a challenging task.

The SHG vision is to reach out and empower poor women through self-reliant and sustainable Self Help Groups. SHG is intended to promote economic development and social empowerment of poor women through a network of Self Help Groups. The "SHG revolution" as it may be termed has been instrumental in increasing participation of women in decision making in households, community and in the local democratic set up, besides helping to prepare women to take up leadership responsibilities.

Economic empowerment is promoted through:

- Greater access to financial resources outside the household.
- Reduced vulnerability of poor women to crisis situations like famine, flood, riots, death/accidents in the family etc.
- Significant increase in women's own income and the power to retain/save such income and use it at her discretion.

- Equal access and control over various resources at the household level.
- Financial self-reliance of women, both in the household and in the external environment.

Capacity building through better awareness, improved functional literacy and numeracy, better communication skills, better leadership skills, self help and mutual help. Such empowerment of the poor and disadvantaged women leads to overall improvement that accrue directly to the individual woman and women's groups; and through a ripple-effect benefits other poor families in the neighbourhood, the community and the village as a whole in the long run.

Under SGSY which is the major poverty alleviation programme of the government there is an emphasis on formation of SHG groups. SGSY will particularly focus on the vulnerable groups among the rural poor. Accordingly, the SC/ST will account for atleast 50 per cent of the Swarozgaris, women 40 per cent and the disabled for 3 per cent.

Fifty per cent of the groups formed in each block should be exclusively for the women. In the case of disabled persons, the groups formed should ideally be disability specific wherever possible; however, in case sufficient number of people for formation of disability specific groups are not available, a group may comprise of persons with diverse disabilities.

Under SGSY Scheme, the total number of Swarozgaris assisted during the year 2000-01 was 9,39,399 (as on March 2001), of this 3,96,757 was women, constituting 42.24 per cent of the total Swarozgaris assisted.

Mahilar Thittam also is an important landmark under which several Self Help Groups have been formed in Tamil Nadu. District Kanchipuram has made much progress in establishing SHG groups. The SHG groups under Mahilar Thittam have a compulsory savings component.

Building partnerships. The SHG approach believes in establishing long term partnerships in the interest of poor women. The project has four main actors, Government, NGOs banks and the poor women themselves. It recognizes that building satisfactory working relationships is a very important step in building the capacities of the poor. Training inputs are provided on team building, communication skills, time management, etc.

NGOs are doing bulk of the field work. Community mobilization through village level meetings and interaction has been their forte. The staff of the SHGs is benefited through interaction with NGOs leading to adoption of participatory practices, besides leading to change in attitudes as NGOs offer Role Models. Banks are also one of the important partners. Participation of women in the process of development has been a step forward in 1999-2000.

Formation of SHGs is a critical process with conscientisation and voluntarism as a necessary basis for formation. Identification of families is done with the help of the below poverty line (BPL) lists prepared by DRDAs in each distrust. Steps are being taken to cover each and every habitation while forming groups and preference is given for SC/ST coverage.

SHG Facilitation–Best Practice

Weekly meetings and optional savings are encouraged in order that poor women are able to capture most of their surplus savings. A large per centage of SHGs have switched to weekly meetings (to a lesser extent – weekly savings) in 1999-2000. Efforts are taken to further strengthen groups through adoption of both weekly meetings and compulsory savings. Groups are trained to maintain accounts and registers in a phased manner. Discipline, shared vision, a common identity and sense of unity have been remarkable created through these groups with the practice of joint taking of the Mahilar Thittam pledge. This has clearly given the SHGs a sense of identity and a common mission. Group meetings are convened by SHGs in their respective villages at convenient locations and at convenient times. Each SHG visits the bank to which it is linked by rotation, deposit savings are introduced so that SHGs become familiar with the various bank practices. After completion of one year, it is necessary for SHGs to have their account audited by an external agency and also carried out in between by field staff.

Training for Transformation

The purpose of training under the project is to develop a shared vision. The other purpose is also to bring about transformation in perception through exposure. A strong and cohesive SHG can be formed only by giving systematic training and adopting participatory methods. Impact of training can be easily seen in better communication skills, greater confidence, higher unity and wider mobility of SHG women. However, it is felt that training in the interactive and participatory methodologies need to be strengthened. The use of pictorials and charts is not widespread. As a consequence efforts should be made at the district level to organize trainers' camps where charts and visuals will be prepared and wide use of these thereafter should be ensured.

Under SGSY bankers' orientation was organized in all 21 districts and 2320 bank managers oriented during 1999-2000. This is the first module and is to be repeated in 2000-01 with additional inputs. It is important that more number of branch managers are oriented. Foremost impact of such orientation has been the ease with which SHGs are able to open accounts. Increased interest shown by bankers in credit linkage to eligible SHGs is also a matter of great significance. Bankers now look at lending to women SHGs as a promising business segment, with 100 per cent repayment rates. Banks have been closely associated with Ma Thi/SGSY.

Economic empowerment of women starts with savings and internal lending. But this does not take the rate of growth to sustainable levels to raise family incomes above poverty. External credit linkage is, therefore, a necessary event in the accelerated path to financial sustainability of each SHGs and thereby of each household. After successful completion of 6 months of effective performance, credit rating of such SHGs is undertaken to assess credit worthiness of such groups. Group standards set by SHG credit guidelines (satisfying the credit rating parameters) are recommended for linkage under SGSY scheme, NABARD has also evolved some rating mechanisms.

In order to inculcate professional commercial/business skills among SHG members for undertaking economic activities. There is a growing need to orient and build capacity of NGO staff in micro-enterprise facilitation. Business orientation for SHG members is necessary to cultivate entrepreneurship skills. District level and block level workshops should be held with DRDA, NGOs, SHGs to identify business opportunities. There is also a need to facilitate linkages between SHGs and local industry and business networks for marketing and skill upgradation. SHG members are to be motivated to launch income Generating Project activities. SHG members participate in exhibitions and learn how to upgrade their products, business skills, etc., besides getting exposed to the variety of competing products and customer requirements. Exhibition stalls should be located in completely commercial areas to attract customers. SHGs from all districts should be given opportunities to participate in such exhibitions. The quality, packing and branding of the SHG products needs to be improved to attract buyers. Marketing skills of SHGs to be substantially improved by promoting SHG products first locally (among SHGs themselves) and then upgrading to district/state levels. Flexible savings by group members should be allowed so that savings do not become an unnecessary imposition on groups. Groups should declare dividends to members out of accumulated interest on savings on an annual basis. However, this cannot be imposed and will be as per the Byelaws of the group. Also SHGs may consider and develop need-based “financial products” as the group mature and is trained to fulfill financial functions beyond its regular savings and small loan operations.

Following a period of sound credit activities at the group level, linkages between SHG members and commercial banks are to be institutionalized.

Formation of clusters should be undertaken only when groups have been trained appropriately and groups of a similar maturity be clustered into the same federation.

Financial intermediation by agencies in the non-formal sector has gained increasing importance and recognizing that financial services to the asset less poor and disadvantaged particularly to women hold the key to mainstreaming them with the development of the country, we have laid increasing emphasis on micro credit interventions which have been accepted internationally as an effective tool for poverty alleviation, contribute to individual and household security and change social relations for the better. RBI has issued exhaustive guidelines to banks in February 2000 for mainstreaming micro credit and enhancing the outreach of micro credit providers. These guidelines afford banks considerable operational freedom for their effective implementations.

19

Regulation for Micro Finance

1. Introduction

Micro Finance is a cost-effective tool to fight against many dimensions of the poverty challenge. Micro Finance Institutions (MFI's) have proved that it is possible to develop sustainable institutional arrangements to serve a large number of poor clients despite difficult market conditions. MFI's are no longer a 'recent phenomenon'— it has become firmly established in many developing countries. Micro Finance in the world, particularly in Asia and Africa has been passing through a transition of transformation towards establishing a sustainable institution for alleviating poverty and recognizing itself as a specialized sector for providing financial services to the poor. A total of 15 million people are served through Micro Finance institutions around the world and out of this 12 million in Asia, 1.5 million in Latin America and 0.5 million in Eastern Europe. Still there is a huge market for micro-finance. It is estimated that there is a potential market for 100 million Micro Finance clients in the world.

The successful implementation of the group based credit delivery model encouraged many other NGOs to introduce similar programes. The first ever micro-credit summit held in Washington D.C in February 1997 accelerated the growth of micro-credit throughout the world. Many NGOs and other institutions that did not have sufficient previous experiences in managing Micro Finance have come forward. At the same time NGOs who were involved in small-scale micro-credit programes have scaled up their programes both in terms of increasing the number of clients and the portfolio size. There is now a recognition that such widening and deepening of Micro Financial services have both a social and commercial implication.

2. Strategic Challenges

The struggle for increased portfolio and outreach while maintaining a poverty focus is a challenging one. More specifically, the challenge can be broken down into three issues:

Firstly how to reach more poor people through micro-finance particularly, how to access the hard core poor.

Secondly, how to deliver micro-finance services in a sustainable way while serving the poor.

Thirdly, how to balance the social objectives with the financial objectives of micro-finance.

An important common element in addressing these issues is one of resources and the source of funds. Given that traditional support provided by donors to the MFI's in the form of grants or concession loans are limited, MFIs increasingly find the need to access other sources to support their growth and move towards a more diversified resource base. The key policy consideration for Micro Finance institutions interested in widening and deepening their financial services is to explore ways to mobilize non-subsidized sources of funding. The three main sources of private financing that most of the experts of Micro Finance recommended for MFI's are deposit mobilization, bank loan and equity finance. These efforts to access market-driven sources of capital are welcome and a step in the right direction. However, such moves also carry their own risks in terms of protection of savers and the risk factors involved in borrowing money from commercial market.

3. Options

To address this issue, many steps are being considered by the donors, government and practitioner's organisations. A common theme of an appropriate regulatory framework is emerging regulation that on the one hand allows some common understanding to facilitate the entry of new stakeholders and on the other hand does not stifle the innovativeness of the MFIs. Some options that are considered include self-regulation, prudential regulation and supervision by an authority constituted by the Central Bank or Government and Micro Finance institution rating (Credit Rating). One can argue that to overcome the risks and constraints inherent in accessing private capital and maintaining good portfolios, MFIs should be monitored and regulated, as is the case of formal financial institutions. Some academics and professional bankers argue for the need of a legal and regulatory framework for MFIs. They also think that MFIs can derive some benefits from a formal supervisory process. However, all of them also recognize the limitations in the ability of public regulatory authorities to provide adequate oversight over MFIs and the difficulties of creating an enabling environment for them—an environment in which they can continue to innovate, grow and prosper. The cost and practical problems faced by the bank supervisors in regulating and supervising MFIs have been emphasized in the work of Christen and Rosenberg (2000). Sharif (2001) also argues that premature regulation is more likely to stifle innovation in this sector than improve its efficiency or minimize risks. It is suggested that a much more appropriate strategy would be to create a mechanism that will regularly disclose MFIs risks and assess their performance against some basic performance standard. Appropriate performance standards can then evolve through such a system in which MFIs assess themselves against some threshold. A level of profit will be needed to get access to bank loans and mobilize savings deposits.

4. Other Concerns

4.1. *Sustainability of Organization and Borrowers*

Sustainability in a broad spectrum can be defined as the ability of an organization to deliver an appropriate level of benefit for an extended period of time even after major assistance from the donor is terminated. From the borrowers point of view it refers to the attainment of self reliance and income generation activity of the target community even after credit facilities are withdrawn or in other words the obsolescence of credit program as felt by the borrowers.

The relevant issues that need to be addressed by any organization to achieve institution and borrower sustainability are:

Managerial Capacity as of good governance and Profitability not only to address the financial needs of the clients but also to harness and support complementary programes. The whole responsibility is shouldered by the MFI, as the borrowers are incapable of lending a hand in the initial stages. However, with awareness through education and knowledge building the willingness of the borrowers to participate in credit, social and other programes; runs parallel to managerial capacity essential to achieve sustainability.

4.2. Measuring Impact of Microfinance

The success of microfinance programes is perceived in two ways. Firstly, it is very important to measure its impact on the lives of the poor clients who have been receiving repeated credit support from the MFIs. The impact may be seen in respect of the changes which happened in their life at the level of material well-being, social well-being and empowerment in particular focus on women's right and gender inequality. Secondly, it is also equally important to measure the sustainability of the Microfinance institutions as lending organizations. The sustainability of MFIs may be looked at an institutional level and a financial level. The institutional sustainability refers to the prevalence of certain conditions of good governance and management. The financial sustainability of MFIs refers to the ability how it response to the needs of the clients and operate in an environment attaining capacity of dealing risks involved in the whole process. It also includes maintaining a sound financial system to cover all expenses from the income.

An examination of micro-credit programes and models in the context of borrower sustainability, reaching the poorest and removal of poverty in Bangladesh has shown the following. The three model viz. credit-only credit-plus (training, technical assistance) and 'credit along with technical assistance plus social development' are considered. Some empirical evidence was provided and the current achievements and constraints of various micro-credit models were analyzed. Arguments were placed in favoyr of a credit with social development model and suggestions were made on deepening the impact of the micro-credit system.

A good microfinance institution is keen to see always the impact of the programme. This may be seen in different dimension. Using different broad indicators such as (a) material well-being with an additional dimension focusing on the poverty reduction impact of the programe by measuring poverty and its correlates, (b) Vulnerability to seasonality and economic security. (c) Changes in women's lives with a particular focus on empowerment and gender, (d) institutional development of the poor, the impact on the lives of the poor can be measured.

(a) *Material Well-being*

BRAC is a major microfinance programme in Bangladesh to determine the impact of BRAC's development programes on socio-economic well being of the programe participants/clients BRAC inputs which includes mostly micro-finance; training and other technical assistance have been considered. The major explanatory variables that have been used are:

- Changes in the values of assets, savings, housing and non-institutional cash loan - reducing dependency on informal sources.
- Changes in food intake both in terms of quantity and quality.
- Changes in occupation and land holding Investment.

(b) *Vulnerability and Crisis Management*

Vulnerability and crisis management refers to the ability of the programe participants/ clients to coping capacity in case of economic security in terms of vulnerability to seasonal fluctuation in consumption, food stock and mechanism employed to confront unforeseen disaster.

(c) *Empowerment*

Empowerment refers to the ability of attaining power to take care of individual's own affairs and the capacity to act collectively to establish social and economic rights. BRAC's activities arc geared towards empowering poor women and men. The concept of "empowerment" is embodied into the underlying facts that bring change- changes that have been taken place in the lives of the poor particularly, the women. Empowerment of the women is considered as the capacity to reduce their socio-economic vulnerability and their dependency on their husbands or other male counterparts, in terms of their ability to become involved in income generating activities and freely spend the income generated from these activities. This may be visualized in three pathways viz. Material, perceptual and relational. Thus it is seen:

- Greater freedom in the choice of services through enhanced demand
- Growth of more appropriate economic services
- Natural resource rights better secured
- Increased action against pollution
- Control over assets and income
- Use of loan and use of savings particularly, by the women
- Capacity and participation in decision making process in the family as well as in the society
- Improved and balanced relationship with family members and elite
- Government recognition of group legitimacy and voice
- Increased in women's freedom and autonomy
- Greater self-esteem, e.g., inclusion in communal affairs
- Capacity to bargain to ensure social and economic justice

(d) *Institutional Development and Social Issues and its Impact*

The social development programe focusses largely on building human and social assets and changing structures and processes- through institution building awareness training and social action. This is to enable the rural poor especially women to build and secure their assets to improve their role of well being, reduce vulnerability and take advantage of new opportunities, exercise their rights and play a more active role in the public space. This in turn helps to complement the micro credit programe, as women are harnessed with the essentials to participate more actively in credit programes

5. Relevancy of Self-Regulation and other Instruments

Before going for regulatory framework and bank supervision, it is necessary to develop the capacity of NGOs/ MFIs to make them capable and confident enough to demonstrate their transparency and accountability towards having a sustainable and efficient Micro Finance management system. As a part of such a capacity building exercise we should introduce the instruments of self-regulation and credit rating. Self-regulation refers most broadly to a set of enforceable rules and standards that will have to be adhered to by the NGOs/ MFIs and their primary stakeholder in order to facilitate the process of assessment and monitoring against standards. These rules and standards include the conditions of good governance and management and indicators for financial, economic and social aspects.

There are many organizations that need to practice a good audit manual (CGAP), good portfolio assessment system and friendly usable MIS before going for self-regulation. Credit rating instrument will be useful to those organizations that have started practicing these tools already. As the microfinance movement is a network of a diverse range of MFIs with varied models, and scale, such a diversified approach seems to be the right one.

A good example of best practices is available among some MFIs and NGOs in Asia but most of these practices are not easily accessible to the others. They cannot learn from the good ones because of non-availability of information. There is a gap. As a network Self Regulation Organisations (SRO) can make access to information to the others through training, workshop and introducing instruments like self-regulations and credit rating. Self Regulation Organisations could be an entry point where MFIs will be motivated and encouraged to emulate best practices and adopt certain standards developed for this purpose and provide information for dissemination that leads to compare the performance of organization with the performance of peer organizations.

6. Self Regulation Tools and Framework

6.1. *Basically a four Step of Implementation Process Includes*

- Awareness phase involving stakeholders (seminars/ workshop/training) in developing the standards;
- Practicing of standards;
- Counselling and review and
- Making information available to the others for sharing, learning and further refinement.

It is expected that a set of agreed rules and standards for self-regulation would be developed as Rules and Standard for Self-regulation.

SRO being a practitioner led network encourages self-regulating culture and practices. Hence they will be in the process of developing a self-assessment tool, based upon common standards; a combination of financial and social goals. The essence is one of developing a mechanism to build the partners compared to rating by a third party. Members of each country network can be involved in evolving this process.

Various self-appraisal, assessment and regulatory mechanisms will be evolved with the active involvement of members. The focus of the SRO is not only to set standards but also to help the members to achieve these standards through handholding support mechanisms.

The uniqueness of this standard will be that its will combine all three aspects - financial, focial and economic goals. The essence is one of developing a mechanism to build the partners compared to rating by a third party. Members of each country network shall be involved in evolving this process.

6.2. *Standards and Measuring Performance Framework for Self Regulation*

I. Implementations of Standards

Once the concept is made available and acceptable to the participants the resource person will be required to help members implement the indicators in their respective organization.

The MFI will be trained to practice the tools and implement the processes in their organization.

Technical support such as software packages etc; to practice audit exercise of international standard, will be provided to the MFI as and when needed for effective implementation of the standards.

II. Monitoring and Review

The members will be requested to provide the self-generated information based on the format developed. The focus of the self- regulation is not only to set standards but also to help the members to achieve these standards through handholding support mechanisms.

Feed back on good practices needs to be generated. Support will be provided to cover loopholes. Careful assessment will be made for proper and efficient performance.

Benefits of Self Regulation

The whole process of implementation of the standard of self- regulation will help to

- Enhance capacity of the institutional members
- Develop a sound Financial and Management system
- Demonstrate accountable and transparent information system
- Ensure a mechanism to deal with any sort of regulatory frames developed by central bank and Government.

Self Regulation For Demand Stream of Micro Finance Sector

1. Rationale

Micro Finance as a means to reduce poverty has acquired multifaceted dimension going beyond mere extension of financial services. Over time, it has evolved as a pivotal element of the anti poverty strategy. Revolving around this pivot are the other means, which address the myriad causes of poverty. As the world development report 2000-2001 rightly recognizes, poverty is not only low income and consumption but also low level of education, health, nutrition and other facets of human development.

Micro finance includes two distinct streams:

(a) Demand stream: Self Help Groups, Federations of Self Help Groups.

(b) Supply stream: Commercial banks, specialized regional rural banks, MFIs etc.

The demand stream has an intra promotional stream built in to it. It represents the professional organisation otherwise popularly known as NGO facilitators promoting member owned and controlled institutions. It has a two dimensional role of providing an enabling environment - one at the grassroots level for promoting the SHGs and their federations of poor women and another at a regulatory level as an enabler of Self-regulation.

Joining these streams either as a regulator/supervisor and providing an enabling environment and, of course chipping in with Bulk lending/lines of credit are the Ministry Apex banks such as National Bank of Agriculture and Rural Development (NABARD), Small Industries Development Bank of India (SIDBI) and of course Central Banker i.e., Reserve Bank of India (RBI).

From this standpoint, the micro finance sector does not fit into the pure model of credit delivery alone. Varying degrees of diversities characterize MFIs, in regard to context, structure / forms, content etc. This divergence is reflected in two broader categories of MFIs.

(a) NGOs with direct financial intermediation–delivery mode/outreach.

(b) Self managed demand system–owned and controlled by poor people.

While the former belongs to delivery model the latter is an enabled entity with professional support. As the Micro Finance Industry continues to grow and develop more financial intermediation functions, the need for orderly growth in a systematic and guided manner cannot be overemphasized. A system of regulation is required to facilitate this process like for any other financial institutions.

2. Approaches in Microfinance Regulation

Microfinance has been practiced around the world in many forms and by various institutions, ranging from informal ROSCA's

NGOs, credit co-operatives, non-bank financial institutions, and commercial banks. The challenge facing regulators considering appropriate regulatory approaches is complicated by the fact that MFIs range significantly in institutional type, scale of operations, and level of professionalism (Berenbach and Churchill 1977). Given the diversity of economic and legal environments under which microfinance is provided, as well as the motivations of actors involved in microfinance, controversy over the manner of regulation and supervision of microfinance is not surprising.

The variety of legislative proposals, regulatory frameworks, and supervisory practices the world over reflect this reality (Valenzuela and Young 1999). Response to MFIs has ranged from no regulation to full external regulation, outlined in Table presented below.

	Regulator	*Supervisor*	*Features*
Initial steps	None	None	Industry standards
Self-regulation	Federation or SRO	Federation or SRO	Peer pressure to abide incentives/ sanctions
Hybrid	Statutory body	Third party (federation, accountant, etc.,)	Joint appointment
Existing laws	Statutory body	Statutory body	Government mandate
Special laws	Statutory body	Statutory body	Government mandate

All the same, regulation could stifle the growth of MF sector and rob it of its flexibility and informality in operations. The regulation could turn out to be repressive and retardant. Therefore the role of regulation would have to be proactive and development oriented for the growth of MF sector.

As such self regulation is deemed to be an alternative tool, which if structured thoroughly can substitute formal government regulation, nay, contribute to growth of MFIs with order, for, the initiatives are in the hands of MFIs. The norms and rules are set to meet the ground realities and the needs of the sector thereby preventing repressive regulation.

3. Classification Of MFI's For The Purpose of Regulation

Based on the type of financial services extended the MFIs may be divided into the following classes for the purpose of regulation:

(a) MFIs purveying credit only;

(b) MFIs purveying credit and mobilising savings from the clients/loanees

(c) MFIs purveying credit and mobilising savings from the clients/loanees and general public.

The classification as suggested above may be the basis for regulation irrespective of the type of other financial services (like insurance, housing finance) and non-financial services provided by the MFIs alongwith the financial services.

4. Features/Characteristics of Self-Regulation

The regulation and financial institutions are inseparable and also is not a point for argument, what is however arguable is the form of regulation. Further, supervision is an essential part of regulation. While the regulation of the MFIs may cover registration, reserve requirements, compliance with prudential norms, directions in respect of microfinance operations, and reporting system to the competent controlling authority. Supervision of the MFIs may comprise on-site inspection and off-site supervision to ensure that the functioning of the MFIs is not detrimental to the interests of the people.

The chief objective of self-regulation in its developmental sense is to increase the outreach and depth of micro finance so as to have unhindered advancement of this sector towards achieving the goal of poverty reduction on a wider scale and spread. The essential features of this approach are:

(a) to ensure target group focus on the poor and gender focus on women

(b) to enhance the image of the sector for orderly growth

(c) to set performance standards in vital parameters – financial, developmental/social

(d) to address the location specific/institution specific concerns of informal institutions/ community based people organisations

(e) to minimize the cost of oversight

Thus self-regulation is not just supervision but an enabling and guiding provision for the micro finance sector. It goes beyond rating/assessment/appraisal.

Given the requirement of self-regulation to function, it cannot work, if it is freewheeling. To enforce compliance, an organisation either existing or new has to be set up backed by legal or quasi legal power to oversee and implement the entire gamut of activities. So in essence, there has to be a regulator to enforce self-regulation, otherwise it will not be effective. In fact, self-regulation is a less stringent form of external regulation.

5. Accountability

Self regulation for the demand stream of the microfinance sector represented, as it were, by member owned and controlled People's institutions rests on the bedrock of its accountability to its members.

This has two basic inviolable premises of accountability.

(a) Economic advancement and (b) Empowerment

The member accountable for development processes would include the following.

(a) Economic Advancement - Improvement in quality of life

Although development activities expect to improve the quality of life of their members, this is possible only if members receive adequate benefits from those activities. Those development efforts, which are member-accountable, provide greater benefits to members and thus are more likely to actually bring improvements in the quality of life. The more member-accountable organisations provided higher economic rewards which had made significant changes, both tangible and intangible, in the lives of women. Some of the benefits included sending daughters to school, better food and nutrition, feelings of security, better clothing and in some cases better housing.

(b) Empowerment of Members

Organisations, which have a high level of member-accountability generally, tend to share power with their members.

The members tend to be more knowledgeable about the day-to-day processes of the organization and are more able to participate in the decision-making processes. However, members are themselves not in a powerful position to demand member-accountability from the organisation. It rests on the willingness of the organisation to create processes which will provide greater opportunities for members to take part in the decision making process. It is expected that through such power sharing processes the members will themselves be able to take over the development activity and sustain it without any external support. Members will thus be able to help themselves and will not need to seek external interventions for their own survival and development.

6. Member Accountability Can be Broadly Defined as Under

(1) Adequately addresses problems and suggestions of members

- Members are encouraged to voice their complaints.
- Suggestions from the members are actively sought
- Organisation attempts to resolve complaints
- Members; suggestions are considered and implemented if appropriate

(2) Shares power with members in managing the organisation

- Dissemination and provides ready access to information related to organisation's activities
- Members are active in management roles
- Disseminates information on progress of organisational activities to members
- Members had shared in the formation and development of the organisation
- Leader (s) is / are receptive to the members and available when needed
- Members' share in making decisions regarding the use of all profits from the activity.
- Funds for the welfare of members are not diverted into other activities without their knowledge.

(3) Timely support to members from the institution

- Provides financial services to the members
- Provides input services on time and in sufficient quantities.
- Creates an infrastructure suitable to meet members' need within available resources
- Establishes linkages with main stream for maximum benefits to members
- Continuous efforts are made to enhance efficiency of the members' efforts (technology / training / others)

7. Specifics of Standards

Standards to measure the performance of MFIs fall into three categories with generally desirable bench-making levels under each of the parameters.

(a) Institutional standards

(b) Financial standards

(c) Social/developmental standards

(a) Institutional standards

I. Governance

- Target group focus
- Vision, Values, Ethics
- Functioning of Governing Board, Members participation, Regularity of meetings, Decision making, Succession Planning etc.
- Legal aspects – compliance with the law of the land.

II. Organisational

- Professional experience and commitment
- Development strategy and services provided
- Degree of focus on microfinance

III. Management

- Quality of managerial and field staff
- Level and adequacy of infrastructure.

- Planning, Monitoring
- HRD Practices

(b) Financial standards

I. Track record of financial performance

- Level and growth of savings of members
- Level and growth of credit of members
- Portfolio quality/value at risk, repayment rate
- Sustainability
- Profitability
- Capital adequacy and liquidity

II. Financial Control System

- Cash flow planning
- Fraud prevention
- Budgeting and Forecasting
  – Quality of Budget
  – Application of Budget
- Tracking system for overdues
- Audit
  – Conduct of Internal and External audit
  – Quality of Audit
- Accounts reconciliation

III. Accounting and reporting

- Recognition of income
- Loan loss provisioning policy
- Management Information System

(c) Development/Social Indicators

(i) Access and control of Land

(ii) Access and control of water

(iii) Access and control of Education

(iv) Access and control of Health

(v) Assets with productivity

(vi) Business Development and Graduation of enterprises

(vii) Graduation of class mobility

(viii) Panchayat Raj Institutions-strong local civic governance

(ix) People's participation/leadership for various community/ local schemes/ projects

(x) People's assertiveness vis-à-vis local/federal governments

The range for the performance standards and also the means of the verification need to be detailed along with the each of the traits/parameters.

8. Making Self-Regulation Operational

With a view to take-up self-regulation we need a vehicle called Self-Regulatory Organisation (SRO). The SROs must be an independent watchdog and thus should not perform the following functions:

- Representing MFIs on various forum and lobbying which can be done by industry bodies;
- Policy advocacy and lobby with donors, government agencies etc.
- Training and technical assistance of MFIs should be done by industry bodies;
- Internal regulation of MFIs should be done through governance and with assistance if necessary by industry bodies.

As has been the experience from the comparable institutions, SROs will have to evolve from MF sector either as a incorporated or unincorporated body of associations with membership from across the sector. Given the variety in the sector, the SROs could evolve as a regional specific, institution specific entities or a combination of both. It could perform the following functions by proactive regulation and supervision and also champion the cause of micro finance in general.

1. Registration and permitting the conduct of business.
2. Setting standards, which could form the ground rules for the sector.

3. Evolving proper systems for accounts and other records
4. Conducting audit and inspection
5. Developing proper systems for reporting, transparency, disclosure etc.
6. Capacity Building through training, workshops, etc.

9. Self Regulatory Organisation (SRO) Network as Facilitator

The SRO being a network of practitioners by practitioners for practitioners comprising of well organised and developed MFIs, could facilitate the process of internalizing self regulation among the member practitioners. It can help build the capacity of the organisations to develop the effective governance structures (a well-functioning board of directors) and various management control systems, including written policies and procedures, internal controls, loan review, compliance, planning, budgeting, internal and external auditing, and management information systems. **It could help design code of conduct, document and disseminate best practices and best standards.**

References

1. Harrington, M. (1991). *Business process improvement*. New York: McGraw-Hill.
2. Hart, S., and Quinn, R. (1993). *Roles executives play: CEOs, behavioral complexity, and firm performance*. Human Relations, 46(3), 115-142.
3. Hoojiberg, R., and Quinn, R. (1992). *Behavioral complexity and the development of effective managers.* In R. Phillips and J. Hunt (Eds.), Strategic leadership: A multiorganizational-level perspective (pp. 44-61). Westport, CT: Quorum.
4. Joseph A. Petrick and John F. Quinn. *Management Ethics Integrity at Work.*
5. Lawrence, P.R., and Lorsch, J.W. (1967). *Organization and environment.* Cambridge, MA: Harvard University Press.
6. Mayo, E. (1933). *The human problems of an industrial civilization.* New York: Macmillan.
7. Petrick, J.A., and Furr, D.S. (1995). *Total quality in managing human resources*. Delray Beach, Fl: St. Lucie.

8. Quinn, R.E., Faerman, S.R., Thompson, M.P., and McGrath, M.R. (1996). *Becoming a master manager* (2nd ed.). New York: John Wiley

9. Quinn, R.E., Spreitzer, G., and Hart, S. (1992). *Integrating the extremes: Crucial skills for managerial effectiveness.* In S. Srivastva and Associates (Eds.) *Executive and organizational continuity: Managing the paradoxes of stability and change* (pp. 92 - 109). San Francisco: Jossey-Bass.

10. Taylor, F.W. (1911). *The principles of scientific management.* New York: Harper and Brothers.

11. Weber, M. (1921). *Theory of social and economic organization.* London: Oxford University Press.

20

Banking Sector Reforms

Banking Sector Reforms coincided with economic reforms. The Government of India (GOI) in 1991 set up the Narasimham Committee on Financial System (NCFS, 1991). The terms of reference of the Committee were to examine all aspects relating to the structure, organisation and functioning of the Indian banking system and the capital markets. The Committee's recommendations made in November 1991 constitute a landmark in the evolution of banking policy in the country. The first stage of banking sector reforms focused on interest rate liberalization, improvement in prudential norms and standards, strengthening banking supervision and liberalizing the banking sector to facilitate the entry of private sector banks and consequently increasing competition in the banking sector. In 1997 the Second Narasimham Committee on banking sector reforms was appointed to review the progress achieved and chart the road map for the second stage of banking sector reforms. The Second Narasimham Committee submitted its report in 1998. The Committee on the Financial System – Narasimham Committee recommendations were implemented by the Reserve Bank of India in large part.

The pace of banking reforms has been a process of gradual and incremental growth giving the casual observer the impression that nothing much has changed. However, if one were to take the totality of banking sector reforms over the last decade into account the change is unmistakable and the achievements thus far are substantial though a great deal still remains to be done. Prior to 1992, interest rates were completely administered by the RBI and were "highly complex and rigid." The RBI stipulated maximum deposit rates on both savings and time deposits (of all maturities), as well as minimum lending rates on loans of different sizes and maturities. This system guaranteed banks a minimum interest rate spread and a measure of protection against mounting losses. Moreover, the same rates were charged by all banks thereby eliminating any scope for price competition between banks. Since 1992, interest rates have been deregulated in a phased manner and by July 1996, banks allowed to set interest rates on all term-deposits of maturity of over one year and on all advances greater than Rs.2 lakh. After initial capitalization by Government, Capital Adequacy norms were introduced. The introduction of capital adequacy norms requires commercial banks, and more recently, non-bank financial companies (NBFCs), to maintain a capital to risk assets ratio (CRAR), of not less than 8 per cent, in line with the BIS norms. This sought to minimize the problem of inadequacy of capital compared to risk exposure that has persistently plagued public sector banks. It was hoped that institution of the BIS norms would provide Indian banks with a comfortable cushion against insolvency, thereby ensuring market stability. Prior to 1991 the rates at which the banks could lend and the rates which they could offer on deposits were also controlled under a strictly administered interest rate regime closely prescribed and monitored by the Reserve Bank of India. Interest rates on Government debt were similarly controlled. The Statutory Liquidity Ratio (SLR) and Cash Reserve Ratio (CRR) were kept high and there were additional mandatory requirements for investment by banks in low interest yielding government securities. Over the last decade RBI has deregulated interest rates. Interest rates on government securities are now determined by the market on the basis of periodic auctions by the RBI. The security market has been considerably widened and deepened. Prudential norms for Income Recognition and Asset Classification have been upgraded in closer alignment with international practices and the Basle Committee recommendations. The objective is full alignment with International Practices and we are moving steadily in this direction towards implementing Basle-II.

External supervision of the banks has been strengthened to monitor and evaluate bank performance in accordance with the key prudential standards. This has made for greater transparency in banking with a sharp focus on the quality of the asset portfolio. The net NPAs of the public sector banks have shown a decline as the stringency of prudential norms has increased sensitivity to the portfolio.

Competition in the banking system has increased leading to significant change as new private sector banks and foreign banks are now being perceived as active competitors for business while Public Sector Banks still dominate the system but greater competition among them is also impacting their behaviour.

These reforms have, no doubt, changed the way banks function. The higher prudential standards are forcing banks actively to seek quality borrowers in order to improve their asset quality. Interest rate liberalization has helped improve operating margins. Due to the competition among banks the blue chip companies and quality borrowers are able to demand credit at better terms. The opening up of domestic and foreign capital markets also enables them to look for cheaper source of credit. Thus the process of disintermediation is also a threat to the banking system. Overall stronger and stricter regulation and unbridled competition is expected to work to the advantage of bank customers and bank borrowers as also lead to the overall allocational efficiency of the system. However, banking reforms have still a long way to go. More importantly, reforms in banking are about changing the way banking institutions function. A liberalized and more open economy with freer flow of capital, places heavy demands on the banking system. Competition and interest rate liberalization will also bring pressure on bank margins. Banks will need much stronger credit appraisal skills than were necessary in the past to reflect the more competitive environment facing borrowers and the consequent higher risk of failure. The liberalized economy also leads to exposure to greater volatility in price, exchange and interest rate movements. Credit appraisal techniques have to take account of the risk uncertainties on this count on banks credit portfolio. Handling emerging challenges will call for a basic restructuring of management system re-engineering in banks and massive investment in upgradation of staff skills. The next stage of banking sector reforms demands parallel improvement in the legal system relating to debt recovery. Efficient banking will require a credible threat of legal action to ensure recovery from defaulting borrowers. Incentives should be there for good borrowers and fear of swift remedial action for defaulting borrowers.

Incentive systems are gradually being changed and the recent liberalization of lending rates will help banks make more commercially oriented lending decisions since reform of the Banking Sector is necessary for stable and long-term growth financial sector restructuring is vital. The Banking System is learning to respond to market incentives. The stricter provisioning norms and non-repressed interest rates are giving banks strong reasons to assess risk more carefully and price loans based on commercial considerations. Given the importance of India's banking sector within the financial landscape, restructuring the banks is a key priority but development of the broader financial sector, including equity and bond markets is crucial as well. This would introduce much needed competition for banks and offer savers a wider range of investment and borrowing opportunities.

From the vantage of 2004 one of the successes of Indian Financial Sector Reform has been the maintenance of financial stability and avoidance of any major financial crisis during the reform period.

A key issue in banking sector reforms in the future relates to government control over public sector banks. The Committee on Banking Sector Reforms had recommended that the government's equity holding should be reduced to 33 per cent in order to free the banks of constraints arising from government ownership. The weight of international experience is also in favour of banks being free from government controls. This will have a great bearing on unshackling the Indian economy. A consensus needs to be built for this to happen. Economic reforms which necessarily include reforms in the banking sector have been dwarfed by ethnic, caste-based affirmative action and religious disputes which have been driving Indian mass politics over the last 15 years. Expressions of 'Indians identity' politics have led to mass mobilization, insurgency, riots and destruction of holy places. In mass perceptions, the significance of the need for assertion of identity has been of far greater significance than the implications of bank reforms/economic reforms. Raging debates on banking/economic reforms remain confined to the English language newspapers, discourses in the internet, India International Centre and the Government Ministries. It is time the issues are made intelligible to the people at large to enable them to fully grasp their significance and to move forward on disinvestment of government controls in the Public Sector Banks. There are no clear templates for Banking/Financial Sector Reform and development. The process is also not free from risk. Policy Makers must not shy away, on this count, but while freeing the Banking Sector face the emerging challenges on an ongoing basis as these arise.

21

Gen Next–Banking Sector Challenges

Banking sector reform assumed a new urgency after the South East Asian crisis which underlined that an open capital account necessitated a strong banking system which would be able to take any hit. It led to a clear appreciation that any endemic weakness of the banking system can engender systemic weaknesses and lead to tremendous vulnerability. Quite simply a fragile banking system is unequal to managing the ebbs and flows of international capital. Hence the crisis brought into sharper focus the shift in the paradigm with the need to strengthen banks worldwide. Internationally the strength of the financial sector /structure is a critical element of evaluating economic performance. Interestingly, in India the process of financial strengthening was not a reaction to the crisis but preceded the Asian crisis and had commenced with the economic reforms unleashed in 1991 with the mantra of globalisation liberalisation which had as its core the financial sector reforms of 1991. Indian banks in tandem with the rest of the world adopted the Basle Committee norms, achieved 8 per cent capital adequacy ratios and implemented the income recognition and asset classification parameters. The achievement of capital adequacy was sequenced through an injection of government capital in some banks. Banks going public and raising capital, banks raising capital through internal resource generation and completing the loop by returning government capital. Thus, the decade of the 90s has marked the emergence of stronger Banks. On performing assets declined balance sheets grew stronger and banks more market savvy and infinitely more gung ho. Though there were significant improvements in several areas of banking which touch customers. No more queues before the public counters, no more 10 to 2 regimens with ATMs and anytime money. Good clean crisp notes with the Clean Note Policy. Banks also ventured heavily into the hitherto uncharted world of retail finance and active management of the treasury.

There was an attitudinal shift. However several caveats remain leading to a need for second generation or Gen Next reforms. Banking is an ongoing battle and there is no room for complacency. The imposition of prudential norms does not mutatis mutandis translate to good banking. It only puts in place prescriptive, Central Bank mandated, internationally accepted standards of evaluation to judge the strengths and weaknesses of a bank. It enables us to see how far the banks are fulfilling the norms laid down and allows us to evaluate them. It thus achieves good ranking not necessarily good banking. The Basle Committee norms had the virtue of simplicity. Without any doubt the accord and subsequent additions and amendments helped to strengthen the soundness and stability of the International Banking System. The widespread acceptance and adoption of the accord in many countries has contributed to the achievement of competitive equality. However the accord was not without an Achilles heel. The risk weighting of assets led, at best, to a crude measure of economic risk as by adopting a broad brush approach it failed to differentiate between borrowers of poor or strong credit quality. Credit to a blue chip and to a retail client merited the same treatment. There was also criticism that the accord did not incentivise banks to the adoption of credit risk mitigation techniques. It had a narrow focus confining itself to credit risk and failing to factor in other risks as liquidity, operational, reputational or market risks. The New Capital Accord Framework (NCAF) is based on a need to redress the weaknesses of the earlier system. The new framework aims to better align regulatory capital with the underlying risks faced by Banks and thereby further strengthen the soundness and stability of the Banking system. The adoption of risk based approach for determining regulatory capital requires Banks to further strengthen their risk management systems. While several banks have their own in house gradation systems for advances these may require to be refined and new risk measurement systems adopted. Good banking compels good quality credit decisions if you subject banks to a financial stress test, the figures alone may not tell the whole story. For instance analysts and examiners often distinguish between the good bad and ugly NPAs and more specifically between Gross NPAs and Net NPAs. If the net NPAs are low the gross NPAs are not construed as being a cause for alarm, which they are as they signal poor quality of credit decisions. High fiscal deficits increase sovereign assets of banks but if the fiscal deficit comes down there would be little scope for Lazy Banking to use Deputy Governor Mohans term. If the fiscal deficit comes down resources will have to be released for investment in the financial sector. Financial strength and profitability will not stem from the comfort of Government security holdings. Thus credit expansion will need the honing of credit skills to enable the Banking system to play its designated role of efficiently allocating resources. With increasing globalisation, Banks will also have to assess whether the enterprises to whom banks are extending credit can withstand globalisation this will lead to a further need to refine Banks credit skills. This will also create an external environment where banks will be compelled to compete. This process of competition has already been unleashed by the new private sector banks. They have a lot of advantages in terms of no legacy of economic infrastructure they have counterbalanced the disadvantages in terms of reach and spread through the use of Information technology and IT Infrastructure. Financial Innovation in terms of product pricing has led to highly competitive Banking. Mutual funds also pose a threat to Banks with booming capital markets they are in a position to offer much higher returns to investors than banks. They are emerging as financial contenders as disintermediation in the financial sector is increasing. To survive and succeed banks will necessarily have to hone their credit skills .In the context of the NCAF and the improvement in risk management the key areas for Gen Next reforms for banks will lie in harnessing technology, building superior MIS and focussing on skilled manpower development .Gen Next reforms will be of overarching importance. The scenario presents both a challenge and an opportunity for Indian Banks and makes the introduction of Gen Next reforms an imperative.

Reference

Dr. Deepali Pant Joshi–*The Financial Express,* April 2004.

22

Corporate Governance

Corporate governance has become a buzz word but it is much more than that. It is a concept which can change our ways of thinking and doing business leading seamlessly to the attainment of 6 sigma in all processes. So what is corporate governance? What does it mean, how do we operationalise it ? In practice what does it imply for the UCB? Today we will try to find answers to all these questions. The word corporate comes from corpus a body and governance is to direct and control. As a concept Corporate Governance has come to the fore only lately but as part of business ethic it has always been there. There are two broad strands of thought, first is the Anglo-American model which we have adopted as most of our institutions and their institutional structures of governance and control are patterned on the Anglo-Saxon model and the Franco-German model which lays stress more on the long-term interests of an institutions core stakeholders. Let us first delve into definition. Its very name is self-explanatory and stands for governance by the Board Milton Friedman the American Nobel prize winning economist defines it in terms of market maximization. To conduct business in accordance with share holders desires make as much money as possible while conforming to the basic rules of society embodied in laws and customs OECD defines it as the system by which business corporations are directed and controlled. It specifies the distribution of rights and responsibilities of different participants in a corporation Board managers shareholders other stakeholders and spells out the rules and procedures for decisions. It provides both structure for setting company objectives and specifies means by which these are to be attained as also the parameters for monitoring performance. It is more rigorous and all encompassing than the American model. In America and UK after Watergate which brought down the presidency of President Nixon and in UK after Nick Leeson a rogue trader nearly brought down the Barings Bank the need to know the necessity of correct of information became paramount leading to Corporate Governance issues. In May 1991 the London Stock Exchange set up a Committee under the chairmanship of Sir Arian Cadbury to help raise the standards of corporate governance and the level of confidence in financial reporting and auditing by setting out clearly what it sees as the respective responsibilities of those involved and what it believes is expected of them. The Committee investigated accountability of the Board of Directors to shareholders and to the society. Corporate Governance has emerged as a set of arrangements that maximize the incentives for value enhancing investments while minimizing inefficient power seeking. It is the issue, quite simply, of how to get managers to work for shareholders and majority shareholders to work for all shareholders. The main function of all Banks and naturally of Urban Cooperative banks is to mobilize savings, i.e., deposits and channelise them into productive investments to earn returns. Thus it is incumbent upon them to screen credit worthy borrowers and projects by filtering and through an appropriate lending policy. To monitor the use of borrowed funds as intended through the exercise of judicious pre sanction survey and effective post credit disbursal. Through appropriate credit administration which has to be buttressed through sound corporate governance so as to ensure recovery of loaned amounts by enforcing creditors' rights thus Banks play a critical role in upholding incentives for value enhancing investments. Corporate Governance of Banks is an essential element of a country's governance architecture it can have systemic financial stability implications, it can shape the pattern of credit distribution and overall supply of financial services it can set the tone foe corporate governance in the non financial sector the crucial question then is Who is to guard the guards themselves Quis Custodiet Ipsos Custodes? Banks constitute the largest financial intermediaries around the world and possess stupendous powers of leverage. Weak legal systems around the world further impede the ability of small, diffuse shareholders to enforce their contractual rights. Unlike in the Corporate World, Authorities as RBI and Government play a direct role in Bank Governance through Bank Regulation and Supervision. This role is justified by the need to ensure systemic stability, financial stability and by deposit insurance liability considerations. Thus RBI Government becomes almost parallel owners. Shareholders specially in Urban Banks enjoy the benefit of high leverage with the downside protection of deposit insurance which weakens their incentives for strong management monitoring. Let me illustrate further while a ubiquitous form of corporate control, concentrated ownership raises new barriers to effective corporate governance. In particular large investors are large as such they may manipulate the firm to act in their own interests and contrary to the broad interests of the Bank and other stakeholders. For instance large shareholders may pay themselves special dividends and exploit minority shareholders, arrange loans for firms they own or arrange business transactions to profit themselves at the expense of the Bank and also shift the Bank to higher risk activities in which they benefit on the upside but debt holders' minority stakeholders bear the brunt of failure. This leads to the key issue of Who controls management? Boards or Bank Supervisors? Regulatory and Supervisory systems that foster more accurate information disclosure, empower private investors legal rights substantially boost banking system and profitability. The current trends lay stronger emphasis on risk measurement and management by Basel2 and helps monitor management actions. Market discipline is emerging as a complement to Bank Supervision there is still room to enhance shareholder discipline which is essential to further financial stability without stifling financial innovation. Supervisors should help Board and shareholders exercise discipline and not supplant them. Shareholders are essential pillars of market discipline. Their incentives must be made to align with those of authorities. Supervisors must make the Boards the main locus of accountability while keeping open communication challenges with management. Management is to be made accountable to Board and not to supervisors. Supervisors should assess board effectiveness particularly.

The Role of Banks in Corporate Governance–Conclusions

Banks are important stakeholders of corporations.

Their actions can affect corporate performance both positively and negatively.

But their influence as lenders should complement effective shareholder monitoring and protection of minority rights.

Governance of banks is an essential element of a country's governance architecture.

Enhanced role for shareholders and boards, helped by bank supervisors.

Much of the literature asserts that financial intermediaries are more opaque than other sectors of the economy: outside investors know less than bankers about what the latter are doing with their funds. Although information asymmetries plague all sectors this problem is more difficult in finance. In product or other service markets, purchasers part with their money in exchange for something now. In finance, money now is exchanged for a 'promise to pay' in the future. Also, in many product or service markets, if the object sold – from a car to a haircut – is defective, the buyers often find out relatively soon. However, loan quality is not readily observable for quite some time and can be hidden for extensive periods.

Banks and non-bank financial intermediaries can also alter the risk composition of their assets more quickly than most non-financial industries. Moreover, banks can readily hide problems by extending loans to clients that cannot service previous debt obligations. Furthermore, in most sectors when inventories of 'stuff' piles up, be it cars, computers, or software, it is generally a negative sign about firm performance. But when inventories of money piles up in a bank – it becomes more liquid – it is much harder to sort out whether this is a negative signal or a prudent response by management to a risky environment.

Reference

Dr. Deepali Pant Joshi–*The Financial Express*, November 2004.

23

The New Leviathan

In the new competitive economic environment size and focus matter even for mere survival. The survival of small banks in a market that is simultaneously shrinking and getting intensely competitive is close to impossible mergers and amalgamations have become necessary to ensure that banks attain appropriate size. As the financial services industry becomes increasingly international the more narrowly defined and historically protected national financial markets become less significant. Consequently, financial institutions must achieve a critical size to compete.

Proponents of financial sector consolidation argue that institutions need size to spread growing information technology and processing costs over larger revenue bases. Another key factor is the need for greater market capitalization with governments and financial sector regulators accepting financial operators' arguments that greater size is crucial to cost cutting and strong national institutions. The race appears to be for size efficiency synergies and profitability. Competition policy in the financial sector is tending towards an easing of regulations and the elimination of obstacles, in this regard. "The effort has been to eliminate existing controls that had distorted resource allocation and inhibited entrepreneurship. The economy is being nudged towards higher productivity and efficiency." Strong banking systems are required to intermediate substantial flows. Banks need to shore up capital asset size, productivity and profitability.

Size generates economies of scale essential to compete in global markets. Oligopolies are not created as technology has the ability to lower entry barriers to new types of financial service providers somewhat reduces the power of concentration.

Economies of scale (size) and product mix (scope) will lead bankers to operate from a greater resource base. Banks need size and resources to compete globally. Global corporations today expect their bankers to have the expertise, products and presence to serve them anywhere and across a broad range of markets.

Mergers will give greater scale reach and enduring relationships with larger number of customers. They also serve as the springboard to increase profitability through greater economies of scale and improved operational efficiency. As Dr. Rakesh Mohan has expressed it. The significant transformation of the banking industry is clearly evident from the changes that have occurred in the financial markets, institutions and products. While deregulation has opened up new vistas it has entailed greater competition". Deregulation has intensified competition through two mechanisms. Firstly, by opening up the banking sector to new entrants (foreign banks and new banks) and easing the rules previously preventing expansion into various financial segments (retail banking/investment/merchant banking and secondly by encouraging development of new products and convergence in services provided by different types of financial operators.

These developments have intensified competition, thereby reducing operating margins and profitability. Financial institutions compensate for the erosion in margins through a scramble for volumes and easing of credit standards which leads to a deterioration of loan portfolios. Thus, weak banks may proverbially rush in where the strongest fear to tread and generate seismic ripples which can lead to systemic instabilities. As a financial institution is only as strong as its weakest link it is necessary to address issues relating to shoring up weak banks through mergers and amalgamations. Bank failures can have devastating systemic consequences hence the stress on revision of national regulatory frameworks to ensure that financial services adhere to prudential principles and competitive imperatives.

Driven by the need to raise additional capital and to counter growing competition from domestic and foreign banks, mergers have emerged as an alternative option in the context of banking sector reform. In addition if weak banks are allowed to continue in business, competing, squeezing margins, or rushing into areas to increase business without measuring the attendant risks, the stability of the financial system would be threatened. Initially mergers were one way of salvaging inefficient banks. There have been three waves of mergers in India. In the early decades of the sixties the failure of the Palai Bank generated a situation of near panic and led to the amendment of Section 44 of the Banking Regulation Act. Prior to 1961, the act only provided for the voluntary amalgamation of banks, it was amended to include Section 44A which explicitly sets out the procedure for amalgamation of banking companies. Further, Section 45 was inserted. This gives the Reserve Bank power to apply to the Central Government for suspension of business by a banking company and to prepare a scheme of reconstitution or amalgamation. Thus, Section 45 imparts RBI the power to compulsorily reconstruct or amalgamate a weak bank with a stronger bank. In 1961 after the failure of the Palai Bank the Banking Companies amendment act empowered the RBI to formulate and carry out a scheme for the reconstruction and compulsory amalgamation of substandard banks with well managed ones. Of the 42 banks granted moratoria 22 were amalgamated with other banks. Under Section 36 AE of the Banking Regulation Act spells out the power of the Central Government to acquire undertakings of banking companies in certain cases, the Central Government can take over a weak bank on the advice of RBI. When a bank is placed under liquidation the RBI can appoint any other bank as the official liquidator. The first wave of amalgamations came in 1960s then there was a lull in the mid eighties again there was a great deal of activity which arose principally with the need to bail out weak banks. Thus in 1984 the Lakshmi Commercial Bank with its baggage of 230 branches was merged with the Canara Bank, Bank of Cochin with its 108 branches was merged with State Bank of India and Miraj State Bank with its 26 branches merged with Union Bank of India. In 1985 the Hindustan Commercial Bank with its 140 branches became part of the Punjab National Bank, 1987 saw the merger of the Traders Bank with Bank of Baroda and 1988 the meshing of United Industrial Bank with its complement of 145 branches with Allahabad Bank. This was followed by the merger of the Bank of Thanjavur with Indian Bank, Parur Central Bank with its 51 branches which merged with Bank of India, Purbanchal Bank with 40 branches merged with Central Bank of India in 1990-1993 saw the merger of 591 branches of New Bank of India with Punjab National Bank, BCCI merged with State Bank of India, in 1994 Bank of Karad with 48 branches became part of Bank of India, in 1995 the Kashinath State Bank of U.P. merged with the State Bank of India, in 1997 the Bari Doab Cooperative Bank of Punjab became part of the Oriental Bank of Commerce. Benares State Bank merged with the Bank of Baroda.

These were banks in distress which were rescued through the process of amalgamation. The third wave of mergers which we have witnessed in the recent past is qualitatively different the merger of HDFC with the Times Bank and that of ICICI Bank with the Bank of Madura illustrate that merger of sound institutions leads to synergies achieved by a combination of complementary strengths. In the case of ICICI Bank it immediately secured the Bank of Maduras sound microfinance portfolio and gained a presence and penetrative outreach in the South of India through the branch network of the Bank of Madura. These are the kind of mergers which will enable the banking industry to consolidate. This will lead to a repositioning for competitive advantage and becomes vital as the rapidly evolving markets, RTGS and the new ways of transacting business in the wired web world now demand large outlays in investment technology and communication networks. The Narasimhan Committee on the financial sector reforms had recommended the creation of a four tier structure of Banks 3-4 large banks with global presence 8-10 national banks followed by local banks and rural banks at the base of the hierarchy. The second Narasimhan Committee had reiterated this stance on the plea that it would help promote the much needed consolidation in the banking industry.

Mergers help to maximize shareholders' returns. Creating shareholder value means that the market favours firms that increase the productive use of their assets by increasing turnover ratios, margin and profitability. Strong, efficient and profitable financial institutions are vital to economic success especially as engines of economic viability in creating and maintaining credit systems for other sectors both nationally and globally. The contrary view is that market power and scale economies associated with market dominance fall victim ultimately to insulation from the market and bureaucratic inefficiency that grows with size creates greater complexity in terms of bureaucratic controls, slows the ability of organizations to respond fast to changing market conditions and leads to complacency. Problems in meshing personnel and systems stemming from divergence in corporate culture and management cannot also be wished away. However in playing for the long haul banks have little option but to further buttress themselves through mergers and amalgamations, whether these will proceed in a gentlemanly and sedate fashion or give rise to predatory activity, only time will tell, but as a mode of business consolidation, clearly mergers and acquisitions are here to stay.

Reference

Dr. Deepali Pant Joshi–*The Financial Express*, June 7, 2004.

24

Policies and Programmes for Employment in India

The single biggest challenge for India's Planners and Policy Makers for the first decade of this century is to create employment for a rapidly increasing labour force. The demographic projections made by the Plans indicate that though there is likely to be a steady reduction in the rate of population growth in the country, the growth rate of the labour force will reach a very high peak at about 2.5 per cent per annum and then only it will show a gradual decline. This increase in the labour force is a result of the high rate of population growth experienced in the late 70s and early 80s. The growth rate of the labour force has to be seen against our past record in creation of employment opportunities. During the 1980s and early 1990s the average rate of growth of employment, which is a practice for work opportunities has been around 2 per cent per year. Therefore, if past trends of employment generation are used as a projection for the future, the country faces the possibility of adding another 20 lakh people to the ranks of unemployed every year. Such a situation is clearly insupportable and indefensible. As we are all aware, unemployment not only entails high human costs but also, in time, imposing significant costs on society in terms of social unrest and deterioration of law and order. It is imperative that employment opportunities are created for our growing labour force. It is equally necessary to create jobs and provide adequate income to the people employed in agriculture. We have adverse land man ratios, which have led to a proliferation of small uneconomic land holdings and fuelled migration to cities from rural areas. Too many of our people still live below the poverty line although post-independence we have virtually eliminated famine, hunger, malnutrition and under-nutrition continued to be a source of concern. Our most glaring failure has been in the sphere of social indicators of quality of life. This fact has been driven home most forcefully with the inter-country comparison of the human development index brought out by the UNDP. Whatever be our criticism of the UNDP methodology we have to face the fact that in some of the objectively verifiable social indicators, India ranks below even the world's poorest and most backward countries of Sub-Saharan Africa. There is an urgent and immediate need to redress this position through effective State intervention for creation of jobs and employment opportunities to meet in "Gunnar Myrdals" words the revolution of rising expectations of our people.

As Prof. Amartya Sen has best expressed it development is the process of expansion of human capabilities and human freedoms. Any assessment of development has to be informed by this consideration. Poverty reduction through employment, through growth, through social development is a key goal. Without sustained economic growth poverty will not be reduced let alone eradicated but economic growth must not be jobless, ruthless, voiceless, rootless or futureless. Economic growth requires the pursuit of a three pronged strategy of growth such as (1) economic growth, (2) direct State intervention through programmes of job creation, employment and poverty alleviation and (3) investment in human capital. Agricultural and allied activities continue to be the primary source of livelihood for the majority of our population. Therefore, it is necessary to increase investment in these sectors through development of appropriate technologies to generate higher level of output and greater employment. The empowerment of women and socially disadvantaged groups like scheduled castes/tribes has to be emphasized in our developmental efforts and legislation has to be enforced to ensure this. Inequalities, caste disparities and unemployment cannot be wished away. These have to be addressed through affirmative action. Hence in all efforts of poverty reduction, special care has to be taken to meet the needs of women and other marginalized and vulnerable groups who should be given priority in employment. A large proportion of the labour force as a whole works in the unorganized sector at distinctly lower levels of wages and productivity. For who are able to earn only enough for sustenance, the states must create supplementary employment opportunities and income.

As Prof. Amartya Sen has stated, action is required in order to protect people employment, livelihood and social security are very necessary. Participatory approach to development is very necessary. There are several instances of successful involvement of people in programmes for poverty reduction and employment generation through elected local bodies, user groups and civil society. People's participation is aimed at bringing out greater transparency and accountability through processes of social audit. People's involvement itself will ensure greater success in the implementation of various programmes for their betterment. In short, the whole issue of policies and programmes for employment in India and subsequent security is the primary issue and provides a challenge to Planners, Policy Makers and all those concerned with the well being of the people. The process of employment generation presupposes a cooperative relationship between government, private sector and civil society. The institutional mechanisms and delivery system need to be strengthened. Three things are a constraint to development (1) insufficiency of resources, (2) delivery system and (3) performance accountability. Progress in the area of employment generation requires a major push towards generating additional employment opportunities combined with institutional and organizational changes to enforce accountability to ensure these aims.

India has had a number of anti-poverty programmes since the early 1960s. These include among others the National Rural Employment Programme (NREP) evolved in financial year 1980 from the earlier 'Food-for-Work' programme. In the early 1980s Food for Work programme was initiated wherein employment was offered at a low daily wage, usually paid in grain, the rationale being that only the truly needy will take jobs at such low pay. To use unemployed and under-employed workers to build productive community assets the rural landless employment guarantee programme was instituted in 1993. Expanding employment opportunities and building rural infrastructure was seen as means of encouraging rapid economic growth.

By now it is well recognized that the instrument of Rural Works Programme is an important component of strategies to alleviate poverty and hunger and discrimination prevalent in agricultural labour markets and can be avoided in public works programme. NREGP scheme sustain household welfare in the short run through provision of employment and contribute to the development of the economy in the long run through strengthening rural infrastructure.

The National Rural Employment Guarantee Scheme (NREGS) promotes wage employment to every rural household, under which adult members volunteer to do unskilled manual work. Under the new scheme, 'BPL households' has been replaced by 'households'. The scope of the bill has been widened it extends a guarantee of employment for 100 days per year to the poorest villagers. The poor households can also self-select themselves at the Panchayat level. The statutory minimum wages have to be paid.

Through this bill, the government is redeeming its economic pledge to give a job to every rural family. Presenting the bill in Parliament, Congress President Smt. Sonia Gandhi has said that "an economic growth at 7 per cent per year, can and must find the resources to improve the lives of its millions of poor". This employment guarantee will initially be implemented in the 150 poorest districts over the next four years and it has the potential, if implemented well of becoming India's best anti-poverty programme. Within the broad framework of policy the government has undertaken a laudable programme to build up the physical infrastructure necessary for betterment of India's rural population. The new jobs will include construction of roads and embankments, wasteland restoration for agriculture and irrigation development schemes and extension work. This rural infrastructure is a sin qua non for rapid and sustained economic growth.

The National Rural Employment Guarantee Act 2004 has stated as an objective provision for the enhancement of livelihood security of the poor households in rural areas of the country by providing at least 100 days of guaranteed wage employment in every financial year to every households whose adult members volunteered to do unskilled manual work and for matters connected therewith or instantly thereto. It provides for the first time a guarantee of employment in rural areas. It asserts that the save as otherwise provided the State Government shall in such rural areas in the State for such period as may be notified by the Central Government provide to every poor household whose adult members volunteer to do unskilled manual work not less than 100 days of such work in a financial year in accordance with the scheme made under the Act. Every person who has done the work given to him under the scheme shall be entitled to receive wages at the wage rate for each day of work. The disbursement of daily wages shall be on a weekly basis or in any case not later than a fortnight after the date on which the work was done. The Central Government or the State Government may within the limits of its economic capacity and development make provision for securing work to every adult member of each household under the scheme for any period beyond the period guaranteed. There is also a provision for payment of unemployment allowance which says that if an applicant for employment under the scheme is not provided such employment within 15 days of receipt of application seeking employment or from the date on which the employment has been set in the case of an advance application which ever is later he shall be entitled to a daily unemployment allowance. As regards the wage rate, different rates of wages may be specified for different areas by notification of the Central Government notwithstanding anything contained in the Minimum Wages Act of 1948. Until such time as a wage rate is fixed by the Central Government in respect of any area in a State, the minimum wage fixed by the State Government under Section 3 of the Minimum Wages Act, 1948 for agricultural labourers shall be considered as the wage rate applicable to that area. For regular monitoring and review of the implementation of the Act, a State Employment Guarantee Council will be set up at the State-level which will have members from Panchayatiraj institutions, organizations of workers and disadvantaged groups such as women and SC/ST. The Panchayats at district level in every district within which the scheme is being implemented shall constitute a Standing Committee comprising its members and subject to terms and conditions prescribed by the State Government supervise, monitor and oversee the implementation of this scheme. The Standing Committee shall co-opt members of Intermediate Panchayat, Gram Panchayat organizations of workers, women organizations, Non-government Organisations and disadvantaged groups as special invitees. The functions of the Standing Committee at district level shall be (a) to finalise and approve block-wise projects to be taken up under a programme under the scheme, (b) to supervise and monitor projects taken up at block level and district level, (c) to carry out such other functions as may be assigned to do by State Council from time to time. There will be a District Programme Coordinator for the implementation of the scheme at the district which will assist the Standing Committee either the CEO of the District Panchayat or the Collector/Any District level officers of the appropriate rank may be designated as the District Programme Coordinator.

For every block the State Govt. will appoint a programme officer for implementing the scheme who will prepare a plan for the block under his jurisdiction through consolidation of project proposals prepared by Gram Panchayats and proposals received from intermediate Panchayats. He will also be responsible for matching the demand for imployment with the employment opportunities arising from projects under the area of his jurisdiction. It will be his duty to ensure (a) monitoring of projects taken up by Gram Panchayats and other implementing panchayats with the block, (b) sanctioning and ensuring payment of unemployment allowances to eligible poor households, (c) ensuring prompt and fair payment of wages to all labourers employed under the programme of the scheme within the block and (d) ensuring that regular 'Social Audit' of the work is carried out. The Gram Sabha shall monitor the execution of works within the Gram Panchayat and the Gram Sabha will undertake regular Social Audit of all the projects under the scheme taken up within the Gram Panchayat. The Gram Panchayat shall make available all relevant documents including the muster rolls, bills, vouchers, measurement books, copies of sanction orders and other connected books of accounts and papers to the Gram Sabha for the purpose of conducting the social audit. The State Government shall in addition by rules, determine appropriate grievance redressal mechanism at the block level and the district for dealing with any complaint by any person in respect of implementation of the scheme and lay down procedure for disposal of such complaints. The involvement of the Panchayat and the Gram Sabha in overseeing and monitoring the implementation of the programme is a guarantee that the works will be executed as planned. It is also hoped that the implementation of the National Rural Employment Guarantee Scheme (NREGS) will lead to creation of durable assets, strengthen the livelihood resource base of the rural poor, and help to build facilities such as Public Health Care Centres and Schools, etc.

Government Sponsored Schemes for Poverty Alleviation/ Self-employment

Economic growth sub-serving equity concerns, ensuring distributive justice and alleviation of poverty has been the primary objective of Indian Planning since inception in 1951. Several anti-poverty programmes have been in operation focusing on the poor and the unemployed in the rural and urban areas. Over the years the poverty alleviation and employment generation programmes have been strengthened to generate more employment, create productive assets, impart technical and entrepreneurial skills and raise the income levels of the poor. At present the Government of India has the following poverty alleviation and employment generation programmes, which are known as Centrally Sponsored Schemes and are piloted through credit linkage with banks and subsidy allocations through the concerned Ministry's budgetary allocations. They are segmented into:

1. A holistic Rural Poverty Alleviation Programme (Swarnajayanti Gram Swarozgar Yojana (SGSY) implemented by the Ministry of Rural Development through Scheduled Commercial Banks, Regional Rural Banks, Co-operative Banks.
2. An urban poverty alleviation programme (Swarn Jayanti Bhahari Rozgar Yojana (SJSRY) implemented by the Ministry

of Urban Development and Poverty Alleviation through Scheduled Commercial Banks (Excluding RRBs).

3. An all India Employment Generation Programme Prime Minister's Rozgar Yojana (PMRY) implemented by the Ministry of Agro and Rural Industry through Scheduled Commercial Banks (excluding RRBs).
4. An Employment General Scheme for a specific segment (Scheme for Liberation and Rehabilitation of Scavengers (SLRS) implemented by the Ministry of Social Justice through Public Sector Banks.

RBI monitors the performance of banks under the Government Sponsored Programmes through the receipt of quarterly progress reports. Progress under these schemes form part of the agenda for discussion at various for a, from grass root level Block Level Bankers Committee (BLBC) to District Credit Committee (DCC)/District Level Review Committee (DLRC), State Level Review Committee (SLRC) and finally at the national level through Central Level Coordination Committee (CLCC) meetings, etc.

The annual credit mobilization targets in respect of SGSY and physical targets in respect of PMRY are fixed by the central Government. The respective State Governments fix the annual credit targets in respect of SJSRY and SLRS.

A major area of concern in the implementation of these schemes is the issue of inordinate gap between sanction and disbursement of loans. A common complaint is that though loans are quickly sanctioned, the funds are disbursed to the borrowers with agonizing delay.

Swarn Jayanti Gram Swarozgar Yojana (SGSY)

Government of India has restructured IRDP and its allied schemes viz. Training of Rural Youth for Self Employment (TRYSEM), Development of Women and Children in Rural Areas (DWCRA), Supply of Improved Toolkits to Rural Artisans (SITRA), Ganga Kalyan Yojana (GKY) and Million Wells Scheme (MWS) and has launched a new programme known as Swarnjayanti Gram Swarozgar Yojana (SGSY) with effect from 1st April 1999.

The scheme aims at establishing a large number of micro enterprises in the rural areas of the country. The objective of the scheme is to bring every assisted family above the poverty line by ensuring appreciable sustained level of income over a period of time by providing then income-generating assets through a mix of bank credit and government subsidy.

SGSY is a holistic programme covering all aspects of self-employment such as organization of poor into self help groups, training, credit, technology, infrastructure and marketing. The scheme is funded on 75:25 basis by center and states and will be implemented by DRDAs through Panchayat Samitis.

There is no ceiling on the size of the loan amount. Group activities will be given preference and 4-5 key activities will be given major assistance.

Salient Features of the SGSY Scheme

Eligibility. Rural poor such as the landless labourer, small and marginal farmers, those with marginal land, rural artisans and educated unemployed enlisted in the BPL list up to an age limit of 60 years.

Reservation. 50 per cent for SC/ST, 40 per cent for women and 3 per cent for handicapped, .50 per cent of SHGs is formed in each block should be exclusively for the women.

Activities.Identified key/cluster activities with emphasis on group activities. Self Help Groups (SHG) membership within a range of 10-20; for minor irrigation minimum of 5 members.

Revolving Fund. SHGs that are in existence for about six months and have demonstrated the potential of a viable group enters the third stage, wherein it receives the Revolving Fund from District Rural Development Agency (DRDA) and banks as cash credit facility. The DRDAs may release subsidy, which is equal to the group corpus with a minimum of Rs. 5000/- and a maximum of Rs.10,000/- linked with bank credit. The banks would sanction credit, which would be in multiples of the group corpus and could go up to four times of the group corpus as cash credit facility based on the absorption capacity and credit worthiness of the group.

Subsequently, if it is found that the group has not been able to reach the micro enterprise stage and requires further financial support to continue in the micro finance stage for some more time, performance of such groups may be got evaluated. In the evaluation if it is observed that the group has been successfully utilizing the revolving fund, they could be considered for sanction of further doses of subsidy fund up to a maximum of Rs. 20,000/- inclusive of previous doses linked with bank credit. The subsidy of Rs. 20,000/- released by DRDA will be adjusted against the loan at the end of the cash credit period on the request of the group.

The group corpus would be defined as the total amount available with the group inclusive of cash with the group, amount in Savings Bank account of the group, loans outstanding against members of the group and interest earned on the loans as well as deposits.

Project Cost- No ceiling

Subsidy - Back end subsidy

General– 30 per cent of the project cost– max Rs.7,500/-

SC/ST– 50 per cent of the project cost– max Rs.10,000/-

Group– 50 per cent of the project cost subject to per capita subsidy of Rs.10,000/- or Rs.1.25 lakh which is less.

Irrigation– 30 per cent or 50 per cent as the case may be without monetary ceiling.

Security- For individuals– up to Rs.50,000 and for Group up to Rs.5 lakh, assets created out of bank loan would be hypothecated to the bank as a primary security. Mortgage of land/third party guarantee may be obtained as security, if assets are not created as in the case of land-based activities. For individual loans above Rs.50,000 and group loans above Rs.5 lakh, in addition to primary security, suitable margin money/other collateral security may be obtained at banks discretion.

Repayment- Minimum 5 years, instalments as per approved unit cost of NABARD/Dist SGSY Committee. Subsidy eligible only after completion of lock in period.

Recovery- Through personal contacts, joint recovery camps, legal action, etc., failing which forfeiture of subsidy for adjustment of dues may be taken up. NGOs may be used as facilitators for recovery and 0.5 per cent of the loan amount may be charged to the swarozgaris to meet this expenditure. Prompt repayment entitles waiver of this monitoring fee.

Refinance- Banks are eligible for refinance from NABARD for loans disbursed under SGSY.

To Address Urban Poverty

Swarna Jayanti Shahari Rozgar Yojana (SJSRY)

The Government of India has launched a rationalized poverty alleviation scheme namely the SJSRY scheme by replacing the existing three schemes viz., Nehru Rozgar Yojana, Urban Basic Services for the Poor and Prime Minister's Integrated Urban Poverty Eradication Programme which is in operation from 1.12.1997 in all Urban and semi-urban towns of India. The objective of the scheme is to provide gainful employment to the urban unemployed or underemployed poor through encouraging the setting up of self-employment ventures or provision of wage employment. Among other components, the scheme has two sub-schemes where bank credit is involved namely Urban Self Employment Programme (USEP) and Development of Women and Children in Urban Areas (DWCUA). The scheme is implemented by all Scheduled Commercial Banks. The scheme is funded on a 75:25 basis between the center and the State.

Eligibility– Below poverty line families are eligible to avail of benefits under the scheme. The beneficiaries are identified by the Urban local bodies on the basis of house-to-house survey. Under USEP, underemployed and unemployed urban youth whose annual family income is below the poverty line and who are educated upto ninth standard and who have been included in ULB list are to be assisted with bank loans.

Reservation- Under the scheme, women are to be assisted to the extent of not less than 30 per cent, disabled at 3 per cent and SC/STs at least to the extent of the proportion of their strength in the local population.

Project Cost- Projects costing up to Rs. 50,000/- are to be financed by banks.

Subsidy- Subsidy is provided by Government at 15 per cent of the project cost subject to a maximum of Rs.7,500/-. The borrower has to bring in 5 per cent of the project cost as margin money. Interest is charged as per interest rate directives issued by RBI from time to time. Partnerships are also permitted.

Under DWCUA, women beneficiaries may take up self-employment ventures in group. DWCUA group should consist of at least 10 urban poor women. The group is entitled to a subsidy of Rs.1,25,000/- or 50 per cent of the project cost whichever is less. In addition, the group may set itself up as a thrift and credit society.

Repayment- The repayment schedule may range 3 to 7 years after initial moratorium of 6 to 18 months as decided by the banks.

Security- Individual loans up to Rs. 50,000/- and group loans up to Rs.3,00,000/- do not require a collateral/guarantee.

Prime Ministers Rozgar Yojana (PMRY)

The scheme was launched on 2.10.93 and initially was in operation in urban areas. From 1.4.94 onwards, the scheme is being implemented throughout the country. The objective of the scheme is to provide self-employment opportunities to educated unemployed youth in the age group of 18 to 35 years. In North-

Eastern states the eligible age group is from 18-40 . There is a 10-year relaxation for SC/ST Ex-servicemen/Physically handicapped and women, in the upper age limit. To be eligible for assistance under the scheme the family income of the beneficiaries shall not exceed Rs.40,000/- per annum and income of parents of beneficiary also shall not exceed Rs.40,000/-. The banks have been allowed to make parents/Head of the family of unmarried girl as co-borrower, with effect from 21.11.2002. The borrower should be the resident of the area for more than 3 years. The minimum educational qualification fixed is VIIIth pass. It has also been provided that the margin money and subsidy amount would be 20 per cent of the project cost. Ceiling on subsidy amount will be Rs.7500/- in States/UTs other than in North Eastern Region. In the seven states in North East the ceiling on subsidy amount payable will be Rs.15,000/-. This has been extended to Himachal Pradesh, Jammu and Kashmir and Uttaranchal. Hence the margin to be brought in by the borrower will vary from 5 per cent to 16.25 per cent of the project cost. The residency criterion for married men in Mechalaya is relaxed in line with married women in rest of the country. All economically viable activities including agricultural and allied activities but excluding direct agricultural operations like raising of crops/purchase of manure etc., are now being covered under the scheme. Projects up to Rs.1 lakh in business sector and up to Rs.2 lakh in other sectors will be eligible for finance by banks. In case of partnership firm, projects up to Rs.10 lakh can be undertaken and loan amount will be to the extent of individual admissibility. Self Help Groups (SHG) could be considered for financing under the PMRY provided all the members of the SHG individually satisfy the eligibility criteria under the scheme. Membership of the Group would not exceed 10 nos. Maximum loan limit for the Group is Rs.10 lakh.

Assistance will be limited to individual eligibility under the Scheme.

A reservation of 22.5 per cent for SC/STs and 27 per cent for other backward classes (OBCs) has been provided. Preference is to be given to women and other weaker sections. Banks have also been advised to ensure a fair and adequate share to the minorities. No third party guarantee / collateral is necessary for projects upto Rs.1 lakh and the advances under the scheme are treated as advances under priority sector.

For industry sector, project upto Rs. 2 lakhs (loan ceiling under PMRY) are eligible for exemption/obtention of collateral security. For partnership project in the industry sector exemption limit- for obtention of collateral security will be Rs. 5 lakh per borrowal account.

Position of Recovery of Loans under PMRY is as given below:

Recovery Position as on March	*Recovery -General*			
	Demand	*Recovery*	*Over dues*	*per cent*
2002	220350.55	76900.67	143449.88	34.90
2003	223785.70	78710.34	145075.36	35.20
2004	70449.75	94542.81	175906.94	34.96

Scheme for Liberation and Rehabilitation of Scavengers (SLRS)

The Scheme was introduced in 1993 and is implemented by all Public Sector Banks except RRBs. The objective of the Scheme is to liberate and rehabilitate scavengers and their dependants from the existing obnoxious occupation of manually removing night soil and filth and to provide them with alternate dignified occupation. The Scheme covers all scavengers and their dependents (both the scheduled caste scavengers and non-scheduled caste scavengers in the country). The Central Government and the State Government participate in the scheme in the ratio of 50:50.

Under the scheme projects upto Rs.50,000/-can be financed. Subsidy is available to borrowers at 50 per cent of project cost subject to a maximum of Rs.10,000/- . The borrowers can also avail margin assistance at 15 per cent of the projects cost at 4 per cent rate of interest from State Scheduled Castes Development Corporation. All loans upto Rs.6,500/- will be treated as DRI loan at concessional rate of 4 per cent. However, where the amount of loan exceeds Rs. 6500/- the entire loan will carry interest as per RBI directive on interest rates. Security for the loan will be only hypothecation of assets created out of the loan. The State Scheduled Caste Development Corporation will have second charge/ pari-pasu charge over the assets to cover their margin money loan assistance. The loans shall be repaid within 3 to 7 years (inclusive of grace period not exceeding 6 months) depending on the life of the assets created and repaying capacity of beneficiaries.

Differential Rate of Interest (DRI) Scheme

Salient features

The scheme was introduced in 1972 and is being implemented by all Indian Scheduled Commercial Banks.

Objective

To provide bank finance at a concessional rate of interest of 4 per cent p.a to the weaker sections of the community for engaging in productive and gainful activities so that they could improve their economic conditions.

Area of operations

The scheme is being implemented throughout the country.

Target group/Eligibility criteria

The income ceiling for eligibility is annual income of Rs. 7200/- per family in urban or semi urban areas and Rs. 6400/- per family in rural areas. Size of land holding must not exceed one acre of irrigated land and 2.5 acres of unirrigated land. The land holding criteria is not applicable to SC/STs. The important categories of borrowers under the scheme are SC/STs and others engaged on a very modest scale, in agriculture and / or allied agricultural activities, people who themselves collect or do elementary processing of forest products, people physically engaged on a modest scale in the fields of cottage and rural industries and vocation, indigent students of merit etc. The banks are required to lend under the scheme, at least 1 per cent of their aggregate advances as at the end of the previous year. 2/3rd of the total DRI advances must be routed through the banks' rural and semi urban branches.

Loan amount

The maximum assistance per beneficiary has been fixed at Rs. 6500/- for productive purposes. In addition to this, physically handicapped persons can avail of assistance to the extent of Rs. 5000/- (maximum) per beneficiary for acquiring aids, appliances, equipment, provided they are eligible for assistance under the scheme. Similarly, members of SC/ST s satisfying the income criteria of the scheme can also avail of housing loan up to Rs. 5000/- per beneficiary over and above the loan of Rs. 6500/- available under the scheme.

Margin money

No margin money has been prescribed under the scheme.

Capital subsidy/Interest

No capital subsidy is available. Rate of interest to be charged on loans is 4 per cent p.a. Interest on current due is not to be compounded.

Security

No collateral security/ third party guarantee is required. Assets created out of the loan amount would only be hypothecated to the banks.

Repayment

Not exceeding five years including grace period of two years.

Reservation/Preference

The banks are required to ensure that at least 40 per cent of their DRI advances flow to SC/STs.

Major difficulties, which are arising in the implementation of the schemes, are of poor targeting and leakages. The target group of people below poverty line with an annual income up to Rs.11,000/- per annum includes small marginal farmers, landless artisans, vulnerable groups such as scheduled castes/tribes, women headed households. Thus targeting from above becomes a difficult proposition. Hence developing people's participation in rural development and adopting self-selection schemes which will also raise awareness of people is important. In certain areas the Self Help Groups (SHGs) have also shown the way through building a corpus of savings through extension of micro-credit. The poor generally, have a lack of savings and a low access to credit which leads to a dependence on moneylenders. SHG raise awareness and allow for small amounts of regular savings. This helps the poor to come together and pool through savings. On the basis of these monthly savings loans access to micro loans is enabled. Thus they have an easy access to credit. Groups self-select their members and there is a peer pressure which ensures timely repayment of loans. Thus NGOs and SHGs promote access to formal credit for individuals by building their credit worthiness skill and other services leading to eventual social economic development. We spend large amount of resources on anti-poverty programmes. Unfortunately the targeting effectiveness is very low and efficiency poor.

Acceleration in growth that had been experienced during the mid-1990s should have created sufficient employment opportunities not only to absorb the increase in the labour force but also to reduce the backlog of unemployment. The Planning Commission also estimated that the elasticity of employment to GDP growth would be 0.4, (Ninth Plan document). This elasticity and a growth rate of 6.5 percent per annum would create 8 million employment opportunities per year – significantly higher than the increase in the labour force. Planning Commission constituted a Task Force on Employment Opportunities in January 1999 under the chairmanship of Shri Montek S. Ahluwalia, then Member, Planning Commission. The Task Force submitted its report in July 2001.

The Task Force examined the requirement of job creation in terms of additions to the work force on the Usual Principal and Subsidiary Status (UPSS) basis, which turned out to be lower than ten million per year at the assumed labour force participation rates. It also assumed that the recently observed labour intensities in the various sectors of the economy would continue to prevail, and therefore concentrated primarily on the major macroeconomic policy changes that would be required to increase the growth rate of the economy sufficiently in order to generate the requisite employment opportunities to absorb the projected increases in the work force. Its main conclusion was that the growth rate of the economy will have to be increased to at least 8 percent per annum, and that this was a feasible target provided that certain critical policy reforms were undertaken.

Some programmes (discussed above) are administered through loans by the Banking system and subsidies through the concerned ministries. There are about 180 schemes administered through the Ministry of Rural Development in addition to those listed above. Currently the Government commits Rs.11,000 crore per annum to these direct poverty alleviation programs including self employment and wage employment programs under the Centrally Sponsored Schemes (CSS). These equal about 25 per cent of Fiscal costs. In addition, some State Governments have their own poverty alleviation schemes. The multiplicity of the programs is advocated on the grounds of multidimensionality of poverty and regional variations in the efficacy of the delivery system. Studies have shown great inter -state disparities poorer states benefit least from the Centrally sponsored schemes (CSS). Research has shown that there are leakages from 20 per cent to 70 per cent. These leakages have been extensively analysed by various researchers and they have found that the supply driven and top down approach with little concern for the complexities at the grassroots level is the major cause of problems. Focussing greater attention on Community/group and client-oriented schemes, Gram Panchayats and Community based organisations, may to some extent at least help to plug the loopholes in the implementation. Social Sector expenditure in India in the 1990s was much poorer than in the East Asian Countries, poor utilisation or misuse of funds due to leakages and corruption need to be avoided and delivery systems have to be effectively revamped. Growth needs to be rapid enough to significantly improve the absolute conditions of the poor, and to have the maximum impact, there should also be an improvement in the relative position of the poor. The share of the poor in the incremental income should be more than their share in the average. There is a need to go beyond the establishment of social safety nets to focus directly on providing employment and

Performance of Scheduled Commercial Banks under SGSY

Year	*Target (Rs in Crores)*	*No. of Swaroz garis*	*Total Loan disbursed (Rs in Crores)*	*per centof achiev ement*	*No.of SC/ST assisted*	*No.of women assisted*	*No.of Disabled assisted*	*Percentage of physical coverage*		
								SC/ ST	*Women*	*Disabled*
2000-01	1797.32	583051	696.89	38.77	162542	203780	3349	27.89	34.95	0.57
2001-02	1788.55	641000	675.26	37.75	161213	189961	5952	25.15	29.63	0.92
2002-03	1509.40	719293	733.61	48.60	160916	173430	16094	22.37	24.11	2.23
2003-04	1408.55	991062	840.81	59.69	256716	276443	8623	25.90	27.89	0.87
2004-05	1593.39	1084749	958.13	60.13	285395	338391	10126	26.30	31.19	0.93

Data as reported by scheduled commercial banks

Reservation for SC/ST 50 per cent; Women 40 per cent; Disabled 3 per cent

Performance of Scheduled Commercial Banks under SJSRY

(Amount Rs in Lakhs)

Year	*Target (Physical)*	*Loans sanctioned*		*Loans disbursed*		*per cent of Achievement*	*per cent of recovery*
		No.	*Amt*	*No.*	*Amt*		
2001-02	154292	91504	28181.63	65610	19526.46	42.52	40.20
2002-03	123186	87478	25390.74	71919	20366.04	58.38	41.46
2003-04	117568	73887	22756.45	59648	17439.73	50.73	38.43
2004-05	95629	61890	19926.83	48798	15067.08	51.02	44.91 (provisional)

Data as reported by Scheduled Commercial Banks

(Continued) Performance of Scheduled Commercial Banks under SJSRY

Year	*Physical Coverage (Number)*												*per cent of recovery*
	SC/ST				*Women*				*Disabled*				
	Sanctioned		*Disbursed*		*Sanctioned*		*Disbursed*		*Sanctioned*		*Disbursed*		
	No.	*Amt*	*No.*	*Amt*	*No.*	*Amt*	*No.*	*Amt*	*No.*	*Amt*	*No.*	*Amt*	
2001-02	22386	6660.08	16192	4952.30	17452	4750.26	13536	3579.28	824	277.18	641	236.69	40.20
2002-03	24133	6990.56	20459	5824.55	20221	5241.57	17471	4453.24	1504	371.29	1333	329.03	41.46
2003-04	20639	6295.74	17977	5348.60	18148	5177.36	15803	4441.86	975	291.03	836	291.35	38.43
2004-05	16372	5005.09	13675	3983.93	13003	4024.75	10921	3105.33	778	243.67	686	283.48	44.91 (provisional)

Data as reported by Scheduled Commercial Banks

Ach = Achievement:

*Provisional

DWCUA under SJSRY

(Amount Rs in Lakhs)

Year	DWCUA Sanctioned			DWCUA disbursement		
	No.of groups	*No of members*	*Amount*	*No. of groups*	*No of members*	*Amount*
2001-02	1295	9650	1235.08	1003	8593	1022.45
2002-03	1237	10406	1658.84	1142	9769	1352.26
2003-04	1687	18001	2294.43	1525	16553	1838.72
2004-05	1260	12294	1565.02	1028	11453	1300.85

Data as reported by SCBs

Recovery performance by banks under SGSY

Year	*Recovery per cent*
2000-01	45.38
2001-02	43.93
2002-03	44.98
2003-04	45.53
2004-05	52.56 (Provisional)

Data as reported by Scheduled Commercial Banks

Performance of Public Sector Banks under SLRS

(Amount Rs in Lakhs)

Year	Target (Physical)	Loans sanctioned		Loans disbursed		Per cent of Achievement	Recovery per cent
		No.	Amt	No.	Amt		
2001-02	21878	15681	3614.60	13468	22141.92	61.55	33.30
2002-03	14857	12705	2361.75	11467	2016.75	77.18	33.37
2003-04	20725	9556	1870.80	7852	1378.81	37.88	36.22
2004-05	14861	10206	2134.40	8209	1574.22	55.23	33.38 (provisional)

Data as reported by Schedule Commercial Banks

raising the income of the poor through explicit poverty interventions We spend large amounts of resources on anti-poverty programs it is therefore essential to improve targeting at present our programmes suffer as their effectiveness is very low and efficiency poor.

The strategy for employment creation through the growth process as recommended by the Task Force is likely to take time and should, therefore, be seen as a medium-run solution. It needs to be complemented by specific short-run strategies of "Policies and Programmes for Employment in India", which can deliver results. As growth with equity is inescapable we have to try to redress the difficulties in the schemes to make them more effective.

References

1. India's Development Scenario – Next Decade and Beyond - K.C. Pant – Academic Foundation, New Delhi 2004.
2. National Rural Employment Guarantee Programme, Text of Draft Bill, Ministry of Rural Development.
3. India's (Maharashtra) Employment Guarantee Scheme: Lessons from Long Experience: S. Mahendra Dev, Centre of Economic and Social Studies, Hyderabad.

Index